AMERICAN
ENTREPRENEUR

AMERICAN

ENTREPRENEUR

HOW 400 YEARS OF RISK-TAKERS, INNOVATORS,
AND BUSINESS VISIONARIES BUILT THE U.S.A.

WILLIE ROBERTSON
AND WILLIAM DOYLE

WILLIAM MORROW
An Imprint of HarperCollins *Publishers*

HarperCollins books may be purchased for educational, business, or sales promotional use. For information, please email the Special Markets Department at SPsales@harpercollins.com.

A hardcover edition of this book was published in 2018 by William Morrow, an imprint of HarperCollins Publishers.

FIRST WILLIAM MORROW PAPERBACK EDITION PUBLISHED 2019.

The Library of Congress has catalogued a previous edition as follows:

Names: Robertson, Willie, 1972– author.
Title: American entrepreneur : how 400 years of risk-takers, innovators, and business visionaries built the U.S.A. / Willie Robertson, William Doyle.
Description: New York : William Morrow, 2018. | Includes index.
Identifiers: LCCN 2018024762 | ISBN 9780062693419 (hardback) | ISBN 9780062693426 (trade paperback) | ISBN 9780062863898 (large print)
Subjects: LCSH: Businesspeople—United States—Biography. | BISAC: BUSINESS & ECONOMICS | Entrepreneurship. | BIOGRAPHY & AUTOBIOGRAPHY / Personal Memoirs. | HISTORY / United States / General.
Classification: LCC HC102.5.A2 R63 2018 | DDC 338/.04092273—dc23
LC record available at https://lccn.loc.gov/2018024762

ISBN 978-0-06-269342-6 (pbk.)

19 20 21 22 23 LSC 10 9 8 7 6 5 4 3 2 1

AMERICAN
ENTREPRENEUR

HOW 400 YEARS OF RISK-TAKERS, INNOVATORS, AND BUSINESS VISIONARIES BUILT THE U.S.A.

WILLIE ROBERTSON
AND WILLIAM DOYLE

wm

WILLIAM MORROW
An Imprint of HarperCollins*Publishers*

HarperCollins books may be purchased for educational, business, or sales promotional use. For information, please email the Special Markets Department at SPsales@ harpercollins.com.

A hardcover edition of this book was published in 2018 by William Morrow, an imprint of HarperCollins Publishers.

FIRST WILLIAM MORROW PAPERBACK EDITION PUBLISHED 2019.

The Library of Congress has catalogued a previous edition as follows:

Names: Robertson, Willie, 1972– author.

Title: American entrepreneur : how 400 years of risk-takers, innovators, and business visionaries built the U.S.A. / Willie Robertson, William Doyle.

Description: New York : William Morrow, 2018. | Includes index.

Identifiers: LCCN 2018024762 | ISBN 9780062693419 (hardback) | ISBN 9780062693426 (trade paperback) | ISBN 9780062863898 (large print)

Subjects: LCSH: Businesspeople—United States—Biography. | BISAC: BUSINESS & ECONOMICS / Entrepreneurship. | BIOGRAPHY & AUTOBIOGRAPHY / Personal Memoirs. | HISTORY / United States / General.

Classification: LCC HC102.5.A2 R63 2018 | DDC 338/.04092273—dc23

LC record available at https://lccn.loc.gov/2018024762

ISBN 978-0-06-269342-6 (pbk.)

19 20 21 22 23 LSC 10 9 8 7 6 5 4 3 2 1

CONTENTS

AUTHOR'S NOTE

One day not long ago, I decided to write a book about how family businesses and entrepreneurs like my family and millions of others have helped build and shape America.

So I huddled up with my buddy and coauthor William Doyle. We got to doing lots of talking and lots of researching, and before you knew it, we came across a whole bunch of stories about great American entrepreneurs, and the book you're holding in your hand was born. We hope you like it.

AMERICAN
ENTREPRENEUR

AN AMERICAN FAMILY BUSINESS

Diligent hands will rule.

—Proverbs 12:24

s long as there's been an America, there have been entrepreneurs.

We started businesses on our kitchen tables and living room couches, and in our backyards, farms, and garages. Sometimes we started with nothing, and sometimes we got a stack of seed money from a friendly bank or family member.

We sweat, strain, cry, laugh, and work our tails off to make something from nothing and build a better life for our families and ourselves. Sometimes we've gone bust and sometimes we've succeeded far beyond our wildest dreams. Even the biggest companies start out small, and we're the ones who started them.

In the process, we founded this nation, built it into the world's economic superpower, and inspired the world with our achievements.

America has always been a land of business visionaries, risk-takers, and doers, of growers, makers, wheeler-dealers, traders, sellers, merchants, and go-getters. American economist William

Baumol described an entrepreneur as "the individual willing to embark on adventure in pursuit of economic goals." Management expert Peter Drucker described entrepreneurship as "the act that endows resources with a new capacity to create wealth."

According to historian John Steele Gordon, "The first patent awarded to an American resident was given to Joseph Jenks in 1646 for a device that improved the manufacture of edged tools, such as sickles. It was the beginning of the 'Yankee ingenuity' that has characterized America's economy ever since, from that first machine tool to bifocal glasses, the cotton gin, automated flour mills, the high-pressure steam engine, interchangeable parts, the McCormick reaper, the oil industry, the airplane, Coca-Cola, the affordable automobile, the digital computer, and Twitter."

America was founded, fed, financed, nurtured, and sustained, in large part, by entrepreneurs.

The spirit of America is the spirit of entrepreneurship—of risk, innovation, ingenuity, grit, and perseverance.

The history of America is largely the history of businesses, most of which started out small and sometimes stayed that way, but sometimes grew far beyond the wildest dreams of their founders.

My inspiration is God, my family is my life, and my business is my family.

I am the CEO of a family business that my father started forty-six years ago in a dilapidated backyard shed when we had nothing except a life of dirt-poor poverty.

It's a business that my mother helped run, my brothers and I grew up in, and my wife, in-laws, and extended family and friends have helped build into a multimillion-dollar powerhouse.

Today that business has launched three successful TV shows,

including *Duck Dynasty*, the most-watched reality TV show in history, sold tens of millions of dollars of products and merchandise, generated hundreds of jobs, and entertained and inspired many millions of people the world over.

But our American dream started out smack in the middle of an American nightmare.

My father, Phil, grew up not far from where we all live today, in a house with no running water and no electricity, and a toilet two hundred feet back in the woods. He attended Louisiana Tech on a football scholarship, started as quarterback over Super Bowl champion-to-be Terry Bradshaw, smoked dope and listened to lots of Jimi Hendrix, married my mother, Miss Kay, when she was eighteen years old and he was twenty, got a master's degree in education, then decided he'd rather hunt ducks than be a teacher. To supplement the family income and just barely scratch out a living, Phil became a commercial fisherman, selling his own net-caught flathead catfish for seventy cents a pound.

One day in 1972, the year I was born, Phil had an idea. He was fed up with the store-bought duck calls he used during duck hunting season. *These things don't sound at all like real ducks*, he thought. *I can build a better duck call.* So he disappeared into the ramshackle work shed in the back of our property and started tinkering around with materials and tools. Weeks went by. Eventually he worked out a sweet design made of two separate cedar-tree-cut reeds rather than the usual one, plus the ingenious twist of carving a dimple in the reeds to hold them separate. It was a design so special that he got a patent for it. He put a lot of hard work and patience into his duck call. He just wanted to make a great duck call for the average hunter.

The result was the backwoods Stradivarius of duck calls, a duck call that sounded more like a duck than a duck did, a sound that reached far up in the sky and invited ducks to come on down, relax, and spend some quality time with new friends, who actually turned out to be the business end of a shotgun. Ducks loved the sweet music the instrument made, and so did the hunters.

To buy a lathe and other gear, Phil took out a $25,000 loan from the Howards, a family of successful local retail entrepreneurs (who eventually became my in-laws), and started cranking out duck calls one by one. My mom pitched in to run the business, handling orders, paying the bills, and balancing the books on the living room couch. Phil and Miss Kay laid the foundation for our family's success. That first year, they made $8,000, and the Duck Commander Company was born. A business was born.

Then, disaster struck.

Just as the duck call business was slowly taking off, Phil decided to make Satan his business partner. There's no other way to describe what happened to him. Phil chugged whiskey straight from the bottle, came home drunk, got in fights, operated a honky-tonk, and kicked the family out of our trailer home for a while. One night he got in a fight with the honky-tonk's owner and his wife, beat up both of them, and threw the lady clear across the bar. He snuck out the back door to escape the police and hid out in the woods to evade the long arm of the law. He spent most of the next eight years as a full-blown heathen, and my parents' marriage started falling apart.

One day, a minister showed up out of the blue, gave my dad a Bible, and told him to put his life in the hands of Jesus. My father turned him down. Until four months later, when he decided it was a really good idea. He begged Miss Kay to take him back, and she did, provided that he stop drinking, lose his old friends, and put his life in the hands of the Lord. He did, and has led a clean life ever since.

As a family, we turned all those mistakes and negative energy into a positive, and we built our business on it.

I've always been entrepreneurial. In fifth grade I was constantly selling and trading things. We were so poor I didn't have an allowance. I needed cash. I had a pretty productive worm farm, and I sold bait worms to the local fishermen every Saturday morning. I filled one of my dad's old boats with cow manure and put every worm I could find in it.

One day, one of my dad's hunting friends, who was a candy distributor, gave me a box of Hubba Bubba bubble gum. This created a dilemma for me. I wanted to consume the entire box. But then I thought, *Well, what if I sold this gum to other kids?*

I took a pack on my school bus, offered each stick for fifty cents apiece, and sold out before we got to school. I thought, *We got something here—we got a real business!*

I got my mom to drive me to the cash-and-carry store, loaded up on inventory, and it wasn't long before I was a full-fledged candy dealer. I did candy deals on the bus, out of my locker, out of my coat—I was practically dealing on the street corner.

Pretty soon I had made hundreds of dollars, which to me was a small fortune! I was like Red in *Shawshank Redemption*—I was "the guy who could get stuff." I did special orders. I had repeat customers. I even offered revolving credit plans.

I was rolling in cash, and I enjoyed living the high life as a ten-year-old. I bought a new pair of sneakers and strolled around like a prize peacock. My fifth-grade teacher called me the Little Tycoon. Business was going wonderfully.

Then I got called in to the principal's office.

"Willie, are you selling gum and candy out of your locker?"

I said, "Yeah, and I'm doing pretty good at it, too!"

He said, "Well, I've had a meeting with the school concession stand, and their sales are way down. So I'm going to shut you down. No more selling stuff at school."

I was crushed.

Now I was desperate for money, since I'd grown accustomed to that lifestyle.

I thought, *What else can I do to make money?* For a while I sold pencils and erasers. For fifty cents, I'd entertain you by popping a june bug in my mouth and eating it raw, as a snack.

Then I came up with an idea that I thought was pretty genius—the Human Jukebox.

We had a long bus ride to school, and I thought, *What if I entertained people and they paid me money?*

So I announced my new career as "the Human Jukebox" and popped up on the back of the school bus seat. Kids would stick a quarter under my arm like I was a jukebox. I'd robotically put the quarter in my pocket, and I'd sing whatever song you wanted to hear. I'd sing all the vocal parts and do the instruments, too. My specialties were Michael Jackson, the Beach Boys, and Molly Hatchet tunes.

But my most popular song by far was "Jukebox Hero," by Foreigner. Those fifth-grade girls loved it.

Norma Jean, the bus driver, would look in her rearview mirror and say, "Willie, get your butt down off that seat!" So I'd just crouch down low and keep singing the whole way. The Human Jukebox didn't make as much money as my gum business, but it was still pretty lucrative.

By trade, neither my father nor my mother was a businessperson. Dad had an education degree, and Mom had a GED. Neither was great at math, and they had little experience in business. Dad was not really a woodworker, didn't have a lot of tools, had no money to speak of, and was paying the bills by commercial fishing, which ain't easy. As soon as we kids could pitch in to help the family business, we all did. As the duck call business slowly grew, Dad was the constant motivational speaker to all of us employees, which in the early days consisted of us four brothers, Alan, Jase, Jep, and me, and Miss Kay. It was a firsthand account of how to start a business, how to run a business, and how to work like crazy to make sure it succeeds. My father would do simple math: "If there are two million duck hunters and we got just 10 percent to buy our duck call, then we would sell 200,000 duck calls."

I don't recommend this to the young folks out there, but my father actually encouraged my brother Jase and me to skip school to pitch in and help the family business. We would skip the maximum number of days possible from school without failing, which was forty back then. We did all the jobs. The worst job of all was to fill catfish traps with socks hand-stuffed with rotten cheese scooped out of a fifty-five-gallon drum. We didn't get paid for our work, though. Dad would always say, "Well, you're getting to eat tonight!" He wouldn't ever pay for worms or bait, either. "Crawfish will eat anything," he said. "Snakes, other fish, they'll eat you if you lay out there long enough!" So if there was a recent roadkill and you could bear the smell, we would take that varmint or whatever it was and I'd chop it up into little pieces and we'd throw it into the crawfish trap. "It's free bait!" my dad would say.

I also sold German carp on the street corner. German carp doesn't sound very appetizing, and it's not the world's tastiest fish, so I borrowed a trick from my dad and called it "the Golden Buffalo, the Pride of the Ouachita River." If you can sell uncleaned German carp, in the middle of August, in the state of Louisiana, boy, you can sell anything! That's how I became a salesman.

A couple of times a week, Dad would go out on the river that runs near our property and rig up 150 hoop nets to catch catfish and crawfish. When we were kids, we all pitched in. My brother Jase, the motorman, would carry the fish to shore in a boat and hand them off to my mom and me, and we'd throw the catch in the back of a truck and take them into town and try to sell them. That's where I got to be the salesman. If the markets would take them, great. If not, we'd go to a street corner and hang out a sign, FRESH FISH FOR SALE.

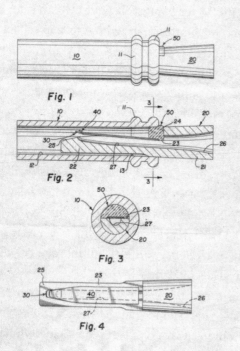

Diagrams from my dad's original patent for his duck call. (Duck Commander)

My dad had big dreams and ambitions, but at first the rest of the family wasn't too sure if this duck call business would work and whether it could grow and succeed over the long term. We'd sit around the dinner table and Phil would grandly announce, "Boys, we're going to sell a million dollars of these duck calls one day." We said, "Well, sure, Dad." We really didn't have any other options at the time, so it sounded like a great idea to us. But it really didn't seem possible. We thought Phil was just telling stories. We were the employees and were churning out duck calls from our two-bedroom house right on the river. Believe it or not, we did it. It took forty years, but we managed to pull it off, and in 2013 we sold not just a million dollars' worth but more than a million duck calls!

When I was a little kid, we had very little money, but I didn't even realize how little we had. I could tell how our family business was doing by the school lunch program. In elementary school, I qualified for the free lunch program, so me and a couple of other little poor kids were always put in the front of the chow line, which was fine with me. Then, around the time I was in junior high school, I was moved back to the "reduced lunch" kids group in the middle of the chow line. I thought to myself, *Hey, we must be selling more duck calls and fish—we're doing all right!*

By the time I moved to high school I had to pay for my lunch. By then I figured we must be multimillionaires. I thought, *We've made it! We made it in life! I'm actually paying for my own lunch!*

The family duck call business grew gradually through the 1970s, '80s, and '90s. One day in the 1980s, Dad had an idea. "Do you think people would want to watch what we do?" He had the idea of filming himself, his family, and his buddies hunting and then selling the footage on VHS tapes in stores. We all argued around the dinner table about it. That's the way our family works: you throw ideas around, you make your case, you get honest feedback, and sometimes it gets loud. It took my wife, Korie, a few years to get used to it and to realize we weren't mad at each other—we were just arguing at a loud level to try to get our point across!

Pretty soon, Dad began producing a series of duck-hunting videos called *The Duck Men*, featuring superauthentic, raw images of hunting, which no one had really done before. They had a kind of bootleg, moonshine feeling to them. They were real fun to watch.

We got a pretty good grassroots following from game hunters, duck hunters, and waterfowl guys around the country. The tapes helped our duck call business because we put our phone number on the back of every VHS box. We started selling more and more duck calls, added T-shirts and hats, and kept growing.

Dad would load up the truck with duck calls and announce, "I'm going on a four-day loop." That meant he was going to drive all around the little towns in the region and pay sales calls on as many hunting shops and sporting goods stores as he could, plus the Walmarts. Back then, you could sell directly into individual Walmart stores, and they had a little section for locally made products like ours. Pretty soon, the duck calls were selling so well that the word went up to Walmart headquarters in Arkansas.

The Walmart buyer called down to our house and asked for Phil. "Mr. Robertson, are you the one who's selling all these duck calls in our stores?" Phil said, "That's me." The buyer asked, "How are you selling into so many of our stores?" He answered, "One at a time!" The Walmart man said, "Mr. Robertson, why don't you come up here to corporate headquarters so I can see your duck calls and meet you in person." Dad went up there, and Walmart wound up putting our duck calls in their national chain of stores. That's what really made it for us as a company. That was a game changer. Eventually, Walmart was selling 500,000 duck calls per year in their stores. And it all came from Dad, out there on the road, busting his butt for days on end and selling into one store at a time. Plus all the help we gave him at home.

My dad was a visionary who always believed in his product and its destiny, and he was also a master salesman. Not only was he a living symbol of our ultimate end users—America's hunters—he understood that selling was show business. When he started the business, he actually carried around a tape recording of what a real mallard duck sounded like in the wild. He played the tape for a sales prospect, then honked on one of his duck calls, which were the best in the business. You couldn't tell the difference. Bang. Sale closed!

Our family business was literally a living room operation. When we got home from school, my brothers and I would watch *The Dukes of Hazzard* on TV while we folded shipping boxes. We'd go in the garage, sweep up the sawdust, dip the duck calls one by one in a barrel of tung oil, and hang them out on racks. My fingers were always stained so brown from the tung oil, I was pretty embarrassed to go to school!

I did customer service, too, at nine years old. If you called the number that was on our videos, or if you called our office, which was our house, I'd answer, "Duck Commander, can I help you?" We'd take the orders and write them on the back of paper plates and napkins, put them in a box for Mom, and she'd ship them out the next day at the post office. By the time I got old enough to run the business, I had done every part of it. It taught me so much about hard work and doing things as a family.

In 2002, when I was thirty years old, Phil made me the company CEO, which made sense, since I was the only one in the family with a college degree, and with a concentration in business. Years earlier, he'd heard about my candy- and gum-selling operation at school when the principal blew the whistle on me and called my dad. Phil didn't get angry. He just put the phone down and said to my mother, "He's the next CEO!" Once I got the CEO job, my main goal was to expand the business and get our products into sporting goods superstores like Bass Pro Shops and Cabela's in all the big hunting markets.

In 2008, we got an offer from the Benelli shotgun company to do a show on the Outdoor Channel. They said it would be a reality show, half about our family and half about shooting their shotguns in the woods.

At first I wasn't sure we should do a TV show, but my wife, Korie, was totally in favor of it. She watched reality TV all the time, and she thought we'd be great for it, because, well, let's face it, we're kind of an odd family.

"You all need a show," Korie said.

"Korie," I replied, "we're not all that interesting. What do we do on a TV show?"

"Willie, you all just aren't normal. I hate to say this, but you're not a normal family. It will make great TV. Just be yourselves!"

I couldn't believe what she was saying. I said, "We're totally normal!"

"Look at you all!" Korie replied. "You're very entertaining! You guys are a TV show!"

"Well, if you think it will work," I said.

I asked my father about it, and he said, "I think it's a terrible idea." I said, "Well, we'll take the meeting, Dad. With a TV show we might sell more duck calls."

Just as we were going into the meeting, Korie announced, "I think they should pay you."

I said, "What?"

"I think they should pay you money."

To tell you the truth, this hadn't occurred to me. And I didn't want to blow the meeting that was about to start. "Wait, Korie! I've got this deal all lined up. They're going to pay for the making of the show, and we're going to sell more duck calls. They're not paying us money, okay? They're not paying us money to be on TV."

This is where it comes in handy to have a wife who's from a family of successful entrepreneurs herself, the Howards. They are a family of entrepreneurs who are used to taking risks, negotiating, and getting their fair share.

To tell you the truth, I didn't always have the confidence in myself that I could actually pull off running a growing business, but Korie always believed in me and my abilities, and she would give me the encouragement to shoot higher. She later said, "I knew whatever he decided, he would do it with all his heart and be successful at it."

Korie made excellent grades and graduated at the top of her class, thrives on challenges and never backs down from one, and is convinced she can figure anything out. We've got six kids, and she put together all the trampolines, toys, and slide sets because she'd actually read the directions, but I was convinced I could look at the picture on the box and just "figure it out."

Korie, you see, has business in her blood. The Howards were supersmart businesspeople who were accustomed to starting businesses, running them, selling them, and sometimes having them flop. Korie's grandfather and his brothers were born and raised poor, and they became some of the most successful and influential folks in our community. Her family owned the retail store I bought toys from as a kid. Her family was critical to the success of our business.

Growing up as poor as I did, I fell into a bit of a trap where I said, "We finally made money; let's make sure we don't lose any!" I didn't want to go back to the way I grew up, wondering: "If the nets run, are we going to eat fish, or are we going to eat bologna sandwiches?"

So the two of us make a great team. Sometimes I'll go with what my wife thinks, and sometimes we go with my gut feeling. Sometimes I'm more of the "out front" guy, and she is behind the scenes. Once we go, we go. All the way. If something works, WE win; if it doesn't, WE lose. No blame, no excuses. We also really believe in people and have a good sense of them. Sure, we've gotten burned a few times, but we invest in people.

Well, my wife sure came through for us that day in the TV meeting. Korie said flatly, "Well, I'm going to ask them to pay you."

I said, "Korie, don't mess this deal up. I've come this far!"

"Let's just ask them," Korie declared.

"Be careful," I warned.

Well, we went into the meeting, and all was going well. The sponsor and TV folks laid everything out and said they were ready to start filming in a month. All we had to do was sign on the dotted line.

Just as the meeting was about to end, Korie said, "One more thing."

Uh-oh, I thought. *Here it comes!*

Korie said, "I think you ought to pay the guys."

Oh shoot, oh, no! I thought to myself. *She's doing it, she's doing it! Korie, what are you thinking? Don't lose it, don't lose the deal!*

One of the TV people asked her, "How much were you thinking?"

Korie said, "Thirty thousand dollars each."

I was thinking, *Did she just say thirty thousand? The deal's over.*

But to my surprise, the TV guy said, "Sure, no problem." I immediately thought, *Shoot, we should have asked for fifty thousand!*

Once we got back home, I strolled into my parents' living room and said, "Guess what? We just got thirty thousand dollars from the Outdoor Channel!" The whole family jumped up and down and told me how brilliant I was. I stole the credit for that a little bit from Korie, to tell you the truth. But now I tell the world how great it is to have a brilliant spouse as your business partner, too.

That show, *Duck Commander,* developed a good following and got us some notoriety in the outdoor industry. Dad became kind of a cult figure in the hunting world. One day a few years later I got an email in the regular Duck Commander corporate in-box from TV producer Scott Gurney in Hollywood, and the email changed our life. He'd had some experience as an outdoorsman and had made a number of shows about the outdoors. Basically the email said, "Hey, I've watched your show. I think y'all have a huge show here that could be way bigger, and give me a holler."

I called him up and we started talking. We put together a "sizzle" reel, which is a tape of test footage of what the show would look like, and he showed it around to TV networks in New York and Hollywood. There was a lot of interest. A&E asked us for two pilot episodes. We knew A&E appealed to both men and women, and we figured we could hit a big audience and show people what we're all about. We just wanted to put out a positive show that the whole family could watch, and it didn't seem like there were a lot of those shows left on TV.

We shot the pilot episodes; they loved it, and A&E bought thirteen more episodes out of the gate. The first season of *Duck Dynasty* was fifteen episodes. We shot the pilots in the summer, and by that December we were in full production. We didn't stop for almost the next five years. The overall story of the show was about a family who stuck together through the power of love and faith, and about me trying to run a business in a normal way, in spite of constant goofball behavior and work avoidance by some of my employees. My employees were always foiling everything I had planned, but we stuck together. Somehow the formula clicked with viewers, and before long the show was a flat-out monster hit.

In our family business I've been skilled at motivating people, orchestrating the process, and getting the most out of my family. They're a really talented group of people, but it can be challenging as heck to keep them on task and motivated. I am pretty good at seeing a vision, setting the vision, and recruiting folks to help achieve the vision, and my father is good at it, too. Korie and her family are great at keeping their nose down and grinding out the real day-in, day-out work we need to be successful.

I could not have accomplished much without Korie's diligent work, intelligence, and companionship. Working this closely with your spouse can be challenging, but it can also be so rewarding. The trick is always knowing how to separate what's happening at work from what's happening at home. On some nights I'll be the

At work in my office. (Duck Commander)

one who wants to talk about work and she doesn't; other nights it will be just the opposite. Sometimes we have to remember it isn't about "me"; it's about "us." Together we've been successful beyond our wildest dreams.

Our family has always been a little bit odd and eccentric, shall we say, and my dad was eccentric enough to be the perfect American character on which to build an outdoor business brand. He was a marketing dream: a big, bearded, Bible-toting, backwoods preacher and storyteller, a hard-core hunter and fisherman who looked and talked like he stepped out of a movie about the early days of America. This guy wasn't just hunting on the weekends. He was out there hunting all day, every day, rain or shine. He was a dyed-in-the-wool original, the kind of guy who seemed like he could psych out a mountain lion in a staring contest and bite the heads off a dozen ducks while taking on a squad of killer beavers in hand-to-hand river combat. He is the real deal, authentic through and through, and even today he doesn't have a computer or a cell phone. If you want to get a hold of him, you've got to go down to his property and try to find out where he's at. His only professional goal was to make a living doing what he liked to do—hunt and fish—and have time to spend with his family.

I ran the business, and my dad was the inspiration and the symbol. It was a great combination. But until the A&E show premiered, we had no idea that we were building something that would become so huge. Pretty soon we branched out into more and more products and sponsorships and licensing deals and our business got bigger and bigger.

Maybe one of our business secrets is that we are an authentic American family business, and what you see is what you get. We're just like the people you see on our TV show. That's us! As a family, we work together, which is positive for the most part. Of course, we're not "Kumbaya" all the time—we argue and fight sometimes—but it's always in the spirit of love. We work together, we eat together, we pray together, we love each other, and our kids are respectful. If people see something positive and attractive in us, I think it's because of our faith in the Lord. He allows us to work together, and He gives us our core. I feel like the Lord has blessed us and put us here and allowed us to do this. He works in mysterious ways. I mean, who would've imagined that through Hollywood, you could have such a popular show that promoted these values? If you'd have told me a few years ago that there was going to be a network television show that was going to have a prayer at the end of each episode, I would've said, "There ain't no way!"

Through it all, I immersed myself in figuring out how the TV business worked, how merchandising and licensing businesses worked, how sponsorships worked, how best to build your brand, and more importantly, how to prepare for the business to plateau, which we knew it eventually would, since nearly all TV shows level off after a few years, and ours would be no exception. I put together deals with sponsors like shotgun companies and camouflage man-ufacturers, and with movers and shakers like former pro baseball players Adam LaRoche, Tom Martin, and Ryan Langerhans, and country music stars Jason Aldean and Luke Bryan. I executive-produced our TV shows. TV is a business, and I had to figure out how to monetize it while we could. We had a rocky moment in 2013 when Phil made controversial remarks in an interview, but our fan base stayed with us and we weathered the storm.

Together, as a family, we have accomplished great things in busi-ness, but I've had some business ideas that my dad said would never work.

When I took over the company, I went to Dad and said, "Look, we need to replace our VHS tapes with DVDs. They're way better. You can just put them in; you don't have to rewind them."

"Forget it," said Dad. "That's the worst idea I've ever heard. Every-body watches VHS!"

I explained, "Well, actually, Dad, that's changing. I don't think a lot of people are watching VHS anymore." He countered, "I watch VHS!"

I said, "I know you do, and you probably will for a long time, but most people are going over to the DVD format. We've got to do it."

"It'll never work!" he declared.

"Let's just try it," I said. I was right on that one.

Then one day I announced, "Dad, I think there's a day coming when people can shop online on the Internet. They'll see a picture, click it, give their credit card number, and order it. They don't even need to leave their computer."

"First," said Phil, "that's never going to take off, and second, that's a dumb idea for us. If people want to order a duck call, they'll pick up the phone and call."

I said, "Let's just try it and see!"

Dad told me to talk it over with Johnny Howard, my father-in-law, who owned the website URL for Duck Commander, duckcommander .com, and was holding on to it for future use by the family business. Johnny was a successful retail and publishing entrepreneur, and he saw the future of the Internet business early on. He'd also been helping my family over the years with business issues like bank loans, patents, and trademarks. My parents sometimes borrowed money from him to get them through the slow periods of the hunting business, which is very seasonal. Johnny and my family worked out a deal where he launched our online business in exchange for the money my parents owed him. We supplied the products and my father-in-law ran the website. Before long, it worked out beautifully. I guess I proved my dad wrong on that one, too!

Then I thought it would be a good idea if we had not just a DVD series but a regularly scheduled TV series to sell our duck calls. Dad replied flatly, "Of all the ideas you've had, that is the worst one. Mark my words, no one will watch us on TV!"

Once we had our TV show, I reminded him of this conversation from time to time—especially when we broke the record for the all-time highest number of TV viewers of a reality show!

But there was one idea I had that was definitely not a good one: I didn't want Uncle Si on the payroll, much less on any TV show. Early in my CEO days, I was tightening up, cutting costs and trimming any fat I could find in the business. My dad's brother Silas, or Uncle Si, was working for us, but technically he probably only worked eighty minutes in the average day. Three or four hours a day he spent sleeping in the office, which was my parents' living room couch. He'd spend much of the day sound asleep, snoring away and talking in his sleep, while I was on the phone and trying to conduct business meetings.

"Dad," I said, "look, I love Uncle Si, but we need to cut him loose. I can't work with this guy."

"You leave Si alone," said Dad. "He'll be fine." He stayed on the payroll.

Then when we started *Duck Dynasty* on A&E, I was against Si being on the show.

"We can't film Uncle Si," I insisted. "He doesn't make sense to anyone! He's so bizarre I don't even want anyone to see him." So it was my bright idea to film around him in the early shows and not show his face.

Well, I was way off on that one! He became a true superstar, one of the most vivid, funny, and downright weird characters in TV history. Nowadays he never misses a chance to let me know that he's the star of the show!

Looking back on our success, I realize that our goal of doing something family-friendly and godly was the culmination of years of struggle in our life and business and a few fortunate events. If Dad had finally left us, if my parents hadn't been able to stick together and work out their problems, there would have been no business. They just would have been another statistic of a broken marriage. We couldn't have done it without each other and without Korie and her family.

The *Duck Dynasty* show broke a bunch of ratings records on A&E and on cable television as a whole. In our third season, we debuted with 8.6 million viewers, the biggest audience in the twenty-nine-year history of the A&E network, which was double the audience from the previous year and second only to *The Walking Dead*. The next year, the fourth-season premiere drew 11.8 million viewers, the most viewers ever for a nonfiction cable series. The show caught on in TV markets around the world, too.

We've appeared on Jay Leno, Jimmy Kimmel, and Conan. Journalist Erik Hedegaard of *Men's Journal* wrote that in the show, we "get into nutty situations—racing lawn mowers, sucking bees out of a hive with a vacuum cleaner, getting busted while nighttime frog hunting on a private golf course—ending each episode with a sweet resolution, a family united in prayer and a meal, all while Willie, in voice-over, enumerates the sundry moral lessons to be derived." It was good clean fun, with no on-screen sex, no curse words, and no marriage breakups.

What's the business power of having a pop culture mega-hit TV show? It's like riding a rocket. In 2012, we sold about 120,000 duck calls. In 2013, the year *Duck Dynasty* premiered, we sold over 1.2 million, becoming by far the bestselling duck call brand in the U.S. We've also sold tons of Buck Commander hunting gear, bobbleheads, hats, T-shirts, apparel, books, food items, you name it. At the Walmart annual shareholders meeting that year, it was announced that their bestselling item of apparel for both men and women in 2014 was our T-shirt!

With the success of the *Duck Dynasty* show, it looked like we became a global phenomenon overnight, but we'd been laying the groundwork for years. We had tremendous growth, and it came really, really fast. It was chaotic, but it was great, and like a runaway freight train—all you can do is hang on! We tried to ramp up and be prepared for it, but it was almost impossible to predict how fast our business would grow. In the first couple of months of the show, our Duck Commander business grew something like 2,200 percent. Our website crashed, we lost orders, we were shipping twenty-four hours a day, and we fell 7,500 orders behind.

After the show first aired, the hunting season, the holidays, and the show all happened at the same time. It was crazy. Paying customers would watch our TV show, where they saw a bunch of goofball characters slacking off on the job. Then they'd call up our warehouse and ask for me, saying, "Hey, Willie, get those guys to work already! My order is late! Go in there and really make them work—I need my duck calls! It's not funny!" It took us months to catch up. We had no idea we would grow so big and so fast.

One of the hardest things for us was running our company while we were in the middle of filming the show. It was basically two different full-time jobs happening at the same time, with hundreds of details to attend to each day. It just got crazier and crazier. But our staff did well, and we definitely prepared them as much as we could. Those days we had about fifty full-time people working for us, but around Christmas we ramped up to around one hundred. We still made all of our duck calls here, but we had to have an outside company handle the shipping for us. We just couldn't keep up with all the growth of that by ourselves.

Off hunting with the family. (Duck Commander)

Our warehouse in West Monroe, Louisiana, has become a regional tourist destination, and people line up to take pictures and visit our company store. They come from all across the United States, Canada, and even overseas. One day, close to two thousand people jammed into the parking lot outside our warehouse. We had to buy extra land around the property to make room for all the tour buses and overflow parking!

In 2014, Duck Commander served as the title sponsor of the NASCAR Sprint Cup Series Duck Commander 500 race in Fort Worth, and college football's Independence Bowl, held each year in Shreveport, which was called the Duck Commander Independence Bowl. In 2017, we held the grand opening of Willie's Duck Diner, a family restaurant in our hometown that features home-cooked recipes by Miss Kay and Phil. The restaurant's slogans are "Where Saying Grace Is Encouraged," "Come as a Guest, Leave as Family," and "Family, Faith, Food." I've just always loved cooking. We had thought about opening a restaurant for years. I love it. I'm there almost every day. I have a room in the back where I eat. I go there and cook sometimes. I was there last Saturday working on this new huge bologna sandwich I'm creating for the menu.

In the spring of 2017, we aired the eleventh and final season of *Duck Dynasty*. To tell you the truth, I'm just amazed at how long it went and how big the show got. For a couple of years there it was pretty out of control.

Our children have become entrepreneurs, too. Our daughter Rebecca has a clothing boutique with Korie called Duck & Dressing right here in Monroe, Louisiana. Rebecca has done all the buying herself and has opened an online store as well, at Duck andDressing.com. Our daughter Sadie has a "daddy-approved" formal dress line that's doing real well, and a successful touring event called Live Original. John Luke and Sadie have both published their own books. They got paid to be on the show, and they both do speaking events. They're making a lot more money than I did at their ages!

Success is how you perceive it. For the Robertson family, we redefined what success means, beyond just worldly goods and riches.

For us, success means you can make a living off hunting and fishing, and being together. To us, that is success.

We do what we love, spend lots of time together, and have made some money. For us, success at work means you can show up to work with no dress code, you can grow your beard as long as you want, you can grow out your hair, you don't even have to bathe regularly.

That's success in our book. It's all how you look at things. I think we are the most successful people ever!

I am an American entrepreneur.

I am the mom-and-pop team who owns the corner grocery store, the old man who shines your shoes, the billionaire who started a megabusiness from scratch, and the twelve-year-old girl who runs a sidewalk lemonade stand while dreaming of opening up her own restaurant someday.

I am the refugee from a faraway land who yearns to achieve the American dream by starting up a small business, being my own boss, putting food on the family table, and giving my kids a shot at a decent life in freedom.

I am the businessman who saved the American Revolution at the moment it was about to fail—by loaning George Washington enough money to get his troops food, guns, and ammo.

I am the grandmother who sells cosmetics to her neighbors out of a display case in her living room.

I am the Native American artisan who sells handcrafted treasures inspired by my ancestors to tourist shops and art galleries, and I am their children, who are destined to create new products, new companies, and new jobs of their own.

I am the Silicon Valley husband-and-wife team who starts a business and changes the world, one click at a time.

I am the Latino immigrant family who runs a fruit-and-vegetable stand on the side of the road and whose sons and daughters will grow up to change the world by launching their own businesses.

I am the African American accountants, insurance brokers, funeral parlor directors, and barber and beauty shop owners who struggled and thrived by serving our own people in the darkest days of segregation. I am their granddaughters and grandsons, the founders and CEOs of companies large and small. I am the woman small-business owner, the Asian American entrepreneur, and the military veteran entrepreneur.

I am the fisherman who drags around tubs of fresh-caught crawfish in the hopes that a market will buy them for the aluminum container at the front of the store—so my own family can have enough cash this week to eat square meals instead of bologna sandwiches.

I am the go-getter who outthinks, outmaneuvers, and outhustles the competition and eventually buys them up, creating more jobs, more products, and more value in the process. I am the rural farmer, the suburban accountant, and the country doctor.

I've started businesses in my brain, in my parents' garage, on the back of paper napkins and plates, and around the kitchen table. Lots of times my own family has provided the muscle, the brains, and the cash to get me started and keep me going. I work around the clock to stock the shelves, balance the books, and make the customers happy, and sometimes I'll give them an item or two on credit when times are tough. I've had some real tough times myself, but I am blessed to live in the United States of America, where you can always find a second chance and a helping hand, especially if you work hard, love your neighbor, and stay true to yourself and whatever divine inspiration guides you.

I am the railroad and steamship operators, blacksmiths, manufacturers, construction contractors, freelancers, architects, and suppliers who helped build the biggest economy the world has ever seen.

I am the countless American men and women, young and old, from every race, religion, and place on earth, who borrowed, sweated, fell on our faces more than once, had doors slammed on our noses, had ideas fizzle, bank accounts dry up, and products fail, but kept on trying, till one day we achieved success.

I am the self-made men and women who forged the West, powered the Industrial Revolution, helped build our cities and factories, created the American middle class, and opened the doors of the Information Age.

I am one of the legions of American entrepreneurs who made this country what it is.

In the pages that follow, you'll meet an amazing bunch of characters who have helped forge our nation.

In the distant past, they established links of commerce across the nations of Native America. In the colonial and post-independence eras, as merchants, tradespeople, and small business owners, they laid the business foundations of a young nation that rocketed onto the world stage.

In the post–Civil War corporate era of Big Business, they rode the new horizons of telegraphy, railroads, and electric power to build the world's biggest economy.

In the era of the global consumer that unfolded from World War II through the present day, they pioneered astonishing new businesses and technologies and inspired the world.

These men and women were every kind of personality, and their families came from every part of the planet.

But they had a few things in common—they were bold, tough, and resilient. They were dreamers and doers. They often failed, but they kept on trying, through incredible trials and impossible odds.

They were all American entrepreneurs. They are the action heroes of business history.

And this is our story.

CHAPTER 1

THE FOUNDING ENTREPRENEURS

What kept them going was the knowledge that everything on the earth has a purpose . . . and every person a mission.

—Mourning Dove, Native American author

Like most epic American stories, this one starts with the first American peoples—the Native Americans.

They invented the earliest forms of American commerce and entrepreneurship. And they had plenty of risks to manage and obstacles to overcome, like brutal weather, rough transportation, and huge distances to markets, just to name a few.

Before the Europeans landed on this continent, there were countless thousands of entrepreneurial men and women among the Native Americans, but due to the lack of written records we'll never know most of their names. When the first French, Dutch, English, Spanish, Scandinavians, and other Europeans first touched shore on North America to seek fame and fortune, they stumbled onto a continent of vast, elaborate, and interconnected commercial trading networks among the native peoples, networks that had thrived for many centuries.

Some tribes were hunters, some were farmers, some fished, and some did all three, but many of them had one thing in common—they collected, traded, and sold goods to other tribes in trading patterns that linked many of the continent's peoples together, in effect, into an international commercial network of suppliers, growers, artisans, traders, brokers, sellers, and repeat customers. From the Pacific and the Rocky Mountains to the Great Plains, Southwest, Canada, and the Atlantic coast, the Native Americans trafficked in flint, knives, arrowheads, animal products, vegetables, copper, marine shells, pottery, and countless other types of goods.

For many centuries, these trading patterns flourished across the northern and southern Plains and far beyond. Thirteen-thousand-year-old flint points cut from quarries in Texas have been discovered in eastern New Mexico, hundreds of miles away. Quarried stone from near Yellowstone in Wyoming made it all the way to the Ohio River Valley around the year 200 CE. Seashells from the Mojave tribe were traded for buffalo hides from tribes of the southern Plains, and the Hohokam tribe in present-day Arizona acted as the middlemen. Historians Emory Dean Keoke and Kay Marie Porterfield wrote that "by between 500 and 200 BCE, North American Indians had established a vital network of trade."

The Native Americans were so entrepreneurial that they even put on their own trade fairs. The land that is present-day Wyoming, for example, was home to the Shoshone, a tribe that staged a regular regional trade fair called the "Shoshone Rendezvous."

This was a big sales and trading event located in the river valleys of southwestern Wyoming west of the South Pass, and it served as a commercial link between the tribes of upper Missouri and those of the Rocky Mountains and Pacific Coast. "We think that the Shoshone were among the great Indian traders in the interior West," said Dudley Gardner, professor emeritus of history and political science at Western Wyoming Community College. Crow In-

Product testing in the field: Snake [Shoshone] Indians Testing Bows, *by Alfred Jacob Miller. (The Walters Art Museum)*

dians came to the rendezvous from the northern Plains; the Nez Perce, Shoshone, and Flatheads came from the Plateau and Great Basin; and Utes came from the Southwest. They all brought goods to trade.

The Shoshone were especially famous for their hunting products, according to Maine-born trapper Osborne Russell, who worked in the Rocky Mountains fur trade in the 1830s, particularly "the manufacture of very powerful bows from the horn of a mountain sheep," which were "beautifully wrought from Sheep, Buffaloe and Elk horns secured with Deer and Elk sinews and ornamented with porcupine quills and generally about 3 feet long."

The business of Native America, you could say, was largely business in the form of trade and barter. Historian Samuel Western explained, "The Shoshone, it seems, traded with everyone, including northwest and southwest tribes. Other Rocky Mountain and central Plains tribes also took goods to the Missouri River valley to trade for corn, pumpkin, squash and native-grown tobacco. Their primary trading partners were the Mandan and Hidatsa of what is now North Dakota and, to a lesser degree, the Arikara, who were located north of the Grand River in present South Dakota. In his journal, William Clark of Corps of Discovery fame noted that the Arapaho conducted business with the Mandan, while the Cheyenne and Sioux traded with the Arikara."

In the 1400s and 1500s, when Europeans started showing up on the eastern Atlantic horizon in fishing boats and bigger ships, few if any of them knew that the Norsemen had tried and failed before them—due to their small numbers and inability to establish friendly relations and trade links with the local native peoples—to settle in what is now Newfoundland around the year 1000. The new European visitors brought their own faiths and business ambitions with them, plus new technologies and products to sell and trade. Sometimes they brought disease, alcohol, overwhelming firepower, and sneaky business practices with them, too.

At first, the wary Native Americans held the Europeans off and literally kept them at arm's length. Early-sixteenth-century Italian explorer Giovanni da Verrazzano wrote, "If we wanted to trade with them for some of their things, they would come to the seashore on some rocks where the breakers were most violent while we remained on the little boat, and they sent us what they wanted to give on a rope, continually shouting to us not to approach the land." Eventually, of course, the Europeans landed, pushed far inland, set up trading posts, and made deals with the locals in exchange for guns and ammo, horses, clothes, cooking utensils, and lots of other goods.

A key part of this sophisticated trading network was the native middlemen, who linked their own trading centers together over vast distances. The Cheyenne were brokers between hunting tribes of the southern Plains and tribes in upper Missouri, and they shuttled European-sourced guns and horses to both. The Plains Crees carried manufactured goods to upper Missouri from Canadian fur traders and brought back corn and horses. In the southern Plains, the Apaches competed with the Comanche and the Jumano tribes for the profitable middleman business between the Pueblos and the Wichitas. Depending on the product and distance involved, markups could range from 100 percent to 300 percent or more.

The arrival of horses in large numbers meant Native American tribes could, for a time, hunt and trade much more effectively and expand their trading territory. "The high tide in typical Plains culture seems to have come in the eighteenth and nineteenth centuries," anthropologist Clark Wissler wrote in a 1914 essay. "This was the era of trade, yet the horse increased the economic prosperity and created individual wealth with certain degrees of luxury and leisure; also it traveled ever ahead of the white trade and white trader." Horses provided Native American commerce with a quantum leap in mobility and the ability to carry trading goods far and wide.

Corn was an especially prized commodity. "For the Sioux, corn was more important than blood," wrote James P. Ronda, professor of western American history at the University of Tulsa, and in August, "as in every other late summer and early fall, Sioux bands flocked to the Arikara towns, bringing meat, fat, and hides from the plains and European-manufactured goods from the Dakota Rendezvous."

For the Europeans, America was often the target of grand money-making schemes and entrepreneurial ventures. Christopher Columbus came in search of new trade routes to Asia for tea and spices. The doomed early-seventeenth-century explorer Henry Hudson was on assignment for the Dutch East India Company to try to find the Northwest Passage, which everyone hoped would become

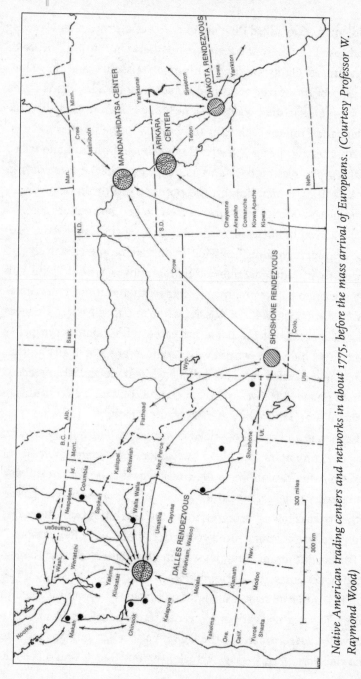

Native American trading centers and networks in about 1775, before the mass arrival of Europeans. (Courtesy Professor W. Raymond Wood)

a business superhighway, when he was set adrift in a small boat by his mutinous crew.

While the Pilgrims journeyed to America mainly to escape religious persecution in England, it was an entrepreneurial venture, too—they planned to launch a fishing business in the New World to pay the bills. They were so inept at first that the Native Americans had to rescue them more than once. Eventually, though, the New England Puritans and their descendants became so good at fishing and shipping that they ushered in a two-century-long economic boom. No wonder there's a big carved wooden sculpture of an Atlantic codfish hanging in a place of honor in the Massachusetts State House.

Many of the English American settlements and colonies, like Massachusetts Bay, Plymouth, and Virginia, were set up by for-profit corporations and were expected to turn a profit. Founder William Penn saw Pennsylvania as a "Holy Experiment" for Quakers to thrive in peace and religious freedom, but he expected a return on his investment, too, declaring flatly, "I want some recompense for my troubles."

Back then, outside of major security issues on the frontier with the increasingly resentful native tribes, America was a great place to start a business, with its seemingly unlimited resources and free market. America was not shackled by feudal systems, aristocrats, entrenched guilds, or dug-in monopolies and cronyism like much of Europe was for many centuries, so the settlers and colonists had an even playing field and unlimited prospects. At least in theory.

The for-profit Jamestown settlement, a venture launched in 1607 by the Virginia Company, was a joint-stock company, a new kind of investment vehicle meant to limit risk and liability for large groups of investors. Historian John Steele Gordon wrote, "By limiting liability, corporations greatly increased the number of people who could dare to become entrepreneurs by pooling their resources

t' Fort nieuw Amſterdam op de Manhatans

From this spot, a nation of entrepreneurs was symbolically born. New Amsterdam, later to become New York City, was the greatest incubator of commerce the world had ever seen. (T'Fort Nieuw Amsterdam op de Manhatans, 1651, New York Public Library)

while avoiding the possibility of ruin. Thus the corporation was one of the great inventions of the Renaissance, along with printing, double entry bookkeeping, and the full-rigged ship."

But the Jamestown entrepreneur-settlers made nearly every mistake in the book—instead of planting crops, they prospected for gold, of which Virginia has none; they tried and failed to launch a glassmaking business; and so on. Many of them starved, and conflict erupted with the Native Americans. By 1618, the time the West Indian tobacco crop took off as a highly profitable business that made Virginia rich, it was too late for the Virginia Company, which had already, as many entrepreneurs do, gone broke.

Modern America got a big burst of entrepreneurial mojo from the energy and cash that flowed in and out of a spot today known as New York City. And the DNA of that city came from the Dutch.

New York was settled in 1624 as "New Amsterdam" by the Dutch West India Company, a national joint-stock company. It was a trading post, with beaver pelts the hot commodity. For the hyper-entrepreneurial Dutch settlers and merchants, profit was the name of the game.

Fur was like gold to a seventeenth-century merchant. As living standards in Europe rose, fur products like hats, coats, collars, muffs, and capes became fashion essentials. Beaver hair was considered the filet mignon of fur, thanks to a unique product feature: beneath the glossy outer layer was another layer of thick, luxuriant short hairs that were turned into felt for warm, superpremium hats. Overall, the business was a good deal for both sides—the Dutch swapped items that the natives wanted, like kettles, axes, needles, and wool, for the precious fur. Tens of thousands of the lucrative pelts were shipped across the Atlantic to European markets.

The Dutch in New Amsterdam didn't even bother building a chapel or a church for seventeen years—if you wanted to worship, you found a spot inside the big fort. Everyone was too busy making deals. And carousing—at one point, the making and drinking of alcohol accounted for fully one-quarter of the city's real estate.

"The Dutch founded New Amsterdam for the sole purpose of making a buck," wrote historian John Steele Gordon. "And the Dutch in this period were very, very good at doing so. The Netherlands was rapidly becoming the wealthiest country in Europe at this point, and it had the most-developed banks, stock market and insurance companies." This new Dutch trading outpost on the edge of the wilderness was a hardworking, hard-partying city. In 1647, incoming governor Peter Stuyvesant described it as "more a mole-hill than a fortress," whose inhabitants had "grown very wild and loose in their morals."

The city of New Amsterdam was a freewheeling hodgepodge of languages and ethnicities—in the 1640s, a French priest reported that at least eighteen languages were being spoken by the town's fewer than one thousand people. By then the city's entrepreneurs were already trading with customers in Europe, Africa, and the Caribbean. The city "didn't care what people there thought about God," according to writer John Sullivan. "It cared about beavers. It cared very, very passionately about beavers. If you didn't get in the way of the beaver-pelt trade with Europe, you were an honorary New Netherlander."

By 1664 the island was a high-profit entrepreneurial cash machine for the Dutch. By then, the city boasted residents from a number of European nationalities, African slaves, some free blacks, and religious minorities including Quakers, Anabaptists, and Jews. This diversity and tolerance may have been the "secret sauce" that nourished the phenomenal growth of New York, and America, ever since. Having a magnificent harbor helped a lot, too.

Suddenly, in the summer of 1664, the party came to an end. Four warships belonging to Great Britain, the Netherlands' chief commercial rival, appeared in the harbor and demanded a surrender, their cannons pointed at the thriving settlement of nine thousand people. The Dutch governor Peter Stuyvesant, who commanded virtually no military force of his own, wisely gave up without any blood being spilled. The British moved in and renamed the area New York, but left much of its freewheeling, deal-making character in place.

Over the next three centuries, the little island, blessed with the entrepreneurial spirit of its long-forgotten Dutch founders, mixed an astonishing diversity of human capital packed into one of the prime business locations on the planet—and became the greatest commercial incubator the world had ever seen. "If what made America great was its ingenious openness to different cultures," wrote author Russell Shorto, "the small triangle of land at the southern tip of Manhattan Island is the birthplace of that idea: This island city would become the first multiethnic, upwardly mobile society on America's shores, a prototype of the kind of society that would be duplicated throughout the country and around the world." By 1774, reported visitor John Adams, the New Yorker's rapid-fire style of street talk had already appeared: "They talk loud, very fast, and all together. If they ask you a Question, before you can utter 3 Words of your Answer, they will break out upon you, again—and talk away."

In 1818, New York started the first regularly scheduled shipping service to Europe, which triggered a boom in transatlantic commerce. Seven years later, the Erie Canal connected the port city with the flourishing American Midwest. In 1825, Governor DeWitt Clinton envisioned that New York would become "the emporium of commerce, the seat of manufacture, the focus of great moneyed operations and the concentrating point of vast, disposable and accumulating capital."

How right he was. Entrepreneurs and investors launched banks and insurance companies. New York became the capital of meatpacking, textiles, finance, fashion, advertising, communications, and the media—and speed-talking! It was, in the words of Oliver Wendell Holmes, the poet and father of a Supreme Court justice, the "tongue that is licking up the cream of commerce and finance of a continent."

New York never forgot its earliest moneymaking roots in the fur trade. Today the city's official seal features two trading partners—a Native American and a Dutch settler—and a friendly beaver.

Before long, the thriving American colonists got fed up with British interference in their business, mainly in the form of increasingly excessive taxes, and they decided to give them the boot. The American merchants, shopkeepers, artisans, farmers, hunters, and workers were, overall, making tons of money, and naturally they

The art of the deal, Manhattan-style: Peter Stuyvesant, governor of New Amsterdam, negotiates a deal with Native Americans, 1660. The Dutch merchants, traders, and entrepreneurs were so busy wheeling and dealing that they didn't build a church for seventeen years. (Getty Images/Alamy)

wanted to hold on to their fair share. "By the time the 13 colonies declared independence, they were, after only 169 years, the richest place on earth per capita," wrote historian John Steele Gordon. As he put it, "No wonder the British fought so hard to suppress the rebellion." The Americans were so prosperous and well fed that on average the Continental Army troops were fully two inches taller than the British enemy troops they fought against.

It was time for America's greatest early entrepreneur to take the stage, and take charge.

He was a tall, powerfully built war veteran, farmer, horseman, slave owner, and experienced frontiersman who hailed from the state of Virginia, where he launched one of America's first and biggest diversified agrobusinesses.

He was the original "buy American-made" man, too. When he was sworn in as president on April 30, 1789, he wanted to encourage American entrepreneurship in a time when imported British goods dominated the fashion market—so he insisted on wearing a plain brown suit made with cloth woven in Hartford, Connecticut.

He went by the name of George Washington.

CHAPTER 2

THE REBEL ENTREPRENEURS

Building the national prosperity is my first and my only aim.

—George Washington

On August 11, 1781, the two greatest entrepreneurs in America held the fate of the nation in their hands.

General George Washington was commander in chief of the Continental Army, and Robert Morris, who was acting as his de facto chief financial officer, was a Philadelphia-based import-export mogul who was believed to be the richest man in the American colonies.

The two men faced a crisis that is common to the founders of many start-up ventures—they were burning through their operating cash faster than they could raise new funds. They couldn't meet their payroll of nearly ten thousand employees (soldiers), and they couldn't feed or supply them, either.

They held an emergency summit meeting at Washington's military camp on the banks of the Hudson River at Dobbs Ferry, New York. Morris raced there from Philadelphia on a fast horse.

As usual, former agribusinessman Washington was terribly worried. He was in his seventh year of commanding the American

Continental Army, a motley collection of troops with mismatched uniforms and weapons who tended to lose many more battles than they won, sometimes went without shoes, food, and pay, and occasionally threatened to stage a mass desertion or even mutiny. They'd fought, escaped, harassed, and worn down the British Army to a stalemate, and now Washington prepared to deliver a death blow to the enemy army's main force, at that point comfortably ensconced in New York City, just two dozen miles to the south.

But as usual, Washington was running out of cash.

To fight a war, you've got to have money, and lots of it, and Washington noted that "in modern wars the longest purse may chiefly determine the event." But as soon as money arrived for the army, it went out, and Washington and his men constantly had to beg, borrow, and scrounge from state governors, merchants, and legislatures to stay afloat as a fighting force. Time and time again, financial crises threatened to collapse the Continental Army, and the dream of American freedom. At this point in the summer of 1781, Washington had thousands of allied French troops camped nearby ready to fight alongside the Americans, but by now the French war chest in North America was nearly empty, too.

"We are at the end of our tether," Washington wrote that April, and "now or never our deliverance must come."

Before he went to war against the British, George Washington was, like Robert Morris and many of their fellow revolutionaries, an entrepreneur. As one writer put it, in 1776 small business was the "backbone of the nation, and the vanguard of the revolution was shopkeepers, merchants, farmers, and small exporter-importers who were tapped into the growing North American trade with the Caribbean and Europe." America was "the first country in the world in which business people got involved in the political system," observed Edwin Perkins, history professor at the University of Southern California.

The American Revolution was, in large part, a rebellion of entrepreneurs, many of them concentrated in fast-growing commercial centers like Newport, Rhode Island; Boston; New York City; Philadelphia; and Charleston, South Carolina; and satellite port cities like Norfolk, Virginia; New London, Connecticut; Savannah, Georgia; and Wilmington, Delaware. "From the earliest American settlements, colonial commerce was the province of diverse groups of settlers," wrote historian Carl E. Prince. "Puritans in Boston, Pilgrims at Plymouth Plantation, Quakers in Philadelphia, Dutch in New Amsterdam (New York City), and Scots in the Chesapeake were all part of the colonial American merchant establishment."

Some of the earliest American small businesses often had simple survival as their goal, and were based on barter and community cooperation and trading exchanges between households, while others were more geared to profit and return on investment. Journalists Christopher Conte and Albert Karr wrote: "By the 18th century, regional patterns of development had become clear: the New England colonies relied on ship-building and sailing to generate wealth; plantations (many using slave labor) in Maryland, Virginia, and the Carolinas grew tobacco, rice, and indigo; and the middle colonies of New York, Pennsylvania, New Jersey, and Delaware shipped general crops and furs. Except for slaves, standards of living were generally high—higher, in fact, than in England itself. Because English investors had withdrawn, the field was open to entrepreneurs among the colonists."

Tragically, much of the colonial economy and its prosperity were powered by the shipment of New World goods like rum, molasses, and sugar to Africa, in exchange for kidnapped human slaves, who were packed on hellish ships and transported for sale in America in the gruesome process of the Middle Passage. Multitudes of innocent souls perished. In Africa, local entrepreneurs helped manage the mass kidnappings, and in America, local entrepreneurs cashed in on the selling of human flesh to end users. By the time the American Revolution erupted, there were nearly 700,000 slaves in the colonies.

Many of the fifty-six signers of the Declaration of Independence were self-made businessmen. Samuel Adams ran the family brewery business in Massachusetts before getting into politics. Philip Livingston from New York was a merchant, importer, philanthropist, and founder of the New York Chamber of Commerce. John Hancock, president of the Continental Congress, made one of the biggest fortunes in the colonies through his family's merchant-shipping business in Massachusetts. Another Founding Father, George Taylor, ran a successful ironworks in Pennsylvania, and another one, Roger Sherman, started off as a shoemaker and shop-keeper.

Benjamin Franklin was a printer, publisher, and early American media mogul who franchised his printing shops all the way from New England to the Caribbean, and championed the American postal service so he and other entrepreneurs could have a distribution system. He was so successful in making money that he was able to retire at age forty-two, exactly halfway through his life, and devote the rest of his years to diplomacy and politics.

Among Franklin's many business insights were: "Remember that time is money," "Credit is money," and the way to wealth "depends chiefly on two words, *industry* and *frugality*." Franklin was a highly creative, disciplined business manager who "was not only one of the first, great entrepreneurs in colonial America, but in many respects he was the archetype of every American manager that followed him," in the words of historian Blaine McCormick.

And then there was colonial businessman George Washington. He was, according to military historian Edward Lengel, "a crafty and diligent entrepreneur," and his executive skills as a military leader and president were forged in his earlier career in business.

He grew up in a single-parent household, did not receive a formal education, and turned a modest family inheritance into what was one of the greatest estates in America at the time he died. "He began early, employing principles imbibed from his parents, family, and friends to build his fortune," Lengel noted. "His first income came from the salary he earned as a surveyor. Saving and investing, he used this to purchase land and grow tobacco. A modest inheritance helped to establish him as a substantial landowner and gifted him with an estate—Mount Vernon—that became his country seat. Marrying Martha Dandridge Custis, a wealthy widow who would become his devoted partner, George acquired the wherewithal to begin operations on an exalted scale."

Washington started off learning the real estate business at age sixteen as an apprentice land surveyor. When he inherited the Mount Vernon plantation, the estate was two thousand acres, and through deal-making and real estate speculation, Washington expanded it to eight thousand acres at the time of his death. Over the years, Washington expanded his business operations into a full-scale industrial village. According to historian Harlow Giles Unger, Washington grew "a relatively small tobacco plantation into a diversified agro-industrial enterprise that stretched over thousands of acres and included, among other for-profit ventures, a fishery, meat processing facility, textile and weaving manufactory, distillery, gristmill, smithy [blacksmith shop], brickmaking kiln, cargo-carrying schooner, and, of course, endless fields of grain." In 1785, with the backing of the Virginia and Maryland legislatures, Washington launched America's first trade development company, the Potomac Company, a partnership of private and public capital that built canals along the river. Like many land-rich plantation owners, however, Washington had liquidity problems and was often cash-poor.

As an entrepreneur, Washington was a hard-core micromanager.

N.W. VIEW OF THE MANSION OF GEORGE WASHINGTON,
MOUNT VERNON.

George Washington's estate at Mount Vernon. (New York Public Library)

He was in constant motion around his estate, checking in on every little detail of his diversified operation, huddling up with his overseers and field managers, rolling up his sleeves to dig soil or tinker with a new piece of equipment. He demanded a constant flow of precise reports and information—numbers, prices, temperatures, measurements, and quantities. Writing in 1965, historian James Thomas Flexner described the hustle and bustle of Washington's life as an entrepreneur: He "was up before dawn, forever on horseback supervising the plantation. In addition to growing tobacco, he had to make the whole operation as far as possible self-sustaining. Pork had to be produced by the thousands of pounds (6,632 in 1762), Indian corn raised to feed the Negroes, fish extracted from the Potomac to be eaten fresh by all and salted down in barrels for the hands. Fruit trees were grafted, cider bottled. Liquor supplied slaves with some incentive; after buying as much as 56 gallons at a time, Washington established his own still, which could in a day change 144 gallons of cider into 30 of applejack. An old mill—

which Washington always referred to as 'she'—had to be supplied with water to turn the wheels, fed with grain, and propped up, as she was very shaky in storms. His own carpenters erected the farm buildings and kept them in repair; his blacksmith was so busy he needed helpers. The mill and the artisans also worked for neighbors. Washington sometimes acted as retailer for his tenants, exchanging goods he had imported from England for tobacco."

To improve efficiency, cut labor, and boost productivity, Washington experimented with new crops and rotation schemes, plows, pumps, seeds, livestock breeding, fertilizers, and tools. He was a technology buff, and scoured the newspapers for the latest gadgets and innovations from overseas. He gave his employees lots of pep talks, sharing nuggets of wisdom like, "Nothing should be bought that can be made," "A penny saved, is a penny got," "The man who does not estimate time as money will forever miscalculate," and "System in all things is the soul of business."

One of Washington's key early decisions as an entrepreneur was to cut his losses and switch his product line by stopping the harvest of Mount Vernon's heavily taxed and soil-damaging tobacco crop and switching to wheat. "By 1766," wrote Mount Vernon director of restoration Dennis J. Pogue, "the disappointingly low prices that he was receiving in return for his tobacco harvest convinced Washington that he would be better off devoting the labor of his workers to producing other commodities that had a more dependable payoff." Washington manufactured his own branded grocery store product—packaged flour, featuring his name right on the label as a sign of quality. The Mount Vernon flour mill was an advanced, three-story operation that manufactured some 275,000 pounds of flour per year, which were sold throughout the thirteen colonies and exported to Europe, too.

Every spring, during the six-week fishing season, Washington operated a profitable commercial fishing operation on the Potomac

River, which ran right past his property. He once explained to a friend that the river was "well supplied with various kinds of fish at all seasons of the year; and in the Spring with the greatest profusion of Shad, Herring, bass, Carp, Perch, Sturgeon." He added, "Several valuable fisheries appertain to the estate; the whole shore in short is one entire fishery." Washington dispatched teams of slaves with rowboats and big nets into the river and they worked round the clock harvesting up to 1.5 million fish, including herring and shad, which were salted and packed in barrels. The unwanted fish scraps were used as fertilizer for his wheat crop. With Mount Vernon as his business and social headquarters, Washington rose steadily in Virginia and national politics until taking charge of the colonial military rebellion in 1775.

The man Washington was to meet with on August 11, 1781, Robert Morris, was born in England, and in 1747, at age thirteen, he moved to Philadelphia, where he went to work in the office of Willing, Morris & Company, an import-export company that became one of the top three wealthiest commercial firms in the American colonies.

By age twenty-three, Morris was showing such promise as a commodities trader that he was made a junior partner, and soon he was a fast-rising star in local politics and social affairs. Eventually he rose to become full owner of the company. At his office on the Philadelphia waterfront, in the days before a commercial banking system, Morris juggled loans, bills of exchange, lines of credit, and shipping schedules in a dizzying symphony of international finance. He did business with buyers and sellers in India, the Caribbean, the Middle East, Spain, and Italy, making him a true global capitalist.

The sheer head-scratching complexity of how Morris conducted business was explained by writer John Dos Passos in this way: "Since American merchants had to deal with the fluctuating pa-

Early American mega-entrepreneur Robert Morris, largely forgotten to-day, was a financial wizard who bailed out the revolution with his own cash and credit at least three times. Of all the revolutionary leaders, George Washington liked him the most. He had it all, including Amer-ica's biggest fortune—until the day it all blew up and he barricaded himself in his house with a shotgun. (Painting by Robert Edge Pine; photograph by cliff1066/Flickr)

per currencies of thirteen separate provinces, transactions were basically by barter. Morris would trade so many hogsheads of to-bacco estimated in Maryland paper currency, say, for a shipload of molasses in St. Kitts estimated in pounds sterling. In default of other currency, bills of lading would have to pass as a medium of exchange, so that half the time he would be using the bill of lading for the shipload of molasses to meet an obligation for a shipment of straw hats held by a merchant in Leghorn. Bills of exchange circulated that could be met part in cash, part in commodities, part in credit. Due to the slowness in communications, years might go by before any particular transaction was completed and liquidated. Add to that the hazards of wartime captures and confiscations, and the custom, so as not to have all their eggs in one basket, of a number of shippers sharing in a shipload of goods." Are you confused yet? Morris explained to a friend a simple truth: "The commonest things become intricate where money has anything to do with them."

With the dangers of piracy, shipwrecks, and long-delayed payments, it was a high-stakes, high-risk way to do business, and as Morris's biographer Charles Rappleye explained, "He spread his stock among various business partners, and in ships plying the sea, so that any given moment might find him flush or strapped, calling in debts or laying large sums out in new ventures. Morris was rich in resources, but rarely in cash." His financial juggling and manipulations were so complex that even he may have sometimes had trouble keeping track of it all. According to one account, "He carried the art of kiting checks and bills of exchange to a high degree of perfection. The fact that sailing ships took so long to cross the Atlantic made it possible to meet an obligation in Philadelphia with a note drawn on some Dutch banker in Amsterdam. That would give him three months to find negotiable paper with which he could appease the Dutchman when he threatened to protest the note."

Before the war started, the gregarious Morris savored his life as one of America's first super-rich citizens. He married a beautiful woman from a respected Maryland family and threw lavish parties at both his town house on Philadelphia's Front Street and his country house across the Schuylkill River, where he kept an impressive fruit-and-vegetable garden and greenhouse. He explained to a friend that "mixing business and pleasure" makes them "useful to each other." According to biographer Rappleye, Morris had a personality as striking as his business success: "He was tall. He was wide. Philadelphia was a great place for feasting and he was often the guy throwing the banquet. He was at home with stevedores as much as he was with fellow merchants and traders." In the springtime, Morris served the finest fresh asparagus and strawberries; in summer it was apricots and plums; and autumn was the season for pears and hothouse grapes. He employed a French chef who served with porcelain settings and silver tableware, and guests knew that the claret and Madeira and roast meats served at Morris's shindigs were of the finest quality.

Like many Americans, Morris grew increasingly angry at British actions that hurt colonial business, and the revolution that he was to help mastermind was itself largely based on a nasty, ongoing business dispute.

Americans wanted unrestricted free enterprise, and the simple ability to make money and keep it, but starting in 1764, the British tightened the screws on American business. They aggressively enforced the old Navigation Acts, which had been around for a century but were largely ignored by the Americans. They imposed the Sugar Act, the Stamp Act, and the Townshend duties, all of which strangled American profits, and the Intolerable Acts of 1774, which based British troops in American port cities, dissolved the troublesome Lower House of the Massachusetts legislature, and shut down the port of Boston. It's little wonder that the First Continental Congress of 1774–75 launched a full-scale boycott of British imports, and before you knew it, the ultimate business dispute broke out—bullets were flying.

George Washington's executive skills as a military commander and president were sharpened by his first career—as an entrepreneur. (Washington's Retreat at Long Island, engraved by J. C. Armytage after an illustration by Michael Wageman)

Afraid of the impact that a break with Great Britain would have on business, and doubtful of the Americans' chances of beating the British Army, Morris, now a member of the Continental Congress, signed the Declaration of Independence only reluctantly, but once the war was on, he was totally on board with the rebel cause. He orchestrated the smuggling of gunpowder from Europe and the Caribbean to the Continental Army, and used his wide international business contacts as a spy network to collect intelligence on British military moves. Morris coordinated a secret arms trade with Europe to supply the American army. He financed a fleet of privateers, ships that ran the British blockades to deliver aid to the colonies.

Morris came to the Dobbs Ferry summit meeting armed with one of the most powerful weapons of war—a balance sheet.

Once again, his good friend Washington was running out of cash, and without cash the revolution was doomed, along with his hopes for a free America. Washington was afraid that large sections of his troops were about to pack up and peel off if they weren't paid, and fast. That was Robert Morris's job.

Unlike the towering, stately Washington, who looked like a Roman god-hero chiseled in stone onto horseback, Robert Morris was a plump, gregarious, ultra-high-energy waterfront merchant and wheeler-dealer who hustled his way into one of the largest fortunes in colonial America through complicated financial improvisation and personal charm. Starting earlier in 1781, Morris almost single-handedly ran Washington's army budget, and the entire financial system of the embryonic American revolutionary government, out of his own pockets and his own brain, with a blizzard of deals, notes, bills, and shipping documents that flew around his Philadelphia office. Historian Terry Bouton called Morris "the most powerful man in America—aside, perhaps, from George Washington," and noted that "the degree of authority he possessed over the economy was probably never matched in the subsequent history of the United States."

Earlier in 1781, the Continental currency had collapsed, the victim of hyperinflation and frantic government overprinting of money. A mock parade was held in Philadelphia by people wearing hats made with now-worthless paper bills. A sad-looking dog marched alongside them, with money pasted all over him. The Continental Congress turned the whole mess over to Robert Morris by appointing him "Superintendent of Finance" of the revolutionary government, a forerunner to the modern job of secretary of the Treasury. To accept the job, the hard-bargaining Morris demanded three conditions: he could hire anyone, he could fire anyone, and he could keep his private business going on the side. The desperate Congress accepted.

Washington and his freezing, starving troops at Valley Forge await de-liverance, or death, in the winter of 1777–78. Twenty-five miles away, entrepreneur Robert Morris was frantically gathering supplies and cash for the Americans before they deserted—or died. (The March to Valley Forge, *by William Trego, 1883, Museum of the American Revolution*)

As soon as he got the job, Morris moved fast to cut waste, tighten accounting, and institute sealed competitive bidding for government contracts. But conditions looked hopeless, and soon Morris was exchanging messages of despair with General Washington, who was desperate for hard currency to pay his troops. He wrote to Morris: "I must entreat you, if possible, to procure one month's pay in specie for the detachment under my command. Part of the troops have not been paid anything for a long time past and have upon several occasions shown marks of great discontent," an understated reference to the possibility of mutinies by various Continental troops.

With the revolution under way, Robert Morris proved himself to be a flat-out financial wizard and management genius who stepped in to assist the rebels whenever he could, sometimes digging into his own pocket while at the same time keeping his own businesses running. In the winter of 1776–77, things got so bad that the Continental Congress, fearing capture by invading British forces, evacuated Philadelphia and fled to Baltimore, leaving Morris behind. He volunteered to run the revolutionary government almost single-handedly as de facto "chief operating officer" for three months.

General Washington and his troops camped out in the frigid woods of Valley Forge, some twenty miles from Philadelphia, and began freezing and starving to death. Morris scrambled around the chaotic docks of Philadelphia, untangled incoming shipments of weapons, food, and clothes, and organized wagon teams to express-deliver the cargo to George Washington and his troops just in time to stage their historic crossing of the Delaware on Christmas Day 1776.

By the end of December 26, Washington had pulled off his first big battle win, a knockout victory over Hessian mercenaries at Trenton that gave the American troops and colonists a critical boost of confidence. A week later, when the Continental troops were stuck on the west bank of the Delaware without food and on the verge of mass desertion, Morris again rushed food, supplies, and payments to them in the nick of time. He helped supply the colonial troops who triumphed at the Battle of Saratoga in 1777, and supported Washington's troops during another savage winter, this time in Morristown, New Jersey, in 1779–80.

Even before Morris was confirmed as superintendent of finance in early 1781, wrote John Dos Passos, "he was beset by Continental officers with pathetic stories of want asking for advances. Sea captains poured out tales of capture and pillage on the high seas. Butchers, bakers, clothiers, drovers, crowded round his desk trying to turn their dog-eared bills into cash."

By now, in the summer of 1781, George Washington and Robert Morris were proving to be a scrappy and highly effective management team. They shared a personal passion for American freedom, and for free-market capitalism unencumbered by high taxes and red tape. Both men had run thriving, sprawling international businesses before the revolution, and so far, they'd kept the American Revolution alive, just barely. But once again, the rebels had blown through nearly the last of their cash, and keeping the food and supplies flowing into the rebel battle camps was, as always, a logistical nightmare.

As he galloped toward the Dobbs Ferry emergency summit meeting, Robert Morris had a partial solution in his mind—George Washington had to cut costs. As the man in charge of Washington's money, and like any responsible chief financial officer, Morris was going to tell the great man he had to streamline the army and somehow stop hemorrhaging red ink.

When the meeting got under way, Washington told his financier he couldn't cut costs. In fact, he needed a new pile of money, and he was going to risk it all in one final major offensive, a desperate gamble to win the revolution and the war. He was going to directly attack the powerful British forces dug into the island of Manhattan in New York City.

The British had two main forces in America, one camped out in nearby New York City led by General Henry Clinton, and a second force under the command of General Lord Cornwallis that was wreaking havoc in the American South, laying siege to Charleston, capturing Savannah, and wiping out much of the American forces in the Carolinas. The good news was that a French expeditionary force of 5,500 troops was arriving in Newport, Rhode Island, and the French fleet was coming within range of the mid-Atlantic to do battle with the British Navy, but there was no guarantee of when or where this would happen, or if it would turn the tide. Meantime, the war could be won if Washington's force of American and allied French land troops could overrun the British on Manhattan—and only if they were paid, fed, and armed.

Escorted by a force of twenty elite mounted troops, his mind no doubt racing with a whirlwind of ideas and fears, Robert Morris raced back toward Philadelphia on a fast-but-dangerous route that took him close to enemy lines. He had to pull together a financial rescue package for Washington and the troops to be able to strike at New York.

But days after the meeting, on August 14, Washington got word that the French fleet would be in position at Chesapeake Bay, Virginia, within just a few weeks, complete with "between 25 & 29 Sail of the line & 3200 land Troops."

Time for a fast, and seemingly impossible, change of plans. Washington now planned an epic "feint" to fake out the British—and knock them out of the war. He would attack at Virginia, not New York.

Washington's plan was to leave a token force outside of New York City, build big army camps and smoking brick bread ovens to make it look like they were digging in for a long stay, spread false intelligence to support the deception, and sneak more than four thousand French and American troops off on an epic march all the way from New York to Virginia. Instead of a fifteen-mile road march to British battle lines north of Manhattan, they would move 550 very long, expensive, hot, and humid miles all the way down to the Virginia coast. Once there, they would surprise-attack Lord Cornwallis's troops at Yorktown and try to seal them off, where their escape would, hopefully, be blocked by the French warships.

If a presumably stunned Robert Morris choked on his tea while learning of this scheme, you couldn't blame him. It seemed impossible. At first, Morris appeared totally flummoxed. On August 21, Morris stalled on Washington's request for a cost estimate for the operation, saying he needed time "to consider, to calculate." The next day, after checking the ledger books, Morris replied to Washington, "I am sorry to inform you that I find Money Matters in as bad a Situation as possible."

But there was no turning back. With or without funds, Washington was already pulling out of camp and the allied troops were hitting the road to Virginia. Robert Morris had to scramble and pull off a miracle. There was barely time to panic. This was the Super Bowl of financial crisis management.

It was at this moment in American history that Morris's skills as an entrepreneur came to the rescue.

On August 22, 1781, Morris sent "begging" letters pleading for money to each one of the thirteen states: "We are on the Eve of the most Active Operations, and should they be in anywise retarded by the want of necessary Supplies, the most unhappy Consequences may follow. Those who may be justly chargeable with Neglect, will have to Answer for it to their Country, to their Allies, to the present generation, and to all Posterity." As usual, this didn't help much, since the feeble Articles of Confederation that then governed the revolutionary cause had no financial teeth in them, no enforcement mechanism to collect funds.

Working round the clock, Morris begged, borrowed, and promised for money. He lined up fleets of small vessels to get the troops across the Delaware and Chesapeake rivers, and he arranged for six hundred barrels of provisions and loans from Spain and France to pay the troops.

He extended his own personal credit to support the supply effort, lined up more loans from the French government, arranged for supplies and funding through sources in Spain and Cuba, and even issued his own currency in $20 and $100 denominations, dubbed "Morris notes," backed up by his own personal reputation and credit. Helping him was Philadelphia bond broker Haym Salomon, who was also notable as an early Jewish American hero of the revolution. It was a desperate race against the clock, and Morris sometimes seemed to come close to cracking under the strain. "It seems as if every Person connected in the Public Service," he wrote in his daybook, "entertains an Opinion that I am full of Money for they are constantly applying even down to the common express Riders and give me infinite interruption so that it is hardly possible to attend to Business of more consequence."

Fortified by the supplies and money orchestrated by Robert Morris and Haym Salomon, and led by General Washington, the American and French forces, now swelled to over ten thousand, arrived at Yorktown in late September. They soon laid siege to General Lord Cornwallis and his eight thousand troops, who were now pinned down by the French fleet offshore, who had blasted away a British Navy force near the mouth of the Chesapeake Bay in early September.

Back in Philadelphia, Robert Morris was at his financial wits' end. He told a friend on September 20, 1781: "The late Movements of the Army have so entirely drained me of Money, that I have been Obliged to pledge my personal Credit very deeply, in a variety of instances, besides borrowing Money from my Friends; and . . . every Shilling of my own."

But finally, fate was on the Americans' side. After a week of bombardment by allied artillery, the trapped British, unable to obtain supplies or reinforcements, were forced to surrender on October 19. In a stunning display that would have been nearly impossible to envision without the help of Robert Morris, Cornwallis's surrendering troops marched out of Yorktown between two mile-long lines of American and French soldiers and stacked their guns in a pile, so the story goes, as a military band played "The World Turned Upside Down." Cornwallis was too embarrassed to join the ceremony. The final formal peace treaty between Great Britain and the United States wouldn't be signed for nearly another two years, but in that moment, the war was essentially over and America was symbolically free.

On November 3, 1781, Robert Morris watched the awe-inspiring

Robert Morris, George Washington, and Haym Salomon, immortalized in a Chicago statue. These two patriots handled Washington's money. Without them, there might not be a United States. (dreamstime.com)

sight of the twenty-four battle flags seized from the surrendering British at Yorktown being paraded into Philadelphia, the capital of the infant nation of the United States. Each flag was carried by a separate American light horseman.

Morris described the triumphant scene that his partnership with George Washington helped engineer: "The American and French flags preceded the captured trophies, which were conducted to the State House, where they were presented to Congress, who were sitting; and many of the members tell me, that instead of viewing the transaction as a mere matter of joyful ceremony, which they expected to do, they instantly felt themselves impressed with ideas of the most solemn nature. It brought to their minds the distresses our country has been exposed to, the calamities we have repeatedly suffered, the perilous situations which our affairs have almost always been in; and they could not but recollect the threats of Lord North that he would bring America to his feet on unconditional terms of submission."

When the war officially ended in 1783, another crisis arose. Many American troops hadn't been paid in a year, as a bankrupt Congress could only afford basic provisions. Robert Morris, true to form, came up with a creative solution, one that the troops agreed to: a down payment, and certificates for three months' pay to be honored by the states in six months, underwritten by Morris's personal credit. Before leaving government in November 1784, Morris saw his scheme for a national bank approved by Congress, and the idea became the Bank of North America, an institution that helped stabilize the colonial economy.

A full-time entrepreneur once again, Robert Morris plunged into a whirl of deals and start-up ventures—canal companies, steam engines, the first iron rolling mill in America, and a scheme to corner the American tobacco market. He and a group of investors loaded up a ship with ginseng, which was cheap to pick in America and highly prized in Asia, called it *The Empress of China*, and sent it from New York to China, yielding a huge profit and launching the age of trade with China.

In 1787, as the first united American experiment under the weak Articles of Confederation proved a failure, Robert Morris returned to national politics, and teamed up with George Washington, James Madison, Alexander Hamilton, and others at the Constitutional Convention at Philadelphia to reengineer the government on the foundations of free enterprise and strong financial authority. Morris was, in fact, one of only two people who signed all three founding documents—the Declaration of Independence, the Articles of Confederation, and the U.S. Constitution.

The U.S. Constitution they created was a blueprint for prosperity, a remarkably forward-looking and enduring document that established a single currency, clear taxing power, a single unified commercial market without interstate taxes or tariffs, a market for government securities, and a central bank. It also protected intellectual property and launched post offices and roads. The document set the stage for an economic boom that continued for the next 230 years, which was powered in large part by entrepreneurs. Robert Morris was George Washington's co-architect of both the American Revolution and the U.S. Constitution, and the most powerful executive in the revolutionary government. And as Robert Morris's biographer Charles Rappleye put it, Morris "laid the foundation that set America on its course to becoming the economic powerhouse it is today."

When the Constitution went into effect in 1789, president-elect Washington wanted Morris to take the job as the new nation's first secretary of the Treasury. But Morris had an even better idea, writing to Washington, "I can recommend a far cleverer fellow than I am for your minister of finance, your former aide-de-camp, Colonel [Alexander] Hamilton." Morris became a senator from Pennsylvania instead.

At the same time the new government was being set up, Robert Morris made the biggest mistake of his life. He decided to become a real estate mogul. He overspent so much on a superluxury town house made of marble and designed by French architect Pierre Charles L'Enfant that the local folks in Philadelphia made fun of him behind his back, even though President Washington lived there during his second administration as Morris's guest. Another architect dismissed the building as a "monster," and it was "impossible to decide which of the two is the maddest, the architect, or his employer," adding, "Both have been ruined by it."

Even worse, Morris gambled everything he had—all his savings and all his credit—on buying six million acres of land throughout the former colonies, in hopes that the value would skyrocket fast in the new nation. It did, but not fast enough for Morris. He was America's biggest landowner, but he couldn't find enough liquid capital to pay his bills. His income could never keep pace with his vastly inflated credit. Morris had trouble collecting back rents and attracting tenants. His health suffered.

In 1787, the world started crashing down on Robert Morris's head. The Bank of England failed and cut off credit throughout the transatlantic markets, leaving Morris vastly overextended. "Who in God's name has all the Money?" Morris lamented. It seemed like he owed everybody. "His complicated system of paper juggling, kiting of promissory notes, interlocking partnerships, land options, loan mortgages and speculation in every conceivable commodity collapsed," wrote journalist Albert Southwick, "leaving him and his partner in arrears by more than 34 million dollars—a vast amount in 1797."

The once-richest man in North America stopped going out in public to avoid being arrested, barricaded his front door, and sat inside his house holding a fowling piece, a precursor to the shotgun. He kept the bill collectors and process servers at bay for three months before surrendering to sheriff's deputies on February 15, 1798. He was hauled off to a squalid prison cell in the debtors' wing of the Prune Street Jail, where he stayed until bankruptcy laws were passed in late 1801.

For nearly three years, Robert Morris suffered a fate like the infamous Bernie Madoff did centuries later—he was a jailbird. It was a terrible fall for a Founding Father. But unlike Madoff, Morris was not a scam artist preying on the innocent, but an entrepreneur who dreamed far too high and, like Icarus, got burned. He took it all stoically, noting while in prison that "a man that cannot hear and face misfortune should not run risks."

Morris died, penniless and in obscurity, in 1803, one of the least-remembered yet most consequential of our Founding Fathers.

By 1795, less than six years after George Washington took charge of a bankrupt, debt-ridden new nation, his government created a roaring engine of economic prosperity.

Washington had a vision for the economic development and prosperity of the United States, and he delivered on it. In the words of the Dutch bankers who handled America's foreign loans, America's credit rating was higher than "any European power whatever." U.S. government bonds sold at a premium in European markets.

How did Washington do it? He engineered the creation of a government with strong tax and customs powers and an effective currency and monetary system, and he appointed a young New York banker named Alexander Hamilton to be secretary of the Treasury. Hamilton proved to be a brilliant choice—and, in 2015, the inspiration for a smash-hit Broadway musical. He also authorized the creation of the Bank of the United States, which helped create a money supply that was more stable than that of most European nations.

In 1794, when rebellious frontier citizens in Pennsylvania rioted to protest a crucial federal liquor tax, Washington, as a sitting president, actually mounted a saddle and led a strike force of thirteen thousand militia troops on a road march out to crush the insurrection, which threatened to cripple the government and the economy. The very thought of the Big Man on horseback was enough to scatter and eliminate the rebellion before Washington ever got there. Problem solved. Clearly, this man meant business.

Washington, in short, put the nation on a path that unleashed the entrepreneurial and free market destiny of the new nation.

Back at Washington's Mount Vernon estate, though, which he

managed part-time by long distance while he was president, things didn't always go swimmingly. Employees boozing on the job was a big problem. In 1793 Washington was forced to fire his farm overseer Anthony Whitting because he "drank freely," "kept bad company at my house," and "was a very debauched person." Earlier, in 1785, Washington had fired his gristmill manager William Roberts for being an "intolerable sot," or alcoholic, then in 1799 rehired him after extracting a promise from him to not have a drop until the day he died. He showed up for work unable to function and half-dead from drink.

When he left the presidency in 1797 and returned to Mount Vernon as a full-time entrepreneur at age sixty-five, Washington added brand-new start-up ventures to his portfolio of breeding sheep, hogs, cattle, and deer for profit, and a whiskey distillery, which soon became one of the biggest distilleries in the new nation. He made the product from crops he grew in his own fields, processed in his own gristmill, and the abundant river water that flowed past the property, and, as a Virginia magazine described it, "rye, malted barley and corn were mixed with boiling water to make a mash in 120 gallon barrels."

Washington had no prior experience in the whiskey business, but he studied it carefully. His timing was lucky, and he cashed in on a big shift in market tastes. Until then, rum was the preferred American drink, but whiskey was experiencing a burst of growth, and Washington's distillery could barely keep up with demand. Within two years he was pumping out eleven thousand gallons of rye whiskey a year and operating five copper-pot stills at full blast for twelve months a year. Washington risked a major investment in the venture, and it soon became his most profitable business segment. By now his land holdings in Virginia, Ohio, Maryland, Pennsylvania, Kentucky, and the Northwest Territories exceeded fifty thousand acres.

When he died in early December 1799, America's founding entrepreneur George Washington was busy with business plans for the new century, his mind abuzz with ideas for livestock management, fertilizers, fencing, building repairs, and crop plantings.

One night in 1798, Washington had stopped by to have a modest meal with Robert Morris, his good friend and cofounder of the United States of America, in Morris's prison cell. "In his new buff uniform and his spanking new epaulets, the general must have been a startling contrast to the prisoner," wrote John Dos Passos, and Washington found Morris "pale and shrunken." Washington, moved by Morris's plight, offered to put him and his wife up at Mount Vernon when the sentence was over, but Washington died before that would come to pass.

Of all the leaders of the American Revolution, George Washington liked Robert Morris the most.

It's easy to see why—without the partnership of these two entrepreneurs, the United States probably never would have happened.

CHAPTER 3

THE PIONEERS

The Americans always display a free, original and inventive power of mind.

—Alexis de Tocqueville, *Democracy in America*, 1836

N ow that America was liberated, its people were free to pursue their dreams of prosperity in a vast, wide-open new market-place of ideas, opportunities, products, ventures—and risks.

There were houses, farmsteads, and factories to build, fields to clear and plant, and transportation and communications networks to lay down. And American entrepreneurs provided much of the brains and muscle power for the incredible burst of energy and achievement that rolled across the land, from the end of the revolution through the beginning of the Civil War.

When the first European settlers penetrated far into the wilderness, many of them were following their destiny as entrepreneurs.

Take the famous Daniel Boone, for example. He was the ultimate Pioneer Man, a Revolutionary War–era hunter, trapper, and real estate speculator who launched moneymaking ventures in remote, little-explored Kentucky and Missouri. According to historian Roger McGrath, "Boone was an entrepreneur, a man on the make. He stretched the boundaries of society and law; he accumulated wealth through discovery and adventure and by violent struggle with the Indians."

Waves of settler entrepreneurs followed Boone into the wilderness, pushed farther west, and forged the Oregon and California Trails across what is now Wyoming, and the Santa Fe Trail, which stretched nine hundred miles, all the way from Missouri to New Mexico. Small family businesses and trading posts popped up along the trails to service the new travelers and populations.

From 1825 to 1840, an annual fur trading fair called the Rocky Mountain Rendezvous was held in present-day Utah and Wyoming, and brought together Native Americans, white trappers, and their families. According to one participant, the big event featured "mirth, songs, dancing, shouting, trading, running, jumping, singing, racing, target-shooting, yarns, frolic, with all sorts of extravagances that white men or Indians could invent."

As American entrepreneurship grew along with a flurry of new inventions, changes came at lightning speed. In 1830 railroads were practically unknown. By 1860 there were more than 36,000 miles of track laid all across the nation. "It's a great sight to see a large train get underway," marveled nineteen-year-old New Yorker George Templeton Strong in 1839. "I know of nothing that would more strongly impress our great-great grandfathers with an idea of their descendants' progress in science." He continued, "Just imagine such a concern rushing unexpectedly by a stranger to the invention on a dark night, whizzing and rattling and panting, with its fiery surface gleaming in front, its chimney vomiting fiery smoke above, and its long train of cars rushing along behind like the body and tail of a gigantic dragon—or like the devil himself—and all darting forward at the rate of twenty miles an hour. Whew!"

Steamboats, pioneered by entrepreneur Robert Fulton, soon linked cities and continents together with speed and reliability. The man-made Erie Canal linked New York City with the Great Lakes, creating a monumental shift in commerce. "You talk of making a canal three hundred and fifty miles through wilderness!" exclaimed Thomas Jefferson when he first heard of the scheme. "It is a splendid project, and may be executed a century hence. It is little short of madness to think of it at this day." Instead of one hundred years to build, it took only seven.

With the biblical phrase "What hath God wrought!" inventor and entrepreneur Samuel Morse introduced the blockbuster technology of the telegraph in an 1844 test communication between Washington and Baltimore, launching the age of instant long-distance communication a full 150 years before the takeoff of the Internet. He earned a fortune on his creation and deserved every penny—he was the symbolic godfather of the telephone, fax machine, and Internet!

Powered by telegraph communications, daily newspapers quickly followed, feeding the appetite of an information-hungry nation. With inventor-entrepreneur Cyrus McCormick's new mechanical reaper, American agriculture was completely transformed, and the Midwest became the nation's breadbasket. "In 1839 only eighty bushels of wheat were shipped out of the infant town of Chicago," wrote historian John Steele Gordon. "Ten years later Chicago shipped two million."

In 1835, a young entrepreneur named Samuel Colt created the Patent Arms Manufacturing Company in Paterson, New Jersey, and registered his first patent. His big idea was a handgun featuring a revolving automatic chamber that fired multiple shots without having to be reloaded. Previously, a single-shot weapon took some twenty seconds to reload, which spelled doom if you were a settler or soldier under attack, for example, by native warriors who in the same amount of time could fire off six arrows or chase you down with a tomahawk.

At first, Colt's guns were prone to misfires, flameouts, and breakdowns, but by the 1850s he'd worked out the bugs with precision manufacturing based on interchangeable parts, automation, and mass production. His revolver became the standard weapon for lawmen, the military, cowboys—and quite a few desperadoes, too. Texas Ranger Samuel Walker called Colt's pistols "the most perfect weapon in the World," and for better or worse, the weapons helped forge the westward expansion of white settlers.

By the 1880s, the obliteration of the Great Plains buffalo herds, powered by firearms technology created by American inventors and entrepreneurs, had destroyed the traditional Native American trading patterns and hastened the collapse of Native American cultures.

"The world is going too fast," wrote one old-timer, a sixty-nine-year-old former mayor of New York named Philip Hone. "Railroads, steamers, packets, race against time," he lamented. "Oh, for the good old days of heavy post coaches and speed at the rate of six miles an hour!"

This giant leap of commerce and expansion transformed the lives of millions of people for the better, but had awful consequences for millions of others, including slaves of African ancestry and the increasingly beleaguered and oppressed Native American populations.

One entrepreneur's labor-saving invention, Eli Whitney's cotton gin, changed the world of agriculture and ignited the South's production of cotton, which soared from 1 percent of the world's total in 1793 to almost 70 percent of the world's total in 1850—but by doing so it helped prolong the horrors of slavery in America.

One day in 1872, seven years after the end of the Civil War, an American entrepreneur in San Francisco came up with a blockbuster idea that capitalized on all that cotton being harvested by Eli Whitney's cotton gins.

Millions of settlers, farmers, miners, laborers, cowboys, and lumberjacks were pouring into the West. They needed pants. Not the hodgepodge of often low-quality khaki, wool, and other choices then on the market. Good, durable pants. Affordable pants.

So Levi Strauss, a Jewish immigrant from Europe who owned a dry-goods store in the city, along with his partner, a tailor named Jacob Davis, invented blue jean pants and waist-high work overalls. They were made of rivet-reinforced, sturdy denim cotton.

The fashion world would never be the same again.

The jeans caught on like wildfire, and achieved immortality as symbols of the freedom, independence, and studly good looks of the rugged American West.

The destiny of an American entrepreneur can sometimes be fixed in a single moment of insight, a moment that changes the world of business.

That's what happened to Isaac Singer, a tall, boisterous, self-styled inventor and notorious womanizer (with no fewer than eighteen children out of wedlock) one day in Boston in 1850, when a machinist asked him to help improve a sewing machine. Singer thought about it for a while, gazed at the machine, and got two Big Ideas. He installed a foot pedal for feeding fabric faster, and a tower arm that held the needle over the worktable.

Bingo. America's first multinational consumer product company was born. Until that point in history, clothes were sewn by hand. The Singer sewing machine could produce nine hundred stitches per minute, more than twenty times faster than the speed of a professional seamstress. Singer hit the road selling the product, appearing at circuses and county fairs, singing a sales song at the top of his lungs while an attractive woman conducted a demonstration of the machine.

Singer made the product more compact and lightweight, and manufacturing innovations enabled him to sell the machine at ten

An original Singer sewing machine. (New York Public Library)

dollars each, affordable to the average housewife. Sales took off in the United States and, eventually, around the world, reaching near-monopoly status. Singer and his partner, Edward Clark, took trade-ins, and set up installment payment plans and sales and service networks.

When Singer died in 1875 at his British estate, he was a rich man—and the lives of many millions of people were improved.

After Robert Morris's flameout into oblivion at the turn of the eighteenth century, America's next genuine tycoon and millionaire was

Stephen Girard, who turned a small shipping business into one of America's biggest fortunes.

The son of a French sea captain, Girard struck out on his own in hopes of prospering as an international trader. In early 1776, when he was twenty-six, his single-masted sloop was chased into the port of Philadelphia by a British warship, and he fell in love with his new land. America, it seemed, offered all kinds of opportunities to an immigrant entrepreneur, so he decided to stick around. He opened a store, then a thriving shipping business, specializing in transporting cargo to the West Indies and New Orleans, where his language skills with French-speaking businessmen came in handy.

After the American Revolution, Girard's trading empire flourished. He cashed in on the booming new American trade with China, and he became a much-admired employer. "Many young boys who served valuable apprenticeships in his counting house praised him," wrote historians Robert Wright and David Cowen. "A successful stint with Girard was the 18th century equivalent of an MBA." They added, "He found just the right mix of fixed salary and bonus incentive to keep employees productive." Girard was a shrewd, highly calculating executive with a knack for hard work and a sharp nose for profitable deal-making.

In 1793, Girard stepped in to serve a heroic role when a deadly yellow fever hit Philadelphia, the U.S. capital, which then had a population of 45,000. Girard stayed in town while most other well-to-do people fled. He set up a hospital, rolled up his sleeves, helped care for the sick and dying, and is credited with helping to save thousands of lives. "Fearlessly, audaciously and defiantly, unselfishly serving others, he had looked death in the eye," wrote his biographer George Wilson.

By 1812, Girard was worth $7 million, the equivalent of some $100 million today. "His sailors were among the healthiest and happiest in the world, allowing him to keep his ships at sea a larger percentage of the time than other merchants," wrote historians Wright and Cowen. "It wasn't unusual for his ships to leave Philadelphia laden with $75,000 worth of produce and to return a year and a half later bearing goods that would sell for $150,000 or more. He purchased sugar from specific hills that he knew to yield only the sweetest canes, and as a connoisseur of coffee and tobacco he was unequaled."

Girard wasn't just a pioneer in shipping and philanthropy; he was a financial genius, too. In 1811, when Girard and his partners bought what was left of the now-failed public First Bank of the United States and relaunched it as a private bank, he created a financing mechanism that kick-started many new entrepreneurial ventures. "It was a simple but brilliant plan," noted author Greg Reid, who explained, "Using his own money and some of the best people in the banking business, he instituted conservative lending policies that allowed him to have less gold and silver on hand than other banks while making more loans to small businesses that were neglected by competitors."

When the U.S. government ran out of money in the wake of the War of 1812, and with no national bank for the government to turn to, Girard came to the rescue by accepting federal deposits, and underwrote much of the war effort. In 1822, he gave a cash-strapped President James Monroe a $40,000 loan. In 1829, he bailed out the Pennsylvania government with a $100,000 loan to avoid bankruptcy. He made profitable early investments in the new American industries of railroads and coal mining.

When he died in 1831, immigrant entrepreneur Stephen Girard had built an estate that was later estimated at the modern equivalent of $200 million.

But he is probably best remembered for starting Girard College, a school that has for 168 years helped educate thousands of children in need. When Girard signed the documents to establish the school, it was the biggest charitable donation in American history.

American entrepreneurs have always had a special knack for bold ideas.

Some of these ideas have seemed, at first, to be downright wacky.

In my family's case, for example, the idea was that people would spend a million dollars on hand-made duck calls. If you'd heard that pitch back in the 1980s, you might be forgiven for thinking we had a few screws loose. But after thirty years of hard work, we did it.

Another case is the amazing story of Frederic Tudor, who, in 1806 at age twenty-three, came up with an equally implausible concept in the days before refrigeration and electricity—"Cut giant blocks of ice out of frozen New England lakes and ship them all over the world and make a bundle of money!" He pulled it off, too.

The third son of a wealthy Boston lawyer and his wife who kept an underground icehouse out back, as many New England families did, Tudor joined the family on a Caribbean vacation, where ice was an unknown commodity. He put two and two together and figured, *Why not just ship ice to the tropics and sell it?* Well, that was a lot easier said than done. His rich father was skeptical, but helped stake him in his first venture, in which he bought a two-masted, square-rigged ship and hauled a cargo of 130 tons of ice down to the tropics, insulated with straw and hay.

It seemed such a nutty scheme that the *Boston Gazette* published the headline "No Joke, Ship Full of Ice Sets Sail for Martinique." The snarky subheading cracked: "Let's Hope This Doesn't Prove to Be a Slippery Speculation!" When Tudor arrived at his destination, some of the ice had already melted. Potential customers there couldn't have cared less, plus there was nowhere to store the stuff.

Tudor took a bath on the deal, losing the equivalent of $90,000 today.

But like many an American entrepreneur ever since, once Frederic Tudor had a big idea, he just wouldn't let go of it. He kept tinkering, tweaking, and trying for the big payoff. And destiny kept slamming the door in his face. Over the next ten years, he lost money, dodged creditors, and wound up in debtor's prison more than once. His biographer Steven Johnson wrote that Tudor "assumed the absolute novelty of ice would be a point in his favor," but he "instead, received blank stares." The depressing pattern of failure repeated itself, with reliably disastrous results. "For most of his early adulthood," wrote Johnson of Tudor, "he was an abject failure, albeit one with remarkable tenacity." He couldn't go back to his father for help, since his father had gambled away the family holdings on bad investments.

Tudor had three big barriers to success. First, few people in the tropics really cared about having ice, and they sure didn't care to pay for it. Second, it's a hugely labor-intensive process to cut big blocks of ice out of a lake that's frozen solid. And last but not least, no one had figured out how to prevent ice from melting on a long ocean voyage.

Through constant experimentation and trial and error, Tudor eventually cracked all three problems. First, to stimulate demand, he gave out free samples to bartenders. "The object is to make the whole population use cold drinks instead of warm or tepid," Tudor wrote in his diary. "A single conspicuous bar keeper, selling steadily his liquors all cold without an increase in price, render it absolutely necessary that the others come to it or lose their customers."

Second, to cut labor costs, Tudor used a new horse-drawn two-bladed ice plow that cut deep into the ice much more efficiently than human-powered handsaws and pickaxes. And third, instead

The Ice King: this dapper fellow, Frederic Tudor, built an early American business empire on an unusual idea— selling ice to global customers in the days before electricity and refrigeration. (Francis Alexander, Museum of Fine Arts, Boston)

of straw and hay, he used layers of sawdust to insulate the ice on long voyages, which worked surprisingly well.

Absorbing the lesson of his Martinique fiasco, a year later he made a deal in Cuba that pre-positioned an icehouse there before he docked his cargo. This time, it worked. Eventually, he got ice-supply monopolies in Cuba and Jamaica, and shipped loads of ice all over the hot, humid American South, too.

As labor-intensive agricultural industries grew in the blazing-hot tropics, so did the demand for icy refreshment, and Tudor cashed in. In 1833, Tudor pulled off a major coup—he managed to ship a 180-ton load of ice from Boston all the way to Calcutta, a 16,000-mile trip that took four months. Most of the stash survived unmelted, and the shipment caused a sensation among the British expat population in Calcutta, who held chilled wine and beer parties to celebrate. Profits rolled in.

By 1856, Tudor's success attracted competition, and the ice-shipping business was booming globally. Over 150,000 tons of ice

ICE CUTTING AT SPY POND, WEST CAMBRIDGE, MASS.

Ice-cutting crews in Cambridge, Massachusetts. (Wikimedia Commons)

per year was being shipped from New England to more than forty countries as far away as Japan, Australia, Singapore, and Brazil, and railroads hauled ice all over the United States.

During the winter of 1846–47, the great writer Henry David Thoreau looked out his window and spotted a team of Tudor's ice-cutters on his beloved Walden Pond, creating chunks of frozen water bound for distant lands. Pondering the weirdness of the scene, he wrote, "The sweltering inhabitants of Charleston and New Orleans, of Madras and Bombay and Calcutta, drink at my well." He added, "The pure Walden water is mingled with the sacred water of the Ganges."

The ice-shipping industry evaporated once refrigeration technology arrived, but by then, the stubborn, tenacious, and multiple failed founder of it all had made a huge impact. "Tudor's big idea ended up altering the course of history, making it possible not only to serve barflies cool mint juleps in the dead of summer, but to dramatically extend the shelf life and reach of food," wrote journalist

Leon Neyfakh. "Suddenly people could eat perishable fruits, vegetables, and meat produced far from their homes. Ice built a new kind of infrastructure that would ultimately become the cold, shiny basis for the entire modern food industry."

Frederic Tudor, the American entrepreneur with what seemed to be a truly wacky brainstorm, died at age eighty, with a net worth of $200 million in today's money.

Some American entrepreneurs weren't above cutting corners or breaking the rules to gain a competitive edge.

One extreme example of this is Francis Cabot Lowell, a Massachusetts merchant who managed to both build a fortune for himself and help launch the Industrial Revolution in America, all based on a single, sneaky act of industrial espionage.

The year was 1811. Lowell, then a leading Boston importer of British textiles, was taking a long, leisurely grand tour around England with his family. Along the way, he stopped frequently to tour textile factories, examining the state-of-the-art high-speed weaving and spinning machines powered by water and steam. At the time, England had strict controls in place to protect its patent-protected trade secrets and advanced industrial technology. It was a serious crime to buy, copy, or share industrial designs. Skilled machinists and textile workers were forbidden from leaving the country. Few outsiders were allowed into the factories.

But the British made an exception for Lowell, who was a big customer of the British textile bosses, and a good friend to boot. Or so they thought. What they didn't know was that the crafty entrepreneur realized he could make more money if he "stole" the British textile-making technology and manufactured clothing himself, back in the States, rather than paying top dollar at full retail prices for finished goods shipped over from the mother country.

During the tours, Lowell carefully studied the British power looms and spinning machines, and took special note of how the Brits outsourced sections of the production system to different teams with specialized tasks. He memorized everything. He didn't use paper and pencil, but he created blueprints in his mind and filed them away. Lowell's behavior eventually got so suspicious that in the summer of 1812, his ocean voyage home to Massachusetts was blocked by British warships, which detained him in Canada. Officials searched his luggage but they found nothing incriminating, of course: it was all tucked away in his brain.

Once back home, Lowell put the stolen technology right to work by building the world's first fully integrated textile mill on the banks of the Charles River in Waltham, Massachusetts. Soon he was shipping finished cotton goods across the country. The idea of a fully integrated factory that processed raw materials into a finished product was brilliant, and it helped trigger the wave of American mass-production manufacturing that transformed the nation. Over the next century, textiles became a dominant industry in New England.

And it all happened thanks to an act of business spycraft. As journalist Howard Anderson put it, "The father of the American Industrial Revolution wasn't an inventor, or even a financier. He was a thief—a Brahmin thief (Exeter, Harvard), but a thief nonetheless. What did he steal? Intellectual property."

One day in 1783, just as the whipped British were packing up and heading home, a young butcher's son from Germany named John Jacob Astor stepped off a ship and hit the streets of New York City, intent on making a fortune.

He carried a suitcase containing seven flutes, and he planned to get into the business of selling musical instruments. When he died sixty-five years later, he was the richest man in the nation. He didn't do it with flutes.

Astor started off hawking rolls and cakes on the sidewalks of Manhattan, then took a job with a fur merchant, scraping and cleaning undressed fur pelts in lower Manhattan, then beating them to scare off the moths.

Astor had a secret weapon that is common to many successful entrepreneurs (myself included!): the support of a strong, brilliant spouse. Two years after arriving in America, he married Sarah Cox Todd, the daughter of Scottish immigrants, a woman who Astor soon realized was smarter than most merchants. She became his behind-the-scenes, hands-on business partner. They opened up a shop on Water Street that traded furs and sold musical instruments. They worked very hard and lived frugally.

Seeing a bigger future in fur than flutes, Astor switched to fur trading full-time, specializing in high-fashion beaver, marten, mink, and otter pelts, which were popular in fashionable society circles in New York and London.

Astor's fur-buying trips took him all over the Midwest and Canada, and he learned the languages of his Native American trading partners. "John Jacob was a canny trader," wrote biographer Axel Madsen. "Few trappers or Indians got the better of him. He did it all himself, hauling the furs back to Albany, baling and loading them on barges down to New York for reshipment to London. The profits were as much as 1,000%."

By 1800, John Jacob Astor was the top American merchant in the fur trade, and he launched a shipping business to capitalize on the booming trade with China. He orchestrated at least one illegal drug deal, in 1816, a profitable shipment of ten tons of opium from the Ottoman Empire to China, making him, in effect, a drug trafficker. With his profits from the fur and shipping businesses, he started dabbling in New York real estate.

In 1808, Astor had an idea. It was the kind of idea that American entrepreneurs have had for centuries—so outlandish that it just might work. Astor thought he could connect America, Asia, Russia, and Europe all together into a global business powerhouse, a new commercial empire based on a special ingredient—animal hair. "His innovation," reported journalist Peter Stark, "was to link the interior North American fur trade over the Rockies with the Pacific coastal fur trade and link that to the Russian Alaskan fur trade, and link that to China, to London, to Paris, to New York. Astor's thinking revolved on entire continents and oceans."

Astor was already a highly successful fur trader, and had started dabbling in New York real estate, but now he saw the promise of fantastic riches in the new territory of the Louisiana Purchase, land that was recently explored by the epic Lewis and Clark expedition.

Astor's brainstorm was to set up a trading center on the remote, little-explored Pacific coast of North America, an area that was rich in high-value beaver, lynx, fox, and bear furs, and especially in sea otter furs, which were highly prized in the Chinese market. Astor's ships would go from New York all the way around Cape Horn to Oregon, and drop off manufactured goods to trade with Native American trappers and suppliers in the Pacific Northwest. Then the ships would take the furs over to China, and carry back Chinese goods like porcelain, silk, and tea to New York, for sale in the U.S. and European markets. Markups were huge. For example, a sea otter pelt could be bought for the modern equivalent of one dollar from coastal Native Americans, then sold for the equivalent of $100 in China.

This early American entrepreneur was thinking on a truly global scale, way ahead of his time. As historian James Ronda put it, Astor was "relentless in the pursuit of wealth" and a business genius who "embraced business techniques far in advance of his contemporaries."

As it happened, President Thomas Jefferson loved the idea of

*John Jacob Astor: America's
first great business tycoon
started off running a store
in lower Manhattan with
his wife that sold furs
and musical instruments.
(Painting by John Wesley
Jarvis)*

a new Pacific trading post and offered his strong moral support.
A successful settlement in Oregon based on the lucrative, booming fur business would strengthen the United States' claim to the
region and muscle out the fast-encroaching Canadians. "The beaver became a factor of empire, and battles were fought and treaties
delayed over who was to control access to prime trapping areas,"
wrote historian James Stokesbury. "The future of North America
depended on the flashing paddle and the beaver trap as much as
it did on muskets and bayonets." President Jefferson was highly
impressed by John Jacob Astor's energy and vision, and pitched in
to help the wheeler-dealer from New York. In a letter to Meriwether
Lewis in 1808, when Astor was planning the logistics of his outpost on the Columbia River, Jefferson called Astor "a most excellent
man," "long engaged in the [fur] business & perfectly master of it."

But from a practical point of view, Astor's plan for the "Pacific
Fur Company" started off as a slow-motion disaster. He sent out

two expeditions, one by land and one by sea, into the largely unknown, often savage wilderness, to link up at the mouth of the Columbia River. In Oregon, the oceangoing contingent carried construction materials to build a settlement and headed around Cape Horn and up the Pacific coast.

Both groups ran into big trouble. Around the area now known as Hell's Canyon on the Snake River in Idaho and Oregon, the overland group faced starvation and tough natural barriers like rapids and endless flatlands. Many members of the ship-bound party were killed by Native Americans. All told, the journeys killed more than sixty of the employees Astor sent to set up the outpost.

Both teams, or what was left of them, eventually made it to the rendezvous point, and by 1811, incredibly, they actually got the business going. The settlement was called Fort Astoria, and soon Astor's complex global trading scheme was raking in money hand over fist.

Then, in an instant, it was over.

In the wake of the War of 1812, a Canadian expedition, commissioned by the British government in Canada, showed up and demanded that Astoria be handed over to a Canadian company, or else. Astor's representative, fearing a military seizure by the Royal Navy of the remote, lightly defended operation, panicked and sold off the fort at a bargain-basement price.

Astor was furious, but there was nothing he could do. He abandoned the Asia venture and got right back to work. During the War of 1812, he bought American ships cheap when they were stuck at the docks, and sold them high when the war ended and business picked up. He also loaned the U.S. government millions of dollars and made a tidy profit on the payback when the war was over. "By the end of the war, the United States government was on the brink of bankruptcy," wrote Stokesbury. "Astor's response, together with a consortium of associates from Philadelphia, was to buy high-interest bonds with debased currency, and he emerged from the war in far better shape than the Federal Government. At the same time, he enlarged his New York City holdings so that by the time peace was made, Astor was immensely wealthy and ready to take over virtually the whole of the American fur trade." In 1816, Congress gave Astor a near monopoly on the fur business in the U.S. by closing down all his foreign competitors.

When the fur business started slowing down in the 1820s, Astor figured it was a permanent trend, so he bailed out and switched to buying real estate in the Midwest, and increasingly in Manhattan, betting that land values would skyrocket as the city moved north. He guessed that New York would become the business capital of the young nation. He guessed right. He became a real estate mogul, the biggest one in early America.

When New York real estate prices plummeted during the financial panic of 1837, Astor scooped up large sections of the city at bargain prices. One deal saw him acquire a full city block, valued at $1 million, for just $2,000. Another saw him acquire a $25,000 interest in a mortgage on financially troubled Eden Farm, a twenty-two-acre property around the site of present-day Times Square. The farmer defaulted; Astor foreclosed, took possession, and sold off pieces of the property for about $5 million.

Through it all, Astor showed a key entrepreneurial skill—he had a remarkable sense of timing, for when to get in and out of a deal, and how and when to invest. "Astor was able to recognize opportunities in a lot of different industries," noted Terri Lonier, a professor of entrepreneurship at Columbia College Chicago. "He knew when political, economic, and market forces were aligned so that he could maximize his investments." Astor's contemporary, New York mayor Philip Hone, said of him: "All he touched turned to gold, and it seemed as if fortune delighted in erecting him a monument of his unerring potency."

Despite his fabulous wealth, Astor led a simple life focused on plain living. He rose early and worked extremely hard. When he died in 1848, just a few weeks short of his eighty-fifth birthday, Astor possessed one-fifteenth of all the personal wealth in the United States, according to one estimate. He was the wealthiest person in America, with an estate estimated at between $10 to $20 million, or around $11 and $22 billion in today's dollars. He had only one regret. "Could I begin life again," he is reported to have said on his deathbed, "knowing what I now know, and had money to invest, I would buy every foot of land on the island of Manhattan." "Every dollar," Astor once said, "is a soldier to do your bidding." Astor's official biographer, James Parton, called him "one of the ablest, boldest, and most successful operators that ever lived," and his *New York Herald* obituary said that he had the "ingenious powers of a self-invented money-making machine."

Like his fellow early American superentrepreneur Stephen Girard, John Jacob Astor left behind one major, lasting legacy to charity. In his will, Astor provided the start-up funds for a library that today has become one of the world's finest centers of knowledge, and a place where much of the research for this book was done—the New York Public Library. New York City socialite Brooke Astor, the widow of John Jacob Astor's great-great-grandson Vincent, was a trustee and honorary chairman of the library until her death in 2007 at age 105.

Today you can take the New York City subway from Astoria, Queens, transfer to the number 6 train, pass directly under the Waldorf-Astoria, and get off at the Astor Place station. All three were named in John Jacob Astor's honor.

When you get off at Astor Place, look up at the tiled artwork on the walls of the station. It features the furry creature that made

Astor's first fortune and was the perfect symbol of the kind of man he was—a busy beaver.

On November 8, 1833, near Hightstown, New Jersey, the axle gear overheated on the forward coach car of a southbound train going 20 miles per hour.

The gearbox caught fire and broke up, causing the car behind it to derail and flip over into an embankment. There were twenty-four people inside.

The accident tossed passengers violently around the inside of the car, smashing limbs, injuring all but one of them and killing two, believed to be the first train-passenger fatalities in history.

One of the passengers in the first car was former president John Quincy Adams, and one of the passengers in the car that derailed was a thirty-nine-year-old up-and-coming steamboat entrepreneur from New York named Cornelius Vanderbilt, who was heading to Philadelphia on business. It was the early days of railroading in America, and just two months after steam locomotives were installed on the line, replacing horses.

A shaken Adams described the scene he witnessed when the train crashed to a stop, writing in his diary: "The scene of sufferance was excruciating. Men, women, and a child scattered along the road, bleeding, mangled, moaning, writhing in torture, and dying, as a trial of feeling to which I had never before been called; and when the thought came over me that a few yards more of pressure on the car in which I was would have laid me a prostrate corpse like him who was before my eyes, or a cripple for life; and, more insupportable still, what if my wife and grandchild had been in the car behind me! Merciful God!"

Cornelius Vanderbilt, who was on his first railroad trip that day, was thrown out of the railroad car to the bottom of the embankment.

His clothes were shredded, his leg was shattered, and one of his ribs had punctured his lung. He coughed up blood. He was sure he was about to die. And he would have died, had a skilled young local doctor not quickly ministered to him. Years later, when Vanderbilt had achieved the position as America's great corporate tycoon, he told the doctor that he had been spared that day "to accomplish a great work that will last and remain." That great work turned out to be laying the foundation for much of the American transportation system in the nineteenth century. As historian Michael Kazin wrote of Vanderbilt, "As a self-taught, self-made entrepreneur, he had no equal."

Vanderbilt was born in 1794 into a poor farming family on Staten Island, from where he could see the booming pre-metropolis of Manhattan on the northern horizon. From ages ten to fifteen, he worked for his father, and for a ferry service shuttling people and cargo between the two islands.

At the age of sixteen, Vanderbilt caught the entrepreneurial bug, and it never left him. He talked his parents into lending him $100 to buy a sailboat and started a discount cargo and ferry business of his own between Staten Island and Manhattan. Mom and Dad agreed, but only if he cut them in on the action. Within one year he was able to pay them off, and give them a healthy slice of the profits as well. At eighteen, Vanderbilt struck a deal with the U.S. government to supply military stations, and by age twenty he had a fleet of vessels shuttling people and cargo all the way from Delaware Bay up to Boston.

In 1817, Vanderbilt signed on as the junior partner in a thriving new steamboat venture called the Union Line, which gave him invaluable experience in running a complex business. Steamboats were a quantum leap forward in waterborne travel, making it much more efficient, reliable—and profitable. Vanderbilt pounced on

the new technology. From 1818 to 1829, Vanderbilt and his partner made a fortune, in part by undercutting the competition by as
much as 75 percent, providing high-quality service, and attracting
huge numbers of customers. The only trouble was that the business
was technically illegal, since by bringing passengers between New
Jersey and Manhattan he was violating an 1808 New York State
government–approved monopoly controlled by Robert Livingston
and steamboat pioneer Robert Fulton. Vanderbilt and his partner
fought the monopoly all the way to the U.S. Supreme Court, which
ruled in their favor and found that only Congress, not state governments, had the authority to regulate interstate business.

By the time his partner died in 1829, the frugal Vanderbilt had
saved enough to build his own personal navy of steamboats, an
empire that eventually numbered one hundred vessels and earned
him the popular nickname "Commodore," which he loved. He expanded his routes all over the Northeast and called his service the
"People's Line," offering cheap fares for all.

In 1851, as the California Gold Rush was taking off, Vanderbilt
launched an ingenious shuttle service between the East Coast and
San Francisco—by running oceangoing steamships to Nicaragua
and using canoes and mule trains, and then a railroad, to haul people, mail, and gold back and forth across the land barrier. By 1861
Vanderbilt dominated both the transatlantic and transcontinental
shipping lines and exerted major influence on the financial markets. Some people considered Vanderbilt to be a speculator, but he
was much more than that. He was a trailblazer, a consolidator, a
builder, and a long-term visionary.

In 1853, Vanderbilt took his first vacation, a grand tour of Europe in a customized personal steamship. While he was gone, he
heard some associates were plotting against him. He sent them
this tight, punchy message: "Gentlemen: You have undertaken to

cheat me. I won't sue you, for the law is too slow. I'll ruin you. Yours truly, Cornelius Vanderbilt." He once explained, "I am not afraid of my enemies, but by God, you must look out when you get among your friends." According to his lifetime assistant, Vanderbilt "thought every man could stand watching," and "never placed confidence in anyone." He confided in few people and made decisions with switchblade speed. One of his business maxims was "Don't tell anybody what you're going to do, until you have done it."

Critics called Vanderbilt a "robber baron" because of his aggressive, take-no-prisoners business style, and he looked the part. Vanderbilt "looked like a conqueror," wrote Louis Auchincloss. "He had a clear complexion, ruddy cheeks, a large bold head, a strong nose, square jaw, a high, confidence-inspiring brow, and thick, long gray hair which turned magnificently white."

Vanderbilt was at the vanguard of an elite new breed of northern businessmen who, according to historian Michael Kazin, thought their hard work helped hold the Union together. "Corporate ethics, however, were honored more in banquet rhetoric than in deeds," wrote Kazin. "Vanderbilt and his cost-conscious brethren naturally preferred friendly negotiations to forceful or dishonest tactics. Yet when polite methods failed, they were quite willing to buy off politicians, double-cross former partners and have the police break up strikes by their workers. Although Vanderbilt habitually dressed in the simple black-and-white outfit of a Protestant clergyman, his only religion was economic power." Historian H. Roger Grant wrote, "Contemporaries, too, often hated or feared Vanderbilt or at least considered him an unmannered brute. While Vanderbilt could be a rascal, combative and cunning, he was much more a builder than a wrecker," who was "honorable, shrewd, and hard-working."

Beginning in 1863 and 1864, when he was already close to seventy years old, Vanderbilt left the shipping business to launch a full-scale assault on the railroad industry, which was where, he thought, the big growth in the transportation business would be. He conducted corporate raids and buyouts of the New York Harlem and Hudson lines and the Long Island Rail Road, then went after the big prize, the New York Central Railroad, which dominated train traffic in and out of New York City. Within ten years Vanderbilt controlled much of the railroad industry that linked New York to Boston, Montreal, St. Louis, and Chicago.

Vanderbilt wasn't mainly a builder of railroads, but a buyer, consolidator, and improver—he kept fares low and upgraded service, and he knew when to play bare-knuckled hardball. In 1867, during

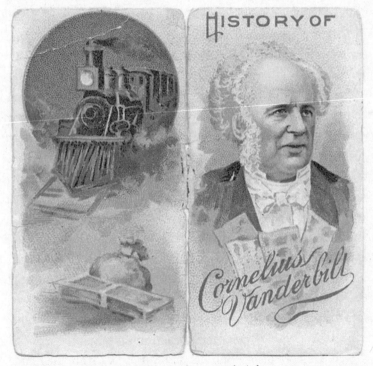

The Commodore: Despite the unfortunate hairdo, mega-entrepreneur Cornelius Vanderbilt pioneered the modern American corporation with two businesses: steamboats and railroads. (Duke Tobacco Company Cigarette Cards Collection, Wake Forest University Library)

a business dispute, he launched a commercial blockade on America's business capital by cutting off all rail service to New York. His enemies caved in quickly, and Vanderbilt won, as usual. In 1869, he both triggered a Wall Street panic and appeared as the hero to stop it, by bailing out companies on the edge of failing with millions of his own dollars. "Vanderbilt," wrote his biographer T. J. Stiles, "was a paradox—both a creator and a destroyer." According to Stiles, "Vanderbilt essentially invented the modern corporation through his purchase and consolidation of New York's major railroads, built the first true corporate conglomerate in U.S. history," and became the "first great corporate tycoon in American history."

With strong management and major investments in train track and equipment, Vanderbilt created efficient railroad passenger service—and pulled the American transportation industry into the modern era.

When Vanderbilt died in January 1877 at age eighty-two, he was, by some estimates, the second-wealthiest person in U.S. history (after Standard Oil cofounder John D. Rockefeller), with a fortune equal to roughly $200 billion in today's dollars. The *New York Times* grandly proclaimed in his obituary, "Every movement of his will was perceptible in the fleets which covered the waters, or in the network of rails which enmeshed the land," and "By him, therefore, the movements of population, the currents of trade and travel, and the requirements of commerce, must have been clearly seen and understood. It was his business, in a large way, to anticipate and meet all these requirements and changes."

No matter how you measure it, American superentrepreneur Cornelius Vanderbilt's impact on America was huge.

Today Vanderbilt's steamboats and railroad cars are long gone, and most of the fortune he left to his descendants vanished long ago from family dissipation, taxes, and overspending.

In 1973, when 120 of Vanderbilt's descendants gathered for their first family reunion, there were no millionaires in the group. "The Fifth Avenue mansions, alas, are long gone," wrote descendant Arthur T. Vanderbilt II. "But today, if you stroll down Fifth Avenue and if the light is just right and you half close your eyes, you might spot a red carpet being unrolled from the door of a limestone chateau down the steps to the curb, watch as a burgundy Rolls-Royce stops in front and guests walk up to the door flanked by maroon-liveried footmen, and hear coming from inside the faraway sounds of an orchestra."

There are two monuments to Vanderbilt that do endure to this day: Vanderbilt University in Nashville, Tennessee, which he funded, and the railroad network of the United States that he shaped, much of which symbolically flows into the architectural masterpiece of New York's Grand Central Terminal, the 1913 version that replaced the original building, which Vanderbilt himself completed in 1871.

On the south side of the building, overlooking Park Avenue from an elevated vehicle viaduct, is a huge bronze statue of the Commodore, weighing ten tons, striking a noble pose in a furry double-breasted coat and comically huge mutton-chop sideburns. He commissioned the statue himself. You can't really see the statue from the street or the sidewalk, though. The view is mostly blocked by the roadway. Shortly after Grand Central opened, the *New York Times*, noting the regularity of railroad accidents, said any Vanderbilt statue should include "the dismembered bodies of men, women and children."

Today, in bronze outside Grand Central, wrote architectural historian Christopher Gray, Cornelius Vanderbilt "stands a hostage, in a haze of exhaust produced by the railroad's most potent enemy, the automobile." The great man left behind another legacy, too. Every weeknight you can tune in to CNN and watch Cornelius Vanderbilt's great-great-great-grandson host his own TV news show. His name is Anderson Cooper.

Back in the 1830s, harvesting grain was nearly as inefficient as it had been since the days of ancient Rome—it took a person fourteen hours to cut one acre of wheat.

Then, along came Cyrus McCormick. He grew up in a prosperous farming family who lived on an 1,800-acre property in Virginia's Shenandoah Valley. His father, who loved to tinker with machines and equipment, worked with young Cyrus to try to make an effective mechanical reaper, but couldn't pull it off. In 1831, he turned the project entirely over to Cyrus, who was twenty-two. Within a year, Cyrus had hammered together a horse-drawn harvester that was able to chop six acres of oats in a single morning. That equaled the work of twelve men working full-out.

Cyrus offered his creation to fellow farmers at the price of about $1,400 in today's dollars, but no one bought the funny-looking device. Farmers had been hand-cutting grain for four thousand years and saw no need for a new approach. "It's a contraption that is seemingly a cross between a wheelbarrow, a chariot and a flying machine," said one skeptic. Cyrus was unfazed and kept on tinkering and selling. He patented his reaper. Years went by. The financial panic of 1837 nearly bankrupted his farm. "In this hour of debt and defeat, Cyrus showed that indomitable spirit which was, more than any other one thing, the secret of his success," wrote biographer Herbert Casson. "Without money, without credit, without customers, he founded the first of the world's reaper factories in the little log workshop near his father's house and continued to give exhibitions."

Still more years went by without great success. McCormick's first models didn't perform too well, so he kept fiddling with them

Cyrus McCormick, who developed and marketed the first widely adopted mechanical reaper. (George Smillie)

to make improvements. By 1840 he had perfected his design, and started demonstrating the new model widely, offering a money-back guarantee, which later proved really popular. By the mid-1840s, he had sold only a relative handful of mechanical reapers, but he was convinced that the westward march of settlers into vast new farmlands and the shortage of labor would eventually pay off for him. He kept plugging away.

To get closer to the growing number of potential customers in the Midwest, Cyrus moved his little factory to the new but fast-rising city of Chicago in 1847. Chicago didn't even have paved streets yet, but it connected to the Great Lakes and to westbound trains, and the move was a logistical masterstroke. The first mayor of Chicago, a man named William Ogden, was so impressed by the potential of plucky Cyrus's product that he chipped in with a $25,000 personal loan, which would be worth about $700,000 today.

In 1848, McCormick sold five hundred reapers. In 1849, the factory turned out 1,500 machines. In 1851, McCormick went to

London to do competitive cutting with his reaper at the Crystal Palace Exhibition, site of the world's first industrial fair, where he won a gold medal and stimulated initial European orders. By 1856, his factory was making four thousand reapers a year for domestic and foreign markets.

The Civil War, from 1861 to 1865, made McCormick's machines essential. "The reaper is to the North what slavery is to the South," declared Secretary of War Edwin Stanton. "By taking the place of regiments of young men in the Western harvest fields, it released them to do battle for the Union at the front and at the same time keeps up the supply of bread for the nation and its armies."

McCormick was a master of mass manufacturing and marketing who pioneered a whole bunch of business-building techniques. He offered fast after-sales service to keep his products working smoothly and his customers happy. He ran ads and pitched product stories to magazines and newspapers. He express-shipped his product by fast rail, in easy-to-assemble sections. He experimented with franchising and hired local partners as sales and service agents and debt collectors. He offered installment payment arrangements and the money-back guarantee, both unheard of until then. He staged product demonstrations before big crowds.

The American Civil War can, in fact, be seen as a battle between the inventions of two American entrepreneurs: Eli Whitney's cotton gin, the tool that powered the economy of the South, and Cyrus McCormick's mechanical reaper, which was widely used in the North. "While the cotton gin had made slavery profitable, the reaper had made the Northern states wealthy and powerful," wrote McCormick's biographer Herbert Casson. "As the war went on, the crops in the North increased, with 200 million bushels being exported during those four years. The reaper thus not only released men to fight for the preservation of the Union, it fed them in the field and kept our credit good among foreign nations at the most critical period in our history."

When he died at age seventy-five, Cyrus McCormick was worth $255 million in today's money, there were some 500,000 McCormick harvesters in operation, and world agriculture had been transformed. Thanks to him, populations all over the world were freed from the danger of famine. The French Academy of Sciences honored McCormick by making him a member and for "having done more for agriculture than any other living man." Historian Christine Heinrichs noted that "his invention made farmers' lives better, released workers for the industrial revolution and made the biggest contribution to ending hunger around the world."

McCormick's final words were, "Work, work!"

The pre–Civil War entrepreneurs were mostly small-business people—traders and merchants, mom-and-pop shops, and family businesses of a few dozen employees at most. They were small, but they pioneered new landscapes and inventions and laid the foundations for a new era of growth that would soon create the world's greatest economy.

It was time for a new breed of entrepreneurs to appear, men and women who would lift America to undreamed-of heights.

They would achieve spectacular wealth and power for themselves, and a few of them would even discover the ultimate secret of life—what God put them on earth for.

CHAPTER 4

THE SUPER-TYCOONS

As soon as the Civil War ended, America made a giant leap to global leadership as the biggest industrial and consumer economy in the world.

American entrepreneurship and business exploded after the war. Factories that had cranked out guns and war supplies stayed open when the war ended, providing a strong platform for a gigantic manufacturing boom.

It was the age when American entrepreneurial giants grew from rags to riches as they dreamed up new markets, new products, and new worlds of business to create.

So many new inventions, innovations, and business ventures blossomed so quickly that this time, roughly between 1870 and the dawn of World War 1 in 1914, became known as the Second Industrial Revolution. Historian Gerald Gunderson reported that in this time, entrepreneurs "found it more attractive on average to develop new products in the United States than in any other economy in the world."

It was like the United States had a sign painted across it for all the world to see: "Come on in and start your own business! Everybody's welcome, the sky's the limit!"

Starting your own business in the booming United States,

compared to the rest of the world, was as easy as apple pie. In European countries and colonies, it often took cutting through a lot of red tape, fancy stamps and seals, political connections, and royal decrees and proclamations to open up a new shop or other business venture. If your business failed, you were considered a social outcast. If you had too many debts, you were thrown in debtor's prison.

But over here in America, starting your own business was a simple legal procedure, going as far back as 1811 when New York State passed an incorporation law that let you do it by filling out a few forms. It was a really smooth operation. Soon the number of corporations skyrocketed. Debtor's prisons in the United States were eliminated by federal law in 1833. Having a bankruptcy or business failure on your record didn't mean permanent failure. You could try again. America gave entrepreneurs a precious gift—the freedom to fail!

The tragic, bloody expulsion of Native American populations across the continent created nation-size areas of fertile land that were now open to be exploited for profit. The American population grew from 40 million in 1876 to 76 million in 1900, with one-third of the increase resulting from immigration. All these people had to be fed, clothed, housed, moved, and entertained, and entrepreneurs stepped right in to meet the opportunity.

Between 1865 and 1900, thanks to railroad magnates and the thousands of entrepreneurs and workers who supplied them with goods and labor, railroads expanded from 35,000 miles of track to nearly 200,000, linking together all the major cities. By the early 1860s, commerce was powered by big railroad ventures, like the networks run by Cornelius Vanderbilt, and the Central Pacific Railroad in California, which was led by a bunch called the "Big Four"—Charles Crocker, Mark Hopkins, Collis Huntington, and Leland Stanford, who also founded Stanford University.

Telegraph lines flanked the railroad tracks, and telephones started appearing in the late 1870s, unleashing instant business communications throughout the country (provided you could afford the long-distance phone charges!). Train tracks were switched from iron to steel, which handled heavier loads of cargo and mail. Farmers could now shop through a product catalog and order the latest tools and equipment for their family business. Food and consumer products crisscrossed the country.

The oil, steel, and copper industries took off, along with many others. Production of steel skyrocketed from under 2,000 tons in 1867 to over 7.2 million tons by 1897, which was more than Germany and Britain combined. Coal, iron, copper, and silver mines opened up across Appalachia and the Midwest and western states. Giant new industrial complexes set up supply chains that created businesses for countless entrepreneurs, some as small as the mom-and-pop sandwich-and-coffee stand parked outside the factory gate.

By the 1880s, America had become a vast, vibrant national market for entrepreneurs with ambition and vision. According to Yale University historian Naomi Lamoreaux, "The half-century or so following the Civil War was a period of extraordinarily rapid economic growth in the United States. Real gross domestic product (GDP) multiplied more than seven times between 1865 and 1920, and real per capita product more than doubled." She added, "Americans have always admired entrepreneurs, but during the years 1865–1920 this attitude was more intense than at virtually any other time in U.S. history." Railroads linked the coasts together, the West fully opened up for business and farming, prospectors rushed west in search of gold, inventors patented a blizzard of new products and technologies, and banks and investors cashed in on the fast-rising tide of entrepreneurship.

This was an age when American entrepreneurs rose to become giants who built empires that shaped the nation, and the world.

Of these giants, three super-tycoons, steel man Andrew Carnegie, banker J. P. Morgan, and oil magnate John D. Rockefeller, stood head and shoulders above the rest, and followed in the path of trailblazer Cornelius Vanderbilt and the transportation networks he pioneered. The three men were friends, enemies, schemers, collaborators, and competitors. Sometimes they were monopolists, and sometimes they created new industries from scratch. Some folks thought they were "robber barons" drunk with power and greed; other people thought they were champions of charity.

These three mega-entrepreneurs were among America's greatest empire builders. They and their fellow entrepreneurs helped lead post–Civil War America into the modern era.

And one of them started off like many American entrepreneurs do—as a penniless immigrant.

He came to this country as a poor twelve-year-old immigrant from Scotland.

He rode the waves of three megatrends—telegraphy, railroads, and steel—to become the richest man on earth, and a founding father of American philanthropy.

Andrew Carnegie was the ultimate American immigrant success story. Though he stood just over five feet tall, he towered over American business history.

Born in 1835, the young Carnegie watched as his beloved father, a handloom weaver, got thrown out of work in Scotland by the new technology of steam-powered handlooms. His mother, a proud, dignified woman, was reduced to mending boots to scrape together enough money to feed and clothe the family, as his father couldn't find a job. "I began to learn what poverty meant," Carnegie recalled. "It was burnt into my heart that my father had to beg for work. And there came the resolve that I would cure that when I got to be a man."

When the desperate Carnegie family immigrated in 1848 across the Atlantic to a slum in what was then the soot-choked, stinking industrial city of Pittsburgh, young Andrew worked twelve-hour days in a textile mill and as a boiler tender. It was hard work, but Carnegie felt proud. "I have made millions since," Carnegie remembered. "But none of those millions gave me such happiness as my first week's earnings." He explained, "The hours hung heavily upon me, and in the work itself I took no pleasure. But the cloud had a silver lining, as it gave me the feeling that I was doing something for my world—our family."

Like Carnegie, I know the feeling of spending twelve-hour days in extremely tough jobs, too. In my younger days, to make a buck before our family business took off, I put in time as a telemarketer, a camp counselor, a janitor, a handyman, and a worker in an ice cream plant, where most of the time, I literally had to work inside a freezer. Boy, did I hate that!

For Carnegie, everything changed when he got his first white-collar job as an office boy for what was then a cutting-edge, high-tech operation: a telegraph company. He was practically in a state of rapture. "There was scarcely a minute in which I could not learn something or find out how much there was to learn and how little I knew," he later recalled. "I felt that my foot was upon the ladder and I was bound to climb."

In those days, working at a telegraph office was as good as working for Google. Carnegie soaked up every bit of information he could. "As the steel pen embossed the dots and dashes of the Morse alphabet on a narrow strip of paper—an electric current moving the pen—the boy learned of international, national and local happenings," wrote Carnegie biographer Peter Krass. "Most important, at age 14, Andy was riding the wave of a new technology and privy to much business correspondence passing through the office. He learned which businesses were buying, which were selling, which were growing and which were failing," which was "all inside information that he eventually used to his benefit."

At night, Carnegie memorized the names and addresses of key business leaders in Pittsburgh, so he could ingratiate himself with them. On the side, he sold news stories that came across the telegraph wires to the local papers. At sixteen, he was his family's chief breadwinner.

Carnegie had a simple dream—of one day becoming an entrepreneur. His plan, he explained to his little brother, was to start a "great" business, one that was successful enough to enable their father and mother to "ride in their carriage." He attended night school to study accounting and double-entry bookkeeping. He was promoted to a full-time telegraph operator, then took a job as a junior manager at the Pennsylvania Railroad, where he learned, in the words of one Carnegie biographer, "the management skills, the financial dealings and the political maneuvers to build an empire."

In 1855, Tom Scott, Carnegie's mentor at the Pennsylvania Railroad, loaned the young go-getter $500 to buy shares in a privately held express-delivery company. When the investment soon began paying him a dividend of $10 a month, or $270 in today's money, Carnegie practically jumped for joy. "I shall remember that check as long as I live," he wrote. "It gave me the first penny of revenue from capital, something that I had not worked for with the sweat of my brow." He hollered out "Eureka!" and thought, *Here's the goose that lays the golden eggs.* This was the start of Carnegie's long career as an investor. With the support of his bosses at the railroad company, he invested in bridges, steel-reinforced rails, sleeper train cars, and oil prospecting.

In 1865, Carnegie left the Pennsylvania Railroad to strike out on his own as a full-time entrepreneur, working for no one but himself, focusing on an industry he knew quite well by now, one that was the lifeblood of America's post–Civil War economic boom: iron and steel. His strategy was to master one business at a time, not to diversify. He decided, in his words, "to go entirely contrary to the adage not to put all one's eggs in one basket. I determined that the proper policy was 'to put all good eggs in one basket and then watch that basket.'" Carnegie explained, "I believe the true road to pre-eminent success in any line is to make yourself master in that line. I would concentrate upon the manufacture of iron and steel and be master in that."

Carnegie took this idea of "vertical integration"—of laserlike focus on a single business—to an extreme, by owning all the steps of production and transportation from the final point of sale all the way back to the original source. Eventually, in the iron and steel business, he controlled a long chain of operations that connected the whole process from start to finish: iron ore mines, vessels that shipped iron ore through the Great Lakes, railroads, coke-burning ovens, and iron and steel plants. In the process, capitalizing on the post–Civil War construction and railroad boom, he dominated the steel industry in less than a generation.

In the 1870s, Carnegie led the industry switch from pig iron to higher-tech, stronger, low-cost steel, which was ideal for railroads, factories, and skyscrapers. "Andrew Carnegie was a brilliant cost analyst," said David Hounshell, professor of technology and social change at Carnegie Mellon University in Pittsburgh. "He knew what were his labor costs, his capital costs and his materials costs, and he knew how to drive the costs down. This was a great advantage." He was also a marketing genius—one time, to prove the strength of his product, he invited the press to watch a hired elephant lope across a bridge made with Carnegie steel. By creating the American steel industry, Carnegie spearheaded America's march into the modern industrial age.

Carnegie was a great businessman, but he was not a saint. In fact, his tactics could be downright brutal. To squeeze maximum efficiency and profit out of his pollution-spewing plants, he always ran them at full capacity, and he ordered his workers to work twelve-hour shifts six days a week in hellishly hot blast-furnace conditions. Carnegie biographer David Nasaw wrote, "The installation of the 12-hour workday had a profound effect on the workforce, turning once proud artisans into animals, too debilitated by exhaustion to live like men." Conditions at his plants were so grim that a visiting Carnegie friend said that "six months' residence here would justify suicide."

The worst episode of Carnegie's career happened in 1892, when he took off for a Scotland vacation and left his partner, the union-busting industrialist Henry Clay Frick, in charge of his steel plants. A 143-day strike unfolded at Carnegie Steel's plant in Homestead, Pennsylvania. Frick ordered in three hundred armed guards from the Pinkerton Detective Agency and a full-blown fracas ensued that turned into a pitched gun battle. A dozen people were killed. Carnegie wasn't directly responsible for the bloodshed—he was in favor of unions—but he was blamed publicly for it. He pushed Frick out of the company. When Carnegie later reportedly sent Frick a note asking to renew their friendship, Frick replied, "Tell him I'll see him in hell, where we are both going." Later, Carnegie created a relief fund for his workers and their families, and became a pioneer for worker pensions.

In 1889, Carnegie championed a radical idea. You could call it "extreme philanthropy," and it was an idea that Bill Gates, Warren Buffett, and other super-tycoons would echo a century later. In a magazine article dubbed "The Gospel of Wealth," he argued that the rich have a moral obligation to give away almost all of their money. Not only should wealthy people contribute to the community, Carnegie declared, but all personal wealth, beyond the basic amount for one's own family, should be considered as a trust fund to create economic opportunity for the less fortunate.

The wealthy person, Carnegie wrote, should "set an example of modest, unostentatious living, shunning display or extravagance; to provide moderately for the legitimate wants of those dependent upon him," and then devote their fortune to "produce the most beneficial results for the community—the man of wealth thus becoming the mere agent and trustee for his poorer brethren, bringing to their service his superior wisdom, experience and ability to administer, doing for them better than they would or could do for themselves." He felt that charity should not be focused on simply giving indiscriminately to the poor, which he feared would "encourage the slothful, the drunken, the unworthy," but should instead be directed to institutions that can help the poor uplift themselves. People who died rich, Carnegie thought, were a disgrace. They should give away their money instead, all of it.

In 1900, Carnegie was getting ready to retire. He got a message from his fellow mega-entrepreneur, the financial mogul J. Pierpont Morgan, who was a latecomer to the steel business and finding it next to impossible to compete with Carnegie's near monopoly. Morgan asked Carnegie to name his price for a full buyout of his steel business. Carnegie replied, $480 million. "Mr. Carnegie, I want to congratulate you on being the richest man in the world!" said Morgan to Carnegie when the deal was closing. Carnegie then asked Morgan if he should have asked for $100 million more instead. Morgan said if he had, he would have gotten it. Morgan turned the business into America's first billion-dollar corporation, U.S. Steel.

Now it was time for Andrew Carnegie to do his greatest deed—to give away nearly his entire fortune, using what he called the

Man of Steel: Andrew Carnegie at the peak of his power. (Theodore C. Marceau, Library of Congress)

"principles of scientific philanthropy," which treated giving as a strategic investment to help people improve themselves.

By 1910, the accrued interest on Carnegie's fortune was accumulating so fast that he simply couldn't give away money fast enough on his own, so he set up the Carnegie Corporation of New York as a philanthropic foundation to take over the process of screening, selecting, and investing in charities worthy of support.

Carnegie's passion for charity gave birth to an amazing number of projects that made America a better place. His favorites were schools, museums, and libraries. Of one of his libraries, he said, "It's the best kind of philanthropy I can think of." His money created the Carnegie Endowment for International Peace, Carnegie Mellon University, the Carnegie Museums of Pittsburgh, the Carnegie Library of Pittsburgh, the Carnegie Institution for Science, the Carnegie Foundation for the Advancement of Teaching, and more than three thousand Carnegie libraries in the United States and globally. When he died, Carnegie had a net worth of over $300 million.

How did he do it? By following a basic, brilliant business philosophy—innovate constantly, invest in the latest technology and equipment, be a low-cost producer, and maximize and retain profits to tide you over when times get tough and competitors stumble.

In my own career as an entrepreneur, I have found that much of the success of our business comes from these principles—innovating with new products and spin-offs, embracing the technologies of DVDs and the Internet, constantly looking for production efficiencies, and reorganizing our finances to maximize profits. I've learned some of these lessons the hard way!

Believe it or not, Andrew Carnegie was the godfather of PBS, Big Bird, and Elmo, too. In the 1960s the Carnegie Corporation of New York championed the creation of the national Public Broadcasting System and nurtured the creation of *Sesame Street*.

"Maybe with the giving away of his money," speculated Carnegie biographer Joseph Wall, it helped him "justify what he had done to get that money."

Carnegie spent his last eighteen years giving away nearly 90 percent of his fortune. After his death in 1919, most of what was left was given to charities.

Carnegie gave away more money than any other twentieth-century American, with the exception of one—a fellow by the name of John D. Rockefeller, whom we will meet in just a few pages.

Unlike Andrew Carnegie, John Pierpont Morgan was not a self-made man who went from rags to riches.

He was born, as they say, with a silver spoon in his mouth. He started his own company at age twenty-four as an extension of the family business, and he went on to become America's greatest investment banker, a man who personally rescued the nation's economy on three different occasions.

Born in 1837, Morgan was raised in the lap of luxury in Hartford, Connecticut, the son of a wealthy investment banker who did most of his business in London. Young Pierpont studied business math at prep school, then studied French, German, and art history in Europe. He went to work for his father at age twenty, then moved to New York City and opened J. Pierpont Morgan & Company in 1861 to act as the family's Wall Street office, and in 1871 he started Drexel, Morgan with partner Anthony Drexel, setting up their office at what soon became the most famous address in American banking: Broad and Wall Street.

As the years passed and he got richer and richer, Morgan, who as a young man was handsome and broad-shouldered, became physically cursed with blotchy skin and a bloated, disfigured nose that was once described as looking like "a purple bulb." It was, according to one historian, a nose "like an over-ripe pomegranate, a flaming, coruscating beak that could stop traffic at 50 paces, the kind of nose usually associated with a non-stop drinker of cheap booze."

J. Pierpont Morgan. (New York Public Library)

In reality, the condition was known as rhinophyma, a condition that causes excess growth of sebaceous tissue. Even with all his money, there wasn't anything Morgan could do about the deformity other than carefully stage his photos and portraits to minimize the startling effect, which must have been intimidating when experienced in person, especially across a conference table during a financial negotiation. He once said of his nose, "It is part of the American business structure."

By the 1870s and 1880s, Morgan was emerging as America's top investment banker, juggling mergers, acquisitions, and consolidations with incredible skill and timing.

Morgan biographer Ron Chernow explained that "[d]uring the 1870s, Pierpont began to style himself as far more than a mere provider of money to companies. He wanted to be their lawyer, high priest and confidant. This wedding of certain companies to certain banks—relationship banking—would be a cardinal feature of private banking for the next century." When he invested in a company, Morgan usually insisted on hands-on powers to stabilize and reorganize the company as he saw fit, so he could maximize returns. He applied the process, which came to be known as "Morganization," to a network of railroad companies that by the early 1900s controlled nearly half of the nation's rail lines. Some of Morgan's business combinations were so huge that critics called them monopolies, or anticompetitive "trusts."

Morgan was, in Chernow's words, "America's most powerful man." "Pierpont differed from most of the Gilded Age robber barons in that their rapacity stemmed from pure greed or a lust for power while his included some strange admixture of idealism," noted Chernow. "He was honest to a fault and had a clear-cut sense of right and wrong, so when he confronted an economy that offended his business propriety, it gave him a revolutionary zeal." In 1892, J. P. Morgan helped launch General Electric Company, underwriting its first stock issue. He believed in the product, too—a decade earlier, he was the first New Yorker to have electricity put into his home. He also helped create industrial giants AT&T and International Harvester.

Not everything Morgan touched turned to gold—his shipping venture, the International Mercantile Marine, tanked after its showcase venture—a transatlantic ocean liner called the *Titanic*—hit an iceberg and sank to the bottom of the ocean during its 1912 maiden voyage, taking more than 1,500 passengers down with it.

Morgan was a devout Episcopalian, but unlike Andrew Carnegie, he had no passion for helping the poor and disadvantaged. He preferred to support the arts, and he collected paintings from Europe, Egyptian antiquities, and rare books, and delighted in throwing lavish parties on his private yacht, the *Corsair*. He cofounded the American Museum of Natural History and served as chair-

The opulent interior of the Morgan Library, which today houses many of J. Pierpont Morgan's collections. (Library of Congress)

man of the board of the Metropolitan Museum of Art, to which he donated a fortune in artwork.

Despite being married, he was said to engage in a wide range of romantic entanglements, especially with famous actresses. He reportedly kept two older actresses in a London apartment, leading one art dealer to quip, "Morgan not only collects Old Masters, he also collects old mistresses."

For nearly twenty years, from 1894 to 1913, J. P. Morgan acted like a one-man financial SWAT team, swooping in to do spectacular deals and rescue entire governments from economic collapse. At the same time, naturally, his company leveraged the emergencies to make huge profits.

In 1894, America's gold system was in danger. Gold reserves had dipped to a scant $9 million, and Morgan warned President Grover Cleveland that $12 million in drafts were about to be presented. According to Morgan biographer Daniel Alef, "In the absence of an income tax, the government's ability to increase its reserves was dependent on its ability to borrow money. But because of a two-year economic collapse, the nation's credit worthiness was essentially nil. Pierpont proposed a daring solution: He would gather $62 million in gold in exchange for $65 million in thirty-year government bonds redeemable in gold or silver and make arrangements that would avoid a dangerous gold outflow happening again." By briefly guiding the flow of gold in and out of the country and rebuilding America's gold stockpile, Morgan stabilized the system.

In 1902, Morgan cooperated with his sometime enemy President Theodore Roosevelt to help settle a coal strike. In 1904, Morgan helped finance the building of the Panama Canal, the biggest real estate transaction in history. In 1907, Wall Street fell into a panic, causing a run on banks. Without a central bank, the federal government turned to J. Pierpont Morgan for salvation.

On Thursday, October 24, 1907, panic spread on Wall Street and state banks and trust companies teetered toward collapse as customers pulled out millions of dollars in cash. That day, J. P. Morgan began an astonishing one-man rescue operation of the American economy.

To stabilize the nation's money supply, Morgan directed the secretary of the Treasury to deposit tens of millions of dollars to pass through to banks and trusts carefully hand-picked by Morgan. He announced to reporters that "if people will keep their money in the banks, everything will be all right." When people successfully withdrew amounts from one key trust company without any problems, the panic at that institution eased.

But the crisis continued—that day, the president of the New York Stock Exchange appeared in Morgan's office and declared that the exchange had to be shut down since its brokers had run out of money from banks to finance margin accounts. Morgan ordered that the exchange stay open, and in five minutes flat he worked out a deal with the nation's leading bankers to pump a critical $27 million into the exchange to keep it running.

That night, Morgan invited the top bankers in the United States to his opulent mansion on New York's Madison Avenue, installed them in his plush library, and encouraged them to find a solution as he sometimes stayed outside the room flipping playing cards, enjoying a game of solitaire. Together, they all patched together more targeted emergency cash injections to prop up vulnerable banks and keep money flowing into the stock exchange.

Morgan issued a veiled threat—any stockbroker who chose to profit from the panic would be "properly attended to." Nobody knew exactly what he meant, and nobody wanted to find out, either. The next day, Friday, came and went without a bank failure, and the pace of withdrawals eased.

By now, J. P. Morgan had choreographed the responses of the federal government, the banks, and the stock market, so there was one more weapon to unleash—the power of God. He summoned the senior religious clergy of New York City to his mansion and told them to preach optimistic sermons from the pulpit on Sunday morning. They did, and the following week, the crisis eased and the nation avoided falling into a severe depression.

It took Morgan, a financial entrepreneur of incredible energy and genius, barely ten days to save the American economy.

When Morgan pulled off this miracle, financier Bernard Baruch called him "the greatest financial genius this country has ever known." By now, some were calling him "the Napoleon of Wall

Street." His biographer Lewis Corey called the 1907 rescue "Morgan's supreme moment, the final measure of power and its ecstasy." The same year, Morgan rescued the city of New York from defaulting on its debt by talking other bankers into purchasing $30 million worth of municipal bonds. "With his financial power," wrote Pittsburgh journalist Donald Miller, "Morgan not only deflected at least three national panics, saving Americans from stock-market losses, but also virtually single-handedly steadied the course of the country's financial development before government agencies grew up to that task."

Like Andrew Carnegie, J. P. Morgan had his share of enemies, too, including a Republican senator who called him "a beefy, red-faced, thick-necked financial bully, drunk with wealth and power, [who] bawls his orders to stock markets, directors, courts, governments and nations." But biographer Jean Strouse noted, "Even some of Morgan's critics said he was a builder and conservator, not a wrecker, liar or cheat." She credited him with thriving "in cycles of expansion and contraction, through panics, depressions, competitive price wars, speculative gambles and government defaults." When a "Morganization" was successful, she wrote, "stock prices rose; when a combination [merger] failed, all his financial and political efforts could not keep share prices from falling." Morgan thought that necessity "had drafted him to do what he could to police the markets and keep the U.S. economy on track, but in the end no one could control money."

Morgan could be cold-blooded when he felt it necessary. Take, for example, his treatment of the great genius, inventor, and fellow entrepreneur Thomas Edison, who, over the course of his lifetime, patented 1,093 inventions and pioneered recorded sound, the alkaline battery, the motion picture camera, the stock ticker, improved X-ray machines and telegraph equipment, the modern R&D lab, the lightbulb, and sustained electric light.

The Wizard of Wall Street: J. P. Morgan at a 1917 war bonds rally in New York. In an odd twist, Morgan's famous nose, described by witnesses as horribly ugly, seems completely handsome in this photo, which must have been taken on a "good nose day" for the master financier. (Library of Congress)

By the late 1880s, Edison had opened up 121 Edison central power stations in the United States, and J. P. Morgan owned a majority of the shares of Edison's firm, the Edison General Electric Company. In 1892, without warning Edison, Morgan abruptly merged Edison's company with another, more profitable company, demoted Edison, and then pulled Edison's name off the company, now known simply as General Electric.

Edison's feelings were hurt, but he continued to thrive. So did one of the engineers in his laboratory, a brilliant young fellow named Henry Ford. Edison liked Ford's idea of a new automobile and let Ford use his warehouse to build two experimental prototypes. Eventually, as a full-time entrepreneur on his own, Ford unleashed the power of mass production and the moving assembly line, creating the affordable Model T "car for the masses" and the Ford Motor Company, which achieved global reach and power.

As for Morgan, in 1913, just before he died at age seventy-five, he championed the creation of the Federal Reserve, which strengthened America's banking system. The idea was to eliminate the need for the kind of private bailouts he'd conducted. On the morning of his funeral, the New York Stock Exchange was shut down in his honor, a move usually reserved for heads of state. At the time of his death, he controlled ten railroads, five industrial companies, including U.S. Steel, and a portfolio of insurance companies and banks. His personal wealth was estimated at anywhere from $1 billion to $40 billion in today's dollars.

It was a lot of money, but one fellow entrepreneur and supertycoon wasn't too impressed.

Upon hearing the figures, this man reportedly quipped, probably half in jest, "And to think he wasn't even a rich man."

Only one person could get away with a crack like that.

His name was John D. Rockefeller. He was the most successful

American entrepreneur of all time—and the richest man in modern history.

If you measure greatness in business by the amount of money you make, then John D. Rockefeller was the greatest entrepreneur in American history.

And if you measure greatness in life by the amount of money you give to others, then Rockefeller was one of the greatest philanthropists who ever lived.

Which is not a bad record for a slightly built, working-class, upstate New York boy, born in 1839, who grew up in a family that experienced extreme economic instability, and whose often-absent father, William, was a traveling salesman who was widely believed to be a con artist, or "flimflam man." William did find time to teach his offspring some basic business lessons, including one he explained this way: "I cheat my boys every chance I get. I want to make 'em sharp." John's long-suffering mother, by contrast, taught young Rockefeller the Christian virtues of thrift, charity, hard work, and self-control. The family moved to Cleveland, Ohio, to escape the shame of rumors that connected the father to alleged sexual impropriety.

As a boy, John D. Rockefeller attended Baptist church services with his devout mother and his siblings. One day, the minister encouraged his congregation to make as much money as possible—and give away as much money as possible. "It was at this moment," Rockefeller recalled, "that the financial plan of my life was formed." Eventually, Rockefeller would live out the biblical concept detailed in Luke 6:38, "Give, and it will be given to you. A good measure, pressed down, shaken together and running over, will be poured into your lap. For with the measure you use, it will be measured to you." Later, looking back on the incredible fortune he made, Rockefeller declared simply, "God gave me the money."

Rockefeller was fascinated with money from an early age. As a boy he bought candy in bulk and sold it at a profit to his siblings. As soon as he turned sixteen, Rockefeller started hustling for a steady income, taking an accounting course (just like Andrew Carnegie) and a bookkeeping job at a small produce shipping company. He worked very hard and loved learning, he remembered, "all the methods and systems of the office." His first day of work was September 26, 1855, a date he celebrated for the rest of his life. "All my future seemed to hinge on that day," he remembered. "I often tremble when I ask myself the question: 'What if I had not got the job?'" He began the lifelong habit of recording all his expenses.

The young Rockefeller soaked up the world of small business like a sponge, earning the de facto equivalent of an MBA in real-world experience by the time he was eighteen years old. "To begin with, my work was done in the office of the firm itself," he remembered. "I was almost always present when they talked of their affairs, laid out their plans, and decided upon a course of action. I thus had an advantage over other boys of my age, who were quicker and who could figure and write better than I. The firm conducted a business with so many ramifications that this education was quite extensive. They owned dwelling-houses, warehouses, and buildings which were rented for offices and a variety of uses, and I had to collect the rents. They shipped by rail, canal, and lake. There were many different kinds of negotiations and transactions going on, and with all these I was in close touch."

From the start, Rockefeller donated 6 percent of his small salary to charity, and was soon tithing to his Baptist church. He declared that his life's ambition was to earn $100,000 and live to be one hundred years old. He achieved his first goal very quickly, and he missed the second by less than three years.

A young John D. Rockefeller. (New York Public Library)

In 1859, at the tender age of eighteen, Rockefeller borrowed $1,000 from his father and, with a partner, started his own company and became a full-time entrepreneur, specializing in trading produce, meat, and grain. "He developed a reputation among bankers for being a devout Christian who was absolutely honest," wrote journalist Scott Smith, "giving his firm an advantage in lining up support."

Rockefeller and his partner made big money on government contracts during the American Civil War. By 1862, their profits totaled some $400,000 in today's currency—but Rockefeller always kept his eye open for new opportunities. "He thought large and lived by the dictum 'never be afraid to give up the good to go for the great,'" noted historian June McCash. "He always had a plan and a clear-sighted goal." At the age of twenty-one, Rockefeller was a prominent businessman in Cleveland. "Business came in upon us so fast that we hardly knew how to take care of it," he later marveled.

In 1864, at age twenty-five, Rockefeller and his partners made one of the best investments in business history: they acquired control of Cleveland's biggest oil refinery, which processed five hundred barrels of crude a day, twice the volume of its closest competitor. According to journalist Scott Smith, "By that time, whale oil had become too expensive for most Americans to use for lighting, so they had turned to tallow, lard, cottonseed oil, coal oil, and the newest—kerosene, which was refined from the only known petroleum fields in the world, in northwest Pennsylvania. Pitched the opportunity to build a refinery in Cleveland, with its easy access to transport by rivers and lakes, Rockefeller seized it."

Rockefeller studied the brand-new oil market carefully. It was just five years since oil was discovered in Pennsylvania, which was pretty close to Rockefeller's home base of Cleveland. He shrewdly predicted that the big money was to be made in the consistent, steady business of refining and shipping, not the speculative business of drilling, where you could lose a lot of money punching dry holes in the ground. "Never one to do things halfway, he plunged headlong into the business," wrote biographer Ron Chernow. "There was humility in his eagerness to learn. Devoid of superior airs, he was often seen at 6:30 a.m. going into the cooper shop to roll out barrels. Since a residue of sulfuric acid remained after refining, he drew up plans to convert it to fertilizer, the first of many worthwhile and extremely profitable by-products from waste materials."

It was the perfect time to jump into the oil business. The American economy was leaping westward along the newly built railroad tracks, and industry was about to take off on an oil-powered boom.

Rockefeller later told of the excitement he felt in being a young, hands-on entrepreneur, and an aggressive competitor in a cutthroat industry: "I shall never forget how hungry I was in those days. I ran up and down the tops of freight cars, I hurried up the boys." Rockefeller and his partners expanded rapidly. "We were being confronted with fresh emergencies constantly," he remembered. "A new oil field would be discovered, tanks for storage had to be built almost overnight, and this was going on when old fields were being exhausted, so we were therefore often under the double strain of losing the facilities in one place where we were fully equipped, and having to build up a plant for storing and transporting in a new field where we were totally unprepared. These are some of the things which make the whole oil trade a perilous one, but we had with us a group of courageous men who recognized the great principle that a business cannot be a great success that does not fully and efficiently accept and take advantage of its opportunities."

In 1867 Rockefeller recapitalized his company with a $100,000 loan from Stephen Harkness, who became a silent partner in the firm and required that his relative Henry Flagler also be brought in as a partner to represent his interests. A few years earlier, Flagler had gone broke in the salt business, but he became a perfect partner for Rockefeller and later became a founding partner and one-sixth owner of Rockefeller's Standard Oil Company. Later, when he cashed out, Flagler had made enough money on his Standard Oil stock that he pretty much created the modern state of Florida, turning it, in the words of historian John Steele Gordon, "from a semi-tropical wilderness into a tourist mecca and agricultural powerhouse."

On December 18, 1867, a week before Christmas, Rockefeller's luggage was loaded onto the eastbound New York Express at Cleveland's Union Terminal train station. The train pulled away at 6:40 that morning, but by chance, Rockefeller wasn't on it. He was a few minutes late and just missed the train. At 3:11 P.M., east of the tiny New York State community of Angola, the two last cars of the speeding train derailed as it crossed the bridge over Big Sister Creek, sending one coach car plummeting down the gorge to the creek bed forty feet below. Ignited by the wooden car's heating stoves and kerosene lanterns, it exploded into an inferno, trapping and killing nearly fifty people inside, many of them burned alive. Rockefeller, who took a later train, sent a telegram back to his wife in Cleveland: "THANK GOD I AM UNHARMED." The event became known as the "Angola Horror," and Rockefeller barely escaped it, just as Cornelius Vanderbilt narrowly escaped a similar railroad disaster decades earlier.

In 1868, Rockefeller secretly cut a deal with the Lake Shore Railway that guaranteed sixty carloads of oil per day in exchange for reducing the freight charge from $2.40 per barrel to $1.65. Both sides kept the deal secret, and Rockefeller gained a huge competitive advantage. He struck similar deals with other railroads that increased costs for his competitors. This type of pricing favoritism, or conspiracy, was outlawed by the federal government twenty years later when it declared railroads to be common carriers for public benefit, but for now, Rockefeller had a wide-open field to secretly cash in on the economies of scale.

As his entrepreneurial venture thrived, Rockefeller bought up some competitors and drove others out of business who simply couldn't compete with him. In 1870, Rockefeller and his partners formed a joint-stock business, Standard Oil Company (Ohio), which he considered a cooperative alliance and critics attacked as a competition-killing cartel, or monopoly. Soon Standard Oil was being publicly attacked as "the most cruel, impudent, pitiless, and grasping monopoly that ever fastened upon a country" by America's largest newspaper, the *New York World*. Biographer Ron Chernow reported that "Rockefeller and other industrial captains conspired to kill competitive capitalism in favor of a new monopoly capitalism."

In what became known as "The Cleveland Massacre of 1872,"

Rockefeller seized control of twenty-two of his twenty-six local competitors. His terms were often generous, but there was an implicit risk for those who refused to play ball—one of Rockefeller's targets lamented that "if we did not sell out we should be crushed out." Historian Charles Morris noted that "Rockefeller may have been unique among oil executives for his understanding of distribution, pursuing tightly integrated marketing and distribution operations from the earliest days, rapidly moving from contractual relationships to mergers." Biographer Chernow wrote that the year 1872 "revealed both his finest and most problematic qualities: his visionary leadership, courageous persistence and capacity to think in strategic terms, but also his lust for domination, self-righteousness and contempt for those who made the mistake of standing in his way."

In 1879, Rockefeller's Standard Oil was indicted by the state of Pennsylvania on charges of running a monopoly, and other states brought suits as well. For Rockefeller, who was, at the same time, borrowing heavily from banks and reinvesting his profits to keep growing, the strain was tremendous. As he labored to create a "national trust," or a vast integrated business empire of pumping, shipping, barrel-making, and warehousing, and plants for manufacturing oil by-products, pipelines, and international wholesaling, he couldn't sleep, fell deep into debt, and constantly worried. "All the fortune that I have made has not served to compensate me for the anxiety of that period," he said.

By 1879, Rockefeller, still a young man at forty, controlled nearly 90 percent of America's oil industry, with 100,000 employees, 20,000 oil wells, 5,000 railroad tank cars, 4,000 miles of pipeline, and a booming overseas business. "By the early 1890s, Standard Oil had achieved virtually complete vertical and horizontal integration of the American petroleum industry—something unusual in American business," observed historian Robert Cherny. "Standard's monopoly proved to be short-lived, however. With the discovery of new oil fields in Texas and elsewhere, new companies tapped those fields and quickly followed the path of vertical integration."

Rockefeller had created the world's first great modern multinational corporation. He moved his business and family to New York City and often took the subway to work, along with regular folks. He eventually built a country retreat in Westchester that was so palatial that one visitor called it "the kind of place that God would have built if only he'd had the money." In 1901, fellow tycoon J. P. Morgan offered Rockefeller and his son spots on the board of U.S. Steel.

Then, at the turn of the twentieth century, at the time his business was going through the roof with the emergence of an automobile industry hungry for Standard Oil's gasoline products, Rockefeller surprised everyone. He stepped away from the stresses and strains of day-to-day management of his empire, turned things over to his partners and his son and designated heir apparent John D. Rockefeller, Jr., and devoted much of his time to giving his money away, just as he'd vowed to do as a teenager. He retained the title of president and still had major influence on the company, but was semiretired from business and now a full-time philanthropist.

For years, Rockefeller had already been donating huge sums to charity. By the 1880s, he was receiving thousands of appeals for money every month, and he discussed the letters with his family around the breakfast table. "Four-fifths of these letters," Rockefeller remembered, were "requests of money for personal use, with no other title to consideration than that the writer would be gratified to have it." He started out by supporting the Baptist Church and education for African Americans.

Rockefeller discovered that the stresses of "do-it-yourself" charity on a meaningful scale could be just as bad as those of running a giant business. "About the year 1890 I was still following the haphazard fashion of giving here and there as appeals presented themselves. I investigated as I could, and worked myself almost to a nervous breakdown," Rockefeller explained in his 1909 memoir. "There was then forced upon me the necessity to organize and plan this department of our daily tasks on as distinct lines of progress as we did with our business affairs."

Rockefeller hired a Baptist preacher to advise him on his donations. The preacher said that Rockefeller's ever-increasing fortune was like "an avalanche," and warned him, "You must keep up with it! You must distribute it faster than it grows! If you do not, it will crush you and your children and your children's children!" Rockefeller agreed, but also worried about the dangers of charity if it was not managed properly. "It is a great problem," he said, "to learn how to give without weakening the moral backbone of the beneficiary." But if people "can be educated to help themselves," he reasoned, "we strike at the root of many of the evils of the world." He concluded, "The only thing which is of lasting benefit to a man is that which he does for himself. Money which comes to him without effort on his part is seldom a benefit and often a curse." Slowly and carefully, Rockefeller hired experts who helped him to become a philanthropist on a scale never before seen in history, a noble calling that occupied most of the last forty years of his life.

During his life and in the decades that followed his death, Rockefeller-funded projects made huge strides toward eliminating hookworm disease, malaria, scarlet fever, tuberculosis, and typhus, and funded research that led to the yellow fever and cerebrospinal meningitis vaccines. Rockefeller founded the University of Chicago, yet insisted that his name appear nowhere on the campus. He said the school was "the best investment I ever made." He supported the Baptist Church in establishing Atlanta's Spelman College, the

American colossus: John D. Rockefeller, the greatest entrepreneur and philanthropist in American history and the richest man in modern history (second from right), inspects "the best investment I ever made," the University of Chicago, on its tenth anniversary in 1901. (University of Chicago)

oldest college historically for African American women, which has educated ambassadors, business leaders, and Pulitzer Prize winners. He named the school after his wife.

Rockefeller founded schools of public health and hygiene at Johns Hopkins University and Harvard. He founded Rockefeller University in New York, a world-class scientific and medical institution. He introduced China to modern medical practices. His funds helped alleviate poverty in the South, provided education to hundreds of thousands of African Americans, and boosted medical and scientific research around the world.

In 1902, Rockefeller created a "General Education Board" that supported high schools, colleges, and universities around the na-

CHAPTER 5

THE WINNERS

Entrepreneurship has no age or time limits . . . it thrives on hope and inspira-

tion. Those who choose to participate can only make the world a better place.

—Debbi Fields, founder of Mrs. Fields Cookies

I f you're ever in need of some inspiration, just think of the American entrepreneur.

And if you ever want a little extra inspiration, think of the millions of women and minority entrepreneurs who have helped build our nation over the last 250 years.

It's tough enough being an entrepreneur. It's all on you. You take the risk, you meet the payroll, you sweat all the details, you stay up at night worrying about your numbers and your customers. Success or failure is in your hands.

But for many decades our American women and minority entrepreneurs had to face not only the usual hurdles of business, but often a shortage of connections and credit and start-up capital, and sometimes even downright hostility from some parts of our government and society.

There's one story that perfectly captures the grit, determination, and flat-out courage shown by countless women and minority entrepreneurs who have graced the pages of American history—the story of Madam C. J. Walker, the first self-made black female millionaire, and a pioneer in the cosmetics industry.

She was a strong, churchgoing, Louisiana-born woman, which makes me like her even more, as I married such a woman myself!

Madam Walker was born under the name Sarah Breedlove in 1867 in a cabin on the Burney plantation in Delta, Louisiana, a small community that's about an hour-and-a-half drive from my house. Four years before she was born, the Burney plantation was a staging area for a turning point of the Civil War, General Ulysses S. Grant's siege of Vicksburg, Mississippi. Walker grew up in a family of share-croppers, in the midst of abject poverty, drudgery, and misery.

Walker's parents were former slaves, and she was the first of her family to be born into freedom. She was orphaned at age seven. She moved in with a sister and her sister's abusive husband, a situation she resolved to escape. "I married at the age of 14 in order to get a home of my own," Walker later explained. Six years later, Walker's own husband vanished from the scene. She was a mother at seventeen, and now at twenty she was a single mother with a little girl to take care of. To put food on the table, she worked as a laundress, scrubbing white people's clothes on a metal washboard.

In 1889, Walker joined legions of other black migrants heading north to seek new opportunities, and she moved to St. Louis, where her four brothers were barbers. She continued being a washer-woman, but when she joined the local African Methodist Episcopal (A.M.E.) church, she was inspired by the many high-achieving African professionals she met there, including teachers, lawyers, and doctors. "That's when she began to envision herself as something other than an uneducated washerwoman," said A'Lelia Bundles, Walker's great-great-granddaughter, who has done extensive re-search into Walker's sometimes mysterious past. She plunged into civic affairs and volunteer work, attended night school, and resolved to improve life for herself and her daughter. "I was at my washtubs one morning with a heavy wash before me," Walker recalled. "As I bent over the washboard, I said to myself, 'What are you going to do when you grow old and your back gets stiff?'"

Walker moved to Denver, Pittsburgh, and Indianapolis, had a failed second marriage, and, as fate would have it, saw her hair start falling out. It may have been stress, or bad nutrition, or it may have been the result of the widespread poor hair hygiene of the time. Many people, especially poor folks, didn't wash their hair more than once a month or so.

There are two versions of what happened next. First, there is Walker's version, in which her inspiration comes from a near-biblical vision. In a 1917 interview, she explained that she prayed to God for a miracle. "He answered my prayer," she reported. "For one night I had a dream, and in that dream a big black man appeared to me and told me what to mix for my hair. Some of the remedy was from Africa, but I sent for it, mixed it, put it on my scalp and in a few weeks my hair was coming in faster than it had ever fallen out." She shared the elixir with friends, who were amazed at its almost magical power to heal and grow hair. Then she began bottling and selling it, and an entrepreneurial empire was born. The truth, however, was a bit more complicated. In St. Louis and Denver, it turns out, she worked as a sales agent for African American cosmetics entrepreneur Annie Pope-Turnbo, selling, among other things, hair products.

Walker changed her name from Sarah Breedlove to the regal-sounding "Madam C. J. Walker," in honor of her third husband, and in 1906 started her own line of products, including the top-selling "Madam Walker's Wonderful Hair Grower," and a hair-straightening product that included coconut oil, beeswax, copper sulfate, sulfur, and perfume. The booming sales of this product may have resulted not so much from any magic powers of its formula but rather from the fact that people started washing their hair more often as hygiene and nutrition were improving at the turn of the twentieth century. The potion's sulfur may have helped heal scalp problems, too.

Blessed with a dazzling personality and a spellbinding sales pitch, Madam Walker started off selling her products door-to-door in Denver's black neighborhoods, then moved to Indianapolis and opened up a manufacturing plant. She held product demonstrations by massaging customers' scalps, pampering them, and making them feel beautiful. Walker hired a strong team of thousands of African American female door-to-door sales agents who became famous for their white blouses, black skirts, and leather satchels and were called "Walker Agents." Money started flowing in by the bucketload.

This was grassroots, direct-to-consumer marketing, and Walker and her agents had a wide-open market, as few people had capitalized on this niche before in a big way. White cosmetics firms couldn't have cared less about black business; they didn't know there was much business to begin with. "Madam Walker fit into a whole pattern of women selling products in localities," explained Kathy Peiss, a history professor at the University of Pennsylvania. "But what was interesting about Walker was how successful she was in building a national company with very high levels of sales. There were many, many women entrepreneurs, but most of them never made it, and she did."

Starting in 1906, Walker ran newspaper ads featuring images of her own luxuriant hair, and before-and-after-treatment shots. She hit the roads through the American South, working with black churches and civic groups, staging demonstrations and classes, signing up sales agents and customers. Within just a few years, her sales force numbered in the thousands, and she was raking in a huge annual income unmatched by all but the most successful white businesspeople.

Walker expanded her business to the Caribbean and Central

Madam C. J. Walker, daughter of slaves, who created a legendary beauty products empire. (Scurlock Studio, Smithsonian Institution)

An early advertisement for Walker's products. (Library of Congress)

America, and pioneered business models later used by cosmetics giants like Avon, Helena Rubinstein, Mary Kay, and Elizabeth Arden, including door-to-door sales, product demonstrations, direct marketing, and money-back guarantees. In 1917, she staged one of the first national meetings of businesswomen in America: the Madam C. J. Walker Hair Culturists Union of America convention in Philadelphia.

In 1913, Madam Walker moved to New York and bought and renovated two combined old-style brownstones on West 136th Street, as she explained, "without regard to cost but with considerable regard for good taste." Her new home featured scalloped pale gray chiffon curtains that flanked stylized Venetian windows, French doors that opened to a downstairs hair salon, Doric columns that marked the entrance to the upstairs living quarters, plus an intricately carved fireplace and English wall tapestries.

Walker also built a spectacular $250,000 three-story stucco Italian Renaissance–style suburban mansion, which she called Villa Lewaro, on a 20,000-square-foot estate in Irvington-on-Hudson, just a few miles down the road from John D. Rockefeller's estate, complete with swimming pool, high ceilings, and marble floors. She explained that the purpose of the mansion was not conspicuous consumption but inspiration: "I am building this home so that I can show young black boys and girls all of their possibilities."

Walker and her daughter A'Lelia became the toasts of black New York, and staged parties and literary salons attended by Langston Hughes, Zora Neale Hurston, dancer Isadora Duncan, and Italian tenor Enrico Caruso. In 1917, Walker traveled to Washington, DC, to present an antilynching petition to the White House. That year, she told a reporter, "I am not a millionaire, but hope to be some day, not because of the money but because I could do so much more to help my race."

Sadly, Walker only got to live in her fantastic estate for a year

Madam C. J. Walker driving her niece and two company employees in 1911. (New York Public Library)

before she died of kidney failure in 1919 at the age of fifty-one. Just before Walker died, her doctor heard her say, "I want to live to help my race." That she did, and much more.

The great sociologist W. E. B. Du Bois eulogized Madam Walker this way: "It is given to few persons to transform a people in a generation. Yet this was done by the late Madame C. J. Walker," who "revolutionized the personal habits and appearance of millions of human beings."

"I am a woman who came from the cotton fields of the South," said Walker in a speech to the National Negro Business League convention a few years before her death. "From there I was promoted to the washtub. From there I was promoted to the cook kitchen. And from there I promoted myself into the business of manufacturing." She announced proudly, "I have built my own factory on my own ground."

What was Madam Walker's formula for success? In short, being proactive. "I got my start by giving myself a start," she said. She explained, "Don't sit around waiting for opportunities. You have to get up and make them." Another time, she said, "There is no royal flower-strewn path to success. And if there is, I have not found it, for if I have accomplished anything in life, it is because I have been willing to work hard."

At the same time that Madam C. J. Walker was achieving her destiny, a black man was writing his own incredible rags-to-riches story of American entrepreneurship in the great state of North Carolina.

John Merrick was born into slavery in 1859, and after emancipation he went to work at a young age as a brick mason to support his parents and siblings. When construction work slowed down, he trained as an apprentice barber. He saw barbershops as a thriving business with a strong future, so at age twenty he went to work in a barbershop in Raleigh as a shoeshiner. In 1880, when a friend opened a shop, Merrick joined as a barber, and within two years he bought the shop. Within ten years he owned six barbershops in Durham and Raleigh, on top of which he sold his own line of grooming products. He accomplished this during the post–Reconstruction era, a time when racial violence and oppression against black citizens were plaguing several southern states.

Merrick was a witty, sociable, outgoing man, a sponge for information and a charismatic networker. He was pals with everyone from the poorest farmers to the wealthiest white business leaders in the city. The barbershop was the perfect stage for his personality, and he loved the barbershop atmosphere of brotherhood, solidarity, and conversation. The shops also enabled him to make valuable connections with white business and community leaders who patronized his business. One of his customers, a wealthy white tobacco man named Washington Duke (who later had a university named after him), gave Merrick hot tips on the Durham property market. By the end of the 1890s, Merrick was one of the biggest real estate owners in the city.

A churchgoing family man with five children, Merrick wasn't just interested in improving himself; he wanted to help uplift the whole African American community. Since black citizens couldn't get insurance policies, Merrick and other Durham black leaders joined together to start a "fraternal insurance society," or "benefit club," whose members pooled funds to cover accidents, funeral costs, and other expenses. Merrick also helped found a black-owned bank, drug company, real estate company, textile mill, newspaper, and hospital. The net effect of all these ventures was to empower black citizens with jobs and economic opportunity, and to fuel the growth of a vibrant, prosperous black middle class in the city of Durham, which came to be known as "Black Wall Street" and the "Capital of the Black Middle Class."

In 1898, using a start-up loan from his mentor Washington Duke, Merrick launched his most profitable and enduring achievement, the North Carolina Mutual Life Insurance Company. This was a dangerous time for a black American to start a business. Racial lynchings were on the rise, and the U.S. Supreme Court had recently legalized segregation with its *Plessy v. Ferguson* decision. At first, the business struggled. In the first year, premiums totaled less than $500. By the third year, five out of seven partners had quit, and the firm was running at a loss.

But like many American entrepreneurs, Merrick had courage and tenacity to spare. He persisted, powered by a desire to help his community, and he gradually grew his insurance business across the American South, and into what was called the "world's largest Negro business" at that point in history.

Merrick became one of the most celebrated and respected

successful black businessmen of the era, and by capitalizing on an untapped market need—until then, black people couldn't get insurance—North Carolina Mutual Life became the largest black-owned business in America. "He was a beacon for African American entrepreneurs," said Kimberly Moore, a modern executive of the company Merrick started. "He was a beacon for African American uplift—economically, socially, educationally. He took a lot of risks. He was saying African Americans needed to be insured. There was an inherent risk of political backlash. But he took a chance. It was pretty revolutionary." When W. E. B. Du Bois visited Durham in 1910, he was so impressed that he wrote, "There is in this small city a group of 5,000 or more colored people, whose social and economic development is more striking than that of any similar group in the nation."

Black American entrepreneurs have been contributing to the economic development of the United States ever since day one of the nation. Even in the darkest days of segregation and discrimination, African Americans have been business owners, sole proprietors, product inventors and developers, innovators, publishers, service providers, merchants, artisans, networkers, and investors.

In fact, the rich African American heritage of entrepreneurship dates all the way back to their ancestral homelands across the Atlantic. The victims of the American slave trade were kidnapped and sold (ironically, often by local black African entrepreneurs who did business with white buyers) from areas in West and Central Africa in what scholar Juliet Walker has called "complex, organized, and structured market economies in which they participated as producers, traders, brokers, merchants, and entrepreneurs." She added that these economies were "propelled by a high degree of both individual and communally based profit-oriented entrepreneurial activities." As a proverb of Nigeria's Yoruba tribe puts it, "The world is a market, the market is the world."

In the early days of American independence, free black entrepreneurs often concentrated in the cities of New England and the upper Atlantic states, but their impact was felt across the nation. In San Francisco, one multiracial entrepreneur, William Alexander Leidesdorff, Jr., was a founding father of the city's business community, built the city's first hotel and a successful shipyard and lumberyard, and operated a real estate business in the early to mid-1800s. The whole time, almost nobody knew the light-skinned Leidesdorff had a black African heritage. He served as the city's first treasurer, and is credited as being America's first millionaire of black ancestry—in 1856 his estate was valued at $1.4 million, or more than $20 million in today's dollars.

By the turn of the twentieth century, black leader Booker T. Washington had formed the National Negro Business League and built it to six hundred chapters, and he encouraged African Americans to uplift themselves and their community by launching their own business ventures. By 1920, the League had given birth to a wide range of offshoot organizations, including the National Negro Bankers Association, the National Negro Press Association, the National Association of Negro Funeral Directors, the National Negro Bar Association, the National Association of Negro Insurance Men, the National Negro Retail Merchants' Association, the National Association of Negro Real Estate Dealers, and the National Negro Finance Corporation.

In both the North and South, many black businesses were often boxed in by social customs to serve black customers only, and this created, by necessity, something of a "golden age" of black entrepreneurship and commerce within the shackles of segregation.

Racial segregation and the geographic concentration of African Americans, in fact, caused many black customers to patronize predominantly black businesses, including black-owned grocery and retail stores, barber and beauty shops, and funeral homes, causing them to flourish and provide a bedrock for the community. For example, explained researchers Vicki Bogan and William Darity, Jr., "in Chicago between 1890 and 1930, the emergence of a considerable Black population and the subsequent segregation of this community facilitated the development of a racially interlocking market on the South Side of Chicago. These Black businesses undertook numerous innovations to overcome the problems of institutional racism, government support of competitors, and other types of discrimination."

But when racial integration came, paradoxically, it had a damaging effect on many black businesses. "When I was growing up, we had black laundromats and drugstores," recalled Oakland accountant Herman Morris of his boyhood in Little Rock, Arkansas. "But integration changed all that. All of a sudden—hallelujah—you could work and shop with whites. People turned away from black economic institutions because that was a way of getting away from the past." Researcher Robert Suggs explained to *Inc.* magazine in 1986 that this was especially true among middle-class blacks: "It was like an insurmountable trade barrier had dissolved overnight. The traditional black business almost immediately lost its most affluent clientele."

One group of black entrepreneurs who played a central role in our history was funeral parlor owners, who, as pillars of many African American communities, helped promote the movement for full equality and civil rights in the 1950s and 1960s.

In 1956, funeral home owner William Shortridge helped create the Alabama Christian Movement for Human Rights to fight segregation and discrimination. Arthur Gaston, who was a highly successful banker, insurance provider, and funeral parlor owner in Birmingham, Alabama, lent Martin Luther King, Jr., a room at his Gaston Motel that became King's headquarters as he led a turning point in the civil rights movement with his arrest in that city in 1963.

Another business that became a center of community life in many black neighborhoods ever since the end of the Civil War was the black-owned barbershop, where neighbors could talk about their struggles and successes freely, in an atmosphere of fellowship, laughter, and safety.

One day in Baltimore in the late 1940s, a six-year-old black boy named Reginald F. Lewis stepped out of the bathtub and into a towel held by his grandma and grandpa.

During the bath, the boy had heard his grandparents talking about job discrimination against black Americans, and how unfair it was.

Toweling off their boy, his grandparents looked at him and said, "Well, maybe it will be different for him." Then they asked him, "Well, is it going to be any different for you?"

"Yeah," said Reginald, "'cause why should white guys have all the fun?"

That question set the tone for the rest of his life, and Reginald F. Lewis went on to become a Harvard-trained lawyer, venture capitalist, and corporate takeover artist, one of America's greatest black entrepreneurs and philanthropists.

Lewis was also inspired by two simple pieces of advice his grandparents gave him: "Know your job and do it well," said his grandfather, and his grandmother gave Lewis a tin can and told him to save everything he earned.

Young Reginald pursued both ideas with a passion. He kept his earnings in a tin can known as "Reggie's Hidden Treasure." Within two years he built up his paper route from ten customers to one hundred, and was saving eighteen out of every twenty dollars per week he made. He sold the business at a profit, his first coup in an entrepreneurial career that would eventually make business history. In high school, Reginald served as captain of the football, basketball, and baseball teams and was elected vice president of the student body. On weekends and nights, he worked jobs with his grandpa.

Like Madam C. J. Walker and countless other American entrepreneurs, Lewis was filled with a passion for self-improvement, and a vision for achieving it. Early on, he decided that his destiny was to have a career that combined the law and business. In 1961, almost as soon as he enrolled at historically black Virginia State University on a football scholarship, he fell in "love at first sight" with the subject of economics. "I quit football after my freshman year and decided to get serious about my studies. The college years were wild. I crammed a lot of living into those four years. After a rotten freshman year, I really started to study. I got straight A's in economics and always went beyond the course. I started reading the *New York Times* and *The Wall Street Journal* every day." One of his classmates recalled, "He always had a purpose. Where other guys were taking courses to get out of school, Reggie had a master plan in mind. When other guys were reading comics, he was reading *The Wall Street Journal*." He graduated from Virginia State University on the dean's list.

In 1965, Reginald Lewis's career path intersected with the legacy of John D. Rockefeller. The Rockefeller Foundation, started decades earlier by the great entrepreneur, financed a summer school program at Harvard Law School to introduce promising African American students to the study of law. Lewis impressed the Harvard faculty so much that they invited him to attend Harvard Law that autumn. He was, in other words, one of the very few students admitted to the law school without even applying! At Harvard,

Lewis developed a passion for securities law and mergers and acquisitions, and upon graduating he landed a job with a prestigious New York law firm.

Lewis recalled in his autobiography, "I did the usual work doled out to beginning associates: setting up corporations, preparing joint venture agreements, securities law filings, some not-for-profit corporate work. I worked on a series of transactions involving small venture capital type deals that were particularly instructive, and on several initial public offerings (IPOs) which were then all the rage."

In 1970, Lewis and a small group of other attorneys started up a black-run New York corporate law firm, and he helped minority-owned businesses obtain badly needed investment capital. Lewis was said to be a tough negotiator and a high-expectations boss, who wanted his employees to give their absolute maximum effort at all times. One of his favorite sayings was "That is not acceptable."

In 1983, his desire to "do his own deals" led Lewis to become a full-fledged financial entrepreneur, and he opened his own investment company, TLC (The Lewis Companies) Group. Within one year, he closed his first major deal by acquiring the McCall Pattern Company, a home sewing-pattern business that he took over with a leveraged buyout. He financed the deal largely with other people's money, leveraging $1 million with his capital plus a $24 million loan. He sold the company four years later at a profit of more than $50 million, a return on his own investment of 90 to 1.

In 1987, he created the Reginald F. Lewis Foundation, which funded philanthropic grants to a wide range of artistic, educational, charitable, medical, and civil rights institutions around the world, including historically black Howard University, and his alma mater, Harvard Law School—to which he gave their biggest donation to date.

Also in 1987, Reginald Lewis orchestrated his greatest triumph—the $985 million takeover of the international division of Beatrice

Foods, which created the first black-owned billion-dollar company, represented the biggest leveraged buyout of overseas assets by an American company in history, and made him one of the wealthiest African Americans in the nation.

Lewis renamed the company TLC Beatrice International, and suddenly he was in charge of a sprawling global collection of sixty-four companies operating in thirty-one countries, ranging from a sausage producer in Spain and an ice cream maker in Germany to a potato chip operation in Ireland. As chairman and CEO, he moved rapidly to pay down the company's debt, improve operations, and increase the profits and value of the company. In the process, he expanded his personal wealth to what *Fortune* magazine estimated at $400 million. With annual sales of $1.5 billion, TLC Beatrice was ranked first on the *Black Enterprise* Top 100 list of African American–owned businesses ranked on the Fortune 500. "By 1990," wrote journalist Irene Silverman, "after selling off assets in Latin America and Asia, he had turned the floundering company around, tripling its previous year's net income and making TLC Beatrice the biggest black-owned company in the U.S."

Lewis, a devoted family man, moved with his wife, an accomplished attorney, and their two daughters to Paris to run TLC Beatrice's global business, moving into a historic town house near the National Assembly building. He studied French and collected paintings by Picasso and Matisse.

Reginald Lewis was mindful and proud of his ethnicity, but modest about his historic achievements as a black entrepreneur. "I'm trying not to take it too seriously," he explained. "It's tough enough to operate without the added pressure that if I make a mistake, I let down 30 million people. I think of myself as an American of African descent who's committed to what he is doing. If that work is an inspiration and helps others of my ethnic background, or any other, I'm delighted. But I don't want it to seep into decisions on how we evaluate our business." On another occasion, he said to the *New York Times*, "Unfortunately, when we label people it tends to circumscribe and define them in ways that cut away from their accomplishments. I decided that particularly in my business career, I would do everything I could to avoid that happening."

In January 1993, after a very sudden onset of brain cancer, Reginald F. Lewis died at only fifty years of age. At his funeral, a statement from his longtime friend, former New York mayor David N. Dinkins, was read. "Reginald Lewis accomplished more in half a century than most of us could ever deem imaginable. And his brilliant career was matched always by a warm and generous heart." Dinkins added, "It is said that service to others is the rent we pay on earth. Reg Lewis departed us paid in full."

One of Reg Lewis's favorite sayings was "Keep going, no matter what."

Oprah Winfrey was awarded a full scholarship to Tennessee State University and proved to be such a powerful, passionate, and empathetic speaker that she rose to host her own morning talk show in Chicago beginning in 1983. It was so popular that it was soon syndicated nationally and became the highest-rated talk show in TV history. In 1988 she launched her own multimedia company, Harpo Studios, and later became the cofounder of Oxygen Media, which operates a twenty-four-hour cable television network aimed at women. She has produced Broadway shows, major motion pictures, and her own magazine. Following in the footsteps of many great entrepreneurs, Oprah shares her wealth with those in need, and has been named by *Businessweek* as the greatest African American philanthropist in American history.

By following her passion to communicate with people and make a difference in the world, Oprah Winfrey transformed herself into a global media brand. She became the first black woman on the *Forbes* "The World's Billionaires" list, with a net worth of over $3 billion, is the richest African American of the twenty-first century, and is today regarded as arguably the most influential woman in the world.

How did she do it? Oprah was an innovator, creating entire new businesses and brands from scratch. "Everybody has a calling," she once explained. "And your real job in life is to figure out as soon as possible what that is, who you were meant to be, and to begin to honor that in the best way possible for yourself." Her calling turned out to be communicating—sharing her authentic curiosity, emotion, enthusiasm, and vulnerability with people around the world.

She was a multimedia operator who understood the synergies of operating in multiple platforms—magazines, movies, theater, and TV, all things she was passionate about. She wrote, "What I know is, is that if you do work that you love, and the work fulfills you, the rest will come."

She was a bold risk-taker, who smashed expectations and stereotypes with equal fearlessness. "I believe that one of life's greatest risks," she noted, "is never daring to risk." Like many supersuccessful people, she discovered that the secret to success is often failure. "Do the one thing you think you cannot do," she explained. "Fail at it. Try again. Do better the second time. The only people who never tumble are those who never mount the high wire." She suggested that you "turn your wounds into wisdom."

And most of all, Oprah Winfrey was a visionary—a woman who dreamed of helping her fellow human beings and channeled all her passion and energy into achieving her dream. "Create the highest, grandest vision possible for your life," she recommended, "because you become what you believe." She explained, "What material success does is provide you with the ability to concentrate on other things that really matter. And that is being able to make a difference, not only in your own life but in other people's lives."

Some of the many pace-setting black entrepreneurs of the twentieth and twenty-first centuries include Berry Gordy, Jr., the founder of powerhouse Motown Records; media mogul and *Ebony* and *Jet* magazine founder John H. Johnson, a former welfare recipient who became one of America's wealthiest, richest, and most powerful African Americans; and Brooklyn-born fashion mogul Daymond John of TV's *Shark Tank* fame, whose global hip-hop FUBU ("For Us By Us") brand has generated sales of $6 billion.

"I started working from the time I was six," John once recalled, "doing everything from selling little pencils in school to shoveling snow in the winter and raking leaves in the fall. When I was 10, I was an apprentice electrician and I used to wire PX cable in abandoned buildings in the Bronx."

John remembered, "I grew up in a lower-middle-class area of New York City, Hollis, Queens. My parents always instilled in m the fact that I had to work hard for everything that I wanted ou life. And then they got divorced. My father left when I was ar 10 years old and I haven't spoken [to] or seen him again sinc making me the man of the house and making my mother mother."

One of the biggest keys to Daymond John's business tr his mother, a diligent and determined flight attendant to keep his head down and "think big," and helped h out of trouble in a neighborhood that had plenty o ences. She provided her son, then age twenty-two, seed capital by mortgaging their home, then le offices and factory. The brand rode the wav which exploded in the 1990s, just as FUBU

man and president of the troubled Freedom National Bank in Harlem, and steered it to profitability within three years.

To achieve his next big win, Llewellyn mortgaged everything he had to stage a leveraged buyout of Fedco Foods Corporation, a failing chain of ten supermarkets in the Bronx and Harlem with sales of $18 million. "For an African American businessman to receive multimillion-dollar financing in the 1970s was a landmark event," marveled investment banker Robert Towbin. Llewellyn tripled the number of Fedco stores and grew sales to $100 million.

In 1985, Llewellyn led a group of black investors to buy Coca-Cola's troubled Philadelphia bottling company. "Llewellyn consolidated plants and warehouses from seven to two, cut the number of employees and increased annual production to 30 million cases, from 9 million when he took over," reported *Forbes*. "Yes, I was the first minority bottler," Llewellyn recalled, "but no, the fact that I was qualified as a buyer with proven experience with finance and retailing had nothing to do with my color." Also in the 1980s, Llewellyn and his partners moved into the TV business, buying Buffalo's WKBW-TV from ABC/Capital Cities for $56 million, and buying Garden State Cable for $420 million.

His success, reported Llewellyn in an interview with *The Black Collegian* in 1997, didn't come easy, but instead was "nerve-wracking, gut-wrenching and pain inducing." He said, "You must act to acquire it with a vengeance and to pursue it with a passion."

"Minorities have to understand that the world revolves around the golden rule," he wrote in a 1990 *Fortune* magazine article that argued that social and political power come from economic power. "Those who have the gold, rule."

In recent years, some sectors of black-owned businesses have shrunk, after being hammered both by economic downturns and by fierce competition from national chain companies, which have affected many nonblack companies as well.

In the March 2017 issue of *Washington Monthly*, "The Decline of Black Business" reported that "[t]he last thirty years also have brought the wholesale collapse of black-owned independent businesses and financial institutions that once anchored black communities across the country. In 1985, sixty black-owned banks were providing financial services to their communities; today, just twenty-three remain." The National Funeral Directors and Morticians Association has seen its membership plunge by 40 percent since 1997. *Black Enterprise* magazine termed the 1990s "a virtual bloodbath" for the black insurance industry, as the number of black-owned insurers dropped by 68 percent, with much of their business lost to mainstream giant insurers, who increasingly catered to the lucrative African American market.

Paradoxically, some of the decline in African American entrepreneurship may have come from greater opportunities opening up for black citizens in many professional fields, giving them more choices beyond starting their own business. The integration of many suburbs, certainly a positive trend, has had the negative effect of weakening black-owned small businesses in black neighborhoods.

Today, black Americans lag behind whites and other minorities in rates of business ownership, but the gap has been narrowing in recent years, and by 2011, African American–owned businesses totaled some two million, and enjoyed the highest growth rate in the number of minority-owned companies from 2002 to 2011.

Overall, African American entrepreneurs have come a long way in recent decades. The total combined revenues of companies on the *Black Enterprise* 100 list now totals over $24 billion, a ninefold rise, after adjusting for inflation, since 1973.

American women have always been key players in American entrepreneurship—as business pioneers in their own right, and in critical leadership and support roles for their husbands and families.

In many cases, like my own, they have acted as inspirers, advisors, sounding boards, and key decision makers for the business careers of their spouses. My wife, Korie, is a full partner in everything I do, and that's especially true when it comes to business. She grew up in a business family.

As a young girl, Korie worked in her grandfather's jewelry store cleaning the glass counters and wrapping Christmas gifts. Her family launched more than twenty business ventures, including Howard Brothers Discount Stores, which is the chain of stores my own mother worked for. The company was very successful, went public, and had seventy-eight stores all across the Southeast before the family sold it in 1978.

The Howards started a new chain in 1984 called the SuperSaver Wholesale Warehouse Club, built it up to twenty-four stores in less than two years, and in 1987 sold the business to Sam Walton of Walmart fame, who turned them into Sam's Clubs. Later, Korie's family started a publishing company, which was eventually sold to Simon & Schuster. For five years in a row, that company won "Best Christian Workplace in America." Not bad! Her family also started a summer camp, and it's a good thing they did, since that's where I met her. Today, Korie's father works for us at our company, on a wide range of management, budget, and contract issues. He is a huge asset to our businesses.

With all this entrepreneurship in her DNA, Korie is way smarter in business than me. She's more of a risk-taker, too, probably because I grew up poor and she grew up a little wealthier. I'm more conservative, and she's more inclined to take a chance.

The American tradition of women as powerful forces in business dates back to the early days of the young republic, when female American entrepreneurs ran retail shops, hotels, and taverns, sometimes because it was the best way to earn a living if a male breadwinner wasn't around. Women started businesses from scratch and they inherited businesses from their relatives and spouses.

The first prominent American female CEO was Rebecca Lukens of Pennsylvania, who, starting in 1825, transformed her family's near-bankrupt Brandywine Iron Works and Nail Factory into a successful steel enterprise that operated into the twenty-first century. "Rebecca was able to build the company up into one of the major players in the iron business, winning commissions for sea-going vessels and contracts for locomotives and Mississippi steamboats," wrote historian Kat Michels.

As a negotiator, Rebecca Lukens was known for being as tough as her factory-produced nails, but she was a kind, benevolent employer who provided housing, good working conditions, and bonuses to her workers. Under her leadership, Brandywine became America's leading producer of boiler plate. In 1994, *Fortune* called Lukens "America's first female CEO of an industrial company," and also inducted her into the National Business Hall of Fame.

In the twentieth century, millions of women entrepreneurs stepped up to the challenge of running their own business. Women won the right to vote and helped achieve victory on the home front in World War II, and women-owned businesses rose from 600,000 in 1945 to nearly one million by 1950, helping to power America's stunning postwar economic boom.

Many of these businesses were started on kitchen tables, amid grocery bags and diaper boxes, as women juggled the demands of domestic life with visions of financial achievement.

In the 1940s, Ruth Handler and her husband began a toy business in their garage workshop in California. Their first hits were the Uke-A-Doodle miniature ukulele, a hand-cranked music box, and the Burp Gun toy weapon. But the success of their Barbie doll line (named after the couple's children Barbara and Ken) and Hot

Wheels toy cars captured the imagination of the world's children and by the 1960s pushed the company into the Fortune 500. Today Mattel has global revenues of over $5 billion.

Lillian Vernon started her catalog business out of her apartment when she was pregnant with her first child. She named the company after herself and built it into the first company founded by a woman to be publicly traded on the American Stock Exchange, and spent fifty-one years as the company's CEO.

Martha Stewart's lifestyle empire began as a catering business in her basement. Liz Claiborne turned her fashion brand start-up into the first Fortune 500 company founded by a woman by catering to the tidal wave of women entering the workforce in the 1970s and 1980s. By the 1980s, women owned 25 percent of American companies.

In 1974, a time when relatively few women had entered technology, Sandra Kurtzig started a business in her spare bedroom that became ASK Computer Systems, which became one of the fastest-growing computer software companies in America. In 1981, she was the first woman to lead a technology company public stock offering. By 1992, sales reached the $450 million mark.

In 1996, at the age of twenty-five, Ecuadorian immigrant Nina Vaca, the daughter of an entrepreneur, started information technology service provider and staffing agency Pinnacle Technical Resources with $300. By 2013, revenues had grown to $200 million. In 2017, she told *Forbes*, "Confidence was instilled in me at a very, very young age. I have two teenage daughters, 16 and 17 years old, and I try to instill that same confidence in them. I tell them, 'Confidence is the best outfit you can wear.' Lack of confidence can be something that holds us back as women. We need to unequivocally, absolutely have confidence in our skills and our worth because people detect a lack of confidence very quickly. We have to be confident in our abilities, in what we represent and in what we bring to the table." She added, "The future of entrepreneurship continues to be very bright. Technology has lowered the barriers to entry for small businesses so we're seeing those numbers grow dramatically. Women and immigrants continue to over-index in starting small businesses. In fact, Latino-owned businesses are one of the fastest growing segments. Entrepreneurship has always been an incredible engine for America and I see no reason why that will change anytime soon."

Mary Kay Ash wrote her own inspiring tale of entrepreneurship, starting off as a single mother at age twenty, eventually building a $1 billion cosmetics and skin-care company, and being named the most outstanding twentieth-century businesswoman by the Lifetime TV network and the top female entrepreneur in American history in a Baylor University study.

Mary Kay was born in Hot Wells, Texas, the daughter of a mother who was the breadwinner for the family. She was married at age seventeen and had three children before her husband divorced her. She worked for Stanley Home Products as national training director, but quit when a man she had trained was promoted above her at twice her salary. She started writing a book about how women could thrive in business by following the Golden Rule: "Do unto others as you would have others do unto you." Then she realized she could build a company on it, too.

She started her business in 1963 with a small start-up budget of $5,000 and the help of her son. "The soothsayers prophesied that I was doomed to failure," she wrote. "However, I was determined to prove them wrong."

Did she ever. By 1973 Mary Kay products were being sold by over 21,000 beauty consultants or independent sales agents. Like Madam C. J. Walker, her corporate philosophy was to empower women by enabling them to generate their own income, and to shower her sales agents with praise, rewards, enthusiasm, and positivity. She gave them incentives like jewelry, vacations, and the chance to drive a Mary Kay career car—including the iconic pink Cadillac—and super-high-energy sales conventions that felt like a biblical revival meeting.

One of the biggest keys to Mary Kay's success was the fact that she took the Golden Rule further than most other business leaders do, to the point where she pictured every person she met as having a sign around their neck that read, "Make me feel important." She explained that her philosophy was to "praise people to success," and "If you let people know you appreciate them and their performance, they'll respond by doing even better." One employee said that "she made everyone feel important whether it was the maintenance man who took care of the building to our top salespeople."

Mary Kay also believed in the positive power of failure. "We fall forward to success," she said. "We learn from our failures." She wrote: "I've found that successful people are never afraid to try because they are never afraid to fail." She shared that inspiration with employees. "Don't limit yourself. Many people limit themselves to what they think they can do. You can go as far as your mind lets you. What you believe, remember, you can achieve."

Today, Mary Kay Inc. is one of the world's biggest direct-sales cosmetics companies, boasting over $3.5 billion in sales and over two million sales agents.

In 1948, a woman from Brooklyn began selling a line of skin-care products at her own counter at New York City's Saks Fifth Avenue luxury superstore.

The products were developed by her uncle, who was a chemist. The woman, a daughter of Jewish immigrants from Europe who was originally named Josephine Esther Mentzer, now called herself Estée

Lauder, which was also the name of her start-up beauty company, which she founded with her husband. She had grown up working in the family's hardware store, where she learned valuable lessons in entrepreneurship and retail business operations. Now she was using a former restaurant kitchen to mix up some of her own skin cream concoctions, which were based on her uncle's formulations.

In the face of Lauder's constant pestering to let her into his store, the Saks Fifth Avenue buyer said he foresaw no demand for her products. She promised to prove she would succeed, if he only gave her a chance. "I have never worked a day in my life without selling," she later explained. "If I believe in something, I sell it, and I sell it hard." He gave in. She sold out her stock in two days, and right away, Saks ordered more.

Lauder had no marketing budget, so she started giving away product samples right in the store. Her competitors thought she was crazy. She was going up against entrenched giants like Revlon and Elizabeth Arden. Everyone was convinced she would run out of product and go broke fast. Instead, she built a multibillion-dollar business that continues to thrive to this day, a business that includes cosmetics and fragrance powerhouse brands Estée Lauder, MAC Cosmetics, Prescriptives, Origins, Aramis, and Clinique.

The company's success was largely based on Estée Lauder's personal energy, enthusiasm, and passion for marketing. "She was devastatingly sincere and insistent about the products, knowing that if people tried them they would glow," wrote authors Harold Evans, Gail Buckland, and David Lefer in their book *They Made America*. "In chance encounters in elevators, on trains, in hotels and stores, trapped under a hair dryer, no woman was safe." Lauder wrote in her autobiography, "Good was not good enough. I know now that obsession is the word for my zeal. I was obsessed with clear glowing skin, shining eyes, beautiful mouths."

In 1998, when *Time* magazine ranked the twentieth century's

*Estée Lauder in the field, demonstrating her lipstick on a customer.
(Library of Congress)*

"most influential business geniuses," Estée Lauder was the only
woman on the list. By the time she died six years later at the age of
ninety-five, her company's annual sales had passed $5 billion.

In 2017, business network CNBC reported that "the Golden Age
for women entrepreneurs has finally begun. The stars have aligned
to help trigger the trend as robust ecosystems churn out enterprising

females equipped with inspiration, know-how, and funding. In recent years, the rate of women entrepreneurs has been growing at a percentage at least double that of their male counterparts."

Between 1997 and 2013, the number of woman-owned firms in the United States rose by 59 percent, which was one and a half times the rate of the national average. Businesses owned by women ethnic minorities are growing especially fast. Today, the 7.7 million American firms that are majority-owned by women employ over 7.1 million people and account for $1.1 trillion in sales, according to the Center for Women's Business Research.

According to 2014 figures from the U.S. Chamber of Commerce Foundation, women-owned enterprises now account for nearly 30 percent of all companies. In 2016, there were an estimated 11.3 million women-owned businesses in the United States—a 45 percent increase since 2007, according to the 2016 State of Women-Owned Businesses Report from American Express.

Latino entrepreneurs have had a rich history in America, even in the centuries before the birth of the United States.

At first, Latino enterprises were concentrated in the American Southwest, plus Florida, Louisiana, and New York. Early Latino entrepreneurs in America included Tomás Menéndez Márquez, owner of the gigantic La Chua Ranch in Florida. He produced over one-third of Florida's cattle stock in the seventeenth century and shipped hides, dried meat, tallow, and trading goods throughout the Caribbean. Márquez and his successors carved out the first trading networks in Florida, often following routes pioneered by Native Americans before them.

Mexican entrepreneurs operated large-scale livestock ranching operations across the present-day American Southwest, in Texas, New Mexico, Arizona, and California, supplying mining and farming customers. Many ranches stayed in business long after the Mexican-American War. "In 1760, for example," wrote historian Geraldo L. Cadava, "Captain Blas María de la Garza Falcón received from the Spanish crown a 975,000-acre land grant in Texas, which he called Rancho Real de Santa Petronila. Much of it later became the King Ranch, which, at half a million acres, was the largest ranch in the U.S."

In the 1800s, the nine-hundred-mile Santa Fe Trail from St. Louis to Mexico was a trading superhighway that provided business and jobs for thousands of Mexican entrepreneurs, including farmers, miners, ranchers, street vendors, general store owners, and other merchants.

Two Mexican American brothers, Bernabé and Jesús Robles, seized the opportunity of the federal Homestead Act of 1862—which offered cut-price land in the West to those who would make it productive—to build a cattle empire that became the Three Points Ranch in southern Arizona and eventually totaled one million acres. Also in the mid-1800s, pioneering Mexican American entrepreneurs like Joaquin Quiroga and Estevan Ochoa operated wagon-hauled freight shipping enterprises that carried products between Mexico and the United States and across the Southwest.

In the twentieth and twenty-first centuries, Latino culture, products, and businesspeople spread throughout the nation, fueled by economic and political immigration from Cuba, Mexico, Puerto Rico, and elsewhere in Latin America. New York City became a mecca for entrepreneurs of Cuban and Dominican heritage, Miami became a capital of Cuban American commerce, and states on the southern border provided a home for many Mexican American small businesses. Today, the impact of Latino American entrepreneurship is felt in cities and communities across the country.

Among the many thousands of successful Latino American entrepreneur stories are those of Los Angeles Angels owner Arturo

Moreno, the first Latino to own a major U.S. sports franchise; Angel Ramos, who founded Telemundo, the second-largest Spanish-language network in the United States; and the Unanue family, who built Goya Foods into the largest Latino-owned food distributor in America.

The Latino share of American entrepreneurs grew from 10.5 percent in 1996 to almost 20 percent in 2012, and in 2014 their combined revenue was over $450 billion, an increase of 100 over the previous six years.

The impact of Asian American entrepreneurs is substantial, too, in American medicine, technology, and many other sectors. "As leading actors in the U.S. economy, Asian American entrepreneurs' contributions cut across all segments," said Dilawar Syed, a member of the President's Advisory Commission on Asian Americans and Pacific Islanders, in 2011. "They are innovators in technology start-ups in Silicon Valley; they operate restaurants and convenience stores in neighborhoods across the U.S.; they run medical clinics, often in underserved communities. Fundamental to this mosaic of entrepreneurial success stories is a set of core characteristics: a strong work ethic, a disciplined pursuit of education, and an unshakeable faith and optimism about the country's future."

Nearly 60 percent of Asian American businesses are headquartered in only four states—Texas, California, Hawaii, and New York. One booming segment is Asian American women entrepreneurs, who already account for 39 percent of the total.

Every morning, millions of these business heroes wake up to chase the American dream—heroes of every background and faith, including men, women, minorities, Native Americans, veterans, millennials, seniors, and disabled citizens.

They are all American entrepreneurs.

They all have a rich, powerful heritage in common—and a fair shot at a great future for themselves, their families, and their communities.

CHAPTER 6

THE GOLDEN AGE OF THE AMERICAN ENTREPRENEUR

Try not. Do! Or do not. There is no try.

—Yoda

The United States is the engine of today's business world, and entrepreneurs provide much of its fuel.

The twentieth and twenty-first centuries have been a golden age for American entrepreneurs, the men and women who powered and sustained much of America's global economic leadership through two world wars, social upheaval and progress, globalizing markets, and the dawn of the space and information ages.

This is a golden age for my own family, too, as we struggled and hustled for over forty years to achieve many of our own dreams by working together in the family business. As the *New York Times* put it in 2013, "Forget the ZZ Top beards and the Bayou accents, the Robertsons of West Monroe, La., are a family of traditional American entrepreneurs: ambitious, rich and spectacularly successful. And that was true even before they were television stars."

A few years ago, we shattered ratings records in the cable TV business when nearly twelve million people tuned in for our season premiere. Our show has aired in more than one hundred countries, pulling in strong ratings on networks from the United Kingdom to Latin America. Someday I'll probably be floating down the Amazon in a tour boat and a local fan on shore will holler, "Hey, aren't you that *Duck Dynasty* guy?" We've achieved success in the businesses of duck and deer hunting gear, rifles and ammunition, outdoor accessories, videos, DVDs, fashion and clothing, shirts, caps, coolers, restaurants, books, music, personal appearances and events, and the music industry.

It's hard sometimes to keep track of all our products. One day, when I was visiting the corporate headquarters of Walmart, I was startled to see my face on a garden gnome. I must say he was a handsome little guy, but I was surprised to see him. I knew I had a Chia Pet and a bobblehead and an action figure, but I didn't know I had a garden gnome. That's awesome, but I thought it was kind of weird—until the day I saw myself on a Pez dispenser.

Beyond my own family, there are scores of modern-age American entrepreneurs who have inspired me with their courage, genius, and tenacity. Here are just a few of my favorite stories.

In 1906, two brothers had a fight over breakfast cereal.

They had been working together for over twenty years, they were having a business dispute, and they were finally at the breaking point. It was a sibling rivalry that *Entrepreneur* magazine later reported "ranks up there with that of Cain and Abel."

The older brother, Dr. John Kellogg, was the boss. He ran a famous health retreat, or "sanatorium," in Battle Creek, Michigan, that was based on principles of healthy living, vegetarianism, and a low-protein, low-sugar, low-fat diet that focused on whole grains, fiber, and nuts. Their family had fourteen children, in an observant

Seventh-Day Adventist household that honored a Saturday Sabbath and abstained completely from meat, coffee, tea, tobacco, and alcohol.

Years earlier, the doctor had hired his brother, Will Kellogg, who was eight years younger, to run the day-to-day business operations of the sanatorium, as well as their mail-order cereal business. He treated Will badly and paid him poorly. John made Will trot alongside him as he bicycled around the sanatorium and required Will to take dictation while he used the toilet. Will's pay was so low that he wasn't sure how he could properly support his family. "I feel kind of blue," Will confessed to his diary. "Am afraid that I will always be a poor man the way things look now."

Despite John's rude treatment, Will quietly flourished as a hands-on family entrepreneur. According to author Howard Markel, "Will was a serious student of the emerging science of business and methodically analyzed, applied, and adopted efficiency techniques and systems espoused by the best commercial gurus of the day. For nearly a quarter century, the quiet, stolid Will was doing more than merely taking orders. He was preparing to become a renowned captain of industry. Just as Henry Ford was figuring out the economies of scale to sell millions of automobiles rolling off his assembly line, Will Kellogg revolutionized the administration of the modern medical center and, later, the mass production and marketing of manufactured food."

By 1900, after fourteen years of expansion by the Kellogg brothers, the sanatorium had become what Markel called "a massive, modern, beautiful and luxurious medical and surgical center; it was so grand that it employed over 1,000 people, cared for seven to ten thousand patients each year, operated dozens of laboratories and radiology units, farmed over 400 acres of land to grow the vegetables, fruit and dairy products the guests consumed daily, and operated a canning and food manufacturing facility, laundry, charity hospital, creamery, and a resort comprising 20 cottages."

For years, the brothers had been making experimental batches of healthy alternative foods. One day in 1898, in an accidental baking discovery, they created a scrumptious, dry, "toasted cereal flake" or "flaked wheat berry" from a batch of boiled wheat paste that had been left out too long. John wanted to serve the flakes crushed up, but Will insisted they be served whole. The Kellogg's corn flake was born. People loved the taste and gobbled up bowls full of it at the sanatorium.

Will thought these tasty flakes were the future of the American breakfast.

His brother John disagreed.

Will quickly discovered that the process worked just as well with oats, rice, and corn. But although it was Will Kellogg who had stumbled upon the creation, it was John who took all the credit, claiming the idea had come to him in a dream.

Will wanted to protect their recipe, move production off-site, and advertise heavily to gear up for bigger sales. John wanted to make it at the sanatorium instead, and show everybody how they did it. One guest patient, C. W. Post, watched carefully, and used the process to create his own company, Postum Cereals, in 1904, which later became General Foods. He soon made a fortune with products like Grape-Nuts, inspired by the Kellogg brothers' idea. John Kellogg didn't mind, but his little brother Will was furious.

This was the last straw. Will, who was often called "W.K.," cut ties with his brother and in 1906 launched his own venture, the Battle Creek Toasted Corn Flake Company, which later became the Kellogg Company. "I sort of feel it in my bones," he told a friend, "that we are preparing a campaign for a food which will eventually prove to be the leading cereal of the United States, if not the world." Boy, did he turn out to be right.

But at first, the going was tough. Real tough. As in: "There are already forty other companies producing cold cereal in the American market, and oh, by the way, our factory is on fire!" tough.

On July 4, 1907, Kellogg watched as his first factory burned to the ground. "He had no capital to rebuild, but with the ruins still smoking, he told his employees to report for work the next morning," wrote Kellogg executive La June Montgomery Tabron in 2014. "By the day's end, he had arranged for an architect to begin plans for a much larger and safer factory. Then, he somehow drummed up the financing to make it a reality."

Will Kellogg rebuilt his factory operations with state-of-the-art assembly line technology, put prizes in his cereal boxes, staged sample giveaways of his new products, and ran ads featuring a farm girl known as the "Sweetheart of the Corn." In 1912, Kellogg unveiled the world's biggest advertising billboard to date, measuring 50 feet high and 106 feet wide. "Mr. Kellogg appreciated the power of the new force that was beginning to be used by progressive businessmen—the force of consumer advertising," wrote biographer Horace Powell. "Visualizing his foods on breakfast tables in millions of homes, he knew that the entrée to these homes was chiefly through advertising."

On a personal level, Will Kellogg wasn't the warmest guy you'd ever met—his employees found him demanding and distant—but he treated them better than many other employers. He gave them health care and a nursery, paid better-than-average wages, helped them through the dark days of the Great Depression, and cut the workday from the normal ten hours to eight. The two Battling Brothers of Battle Creek sued each other over which one could market cereal under the Kellogg name. After court proceedings that dragged on for years, Will Kellogg won, his brother withdrew in obscurity to Florida, and Will's company went on to become wildly successful and led the global market for ready-to-eat cereal.

A Kellogg's advertisement from 1919. (The Oregonian)

Workers in a Kellogg's factory in 1934. (U.S. National Archives)

As a result, Will Kellogg became one of the wealthiest people in the United States. In the great tradition of many successful American entrepreneurs, he put his money to good use—by helping his fellow human beings. In the 1930s, he started the W. K. Kellogg Foundation to support children's health care and education, and eventually endowed it with almost all of his equity in the Kellogg Company. Today, thanks to its 34 percent ownership of Kellogg Company, the foundation is one of the world's biggest private charities.

One of the most colorful American entrepreneurs ever born was a brilliant banker from Boston by the name of Joseph P. Kennedy.

With a genius for marketing and publicity and a massive bank account, Kennedy engineered a family takeover of the most powerful piece of real estate in American history—the Oval Office.

The charming, sandy-haired Kennedy was, in the words of one writer, a "ruthless businessman and investor" who "capitalized on his wealth to become perhaps America's premier social climber, an Irish-Catholic outsider who stormed the bastions of the WASP aristocracy."

Son of a middle-class Boston tavern owner, Joe Kennedy attended Harvard and became a banker and financier, propelled by a hunger for family prestige, wealth, and social and political power. In a brilliant move, Kennedy cashed out most of his stock holdings just before the Crash of 1929, shielding his family's wealth from the ravages of the Great Depression. "From the beginning, Joe knew what he wanted—money and status for his family," said a close friend. Kennedy had a confident, quick smile, a firm handshake, and a meticulous personal style, which featured a wardrobe that was hand-tailored (down to his underwear) in London and Paris.

By the 1930s, Kennedy was well on his way toward amassing a

personal fortune that the *New York Times* valued at $500 million at the time of his death in 1969. He earned his money through a wide variety of entrepreneurial ventures, including banking, real estate, corporate takeovers and consulting, liquor importing, and movie production. Movie superstar Gloria Swanson, who was Kennedy's mistress and management client before he double-crossed and abandoned her, recalled that Kennedy "operated just like Joe Stalin": "their system was to write a letter to the files and then order the exact reverse on the phone." When she met Kennedy, Frances Marion, America's highest-paid screenwriter at the time, thought, "He's a charmer. A typical Irish charmer. But he's a rascal."

In a stunning four-year raid on Hollywood, Kennedy took over three movie studios and ran them each simultaneously, launched the talking-picture revolution, established the prototype of the modern motion-picture conglomerate, and cashed out with millions of dollars in his pocket. Betty Lasky, daughter of Paramount founder Jesse Lasky, observed, "Kennedy was the first and only outsider to fleece Hollywood."

Joe Kennedy was a master manipulator of money and people. In the words of a January 1963 profile in *Fortune*, he was "a smart, rough competitor who excelled in games without rules. A handsome six-footer exuding vitality and Irish charm, he also had a tight, dry mind that kept a running balance of hazards and advantages. Quick-tempered and mercurial, he could move from warmth to malice in the moment it took his blue eyes to turn the color of an icy lake. Friendships shattered under the sudden impact of brutal words and ruthless deeds, yet those who remained close to him were drawn into a fraternal bond." Kennedy had, in the opinion of one colleague, a gift for speculation, based on "a passion for facts, a complete lack of sentiment, a marvelous sense of timing."

Joe Kennedy wanted to be president of the United States, but

Joseph P. Kennedy in 1938, when he was ambassador to the United Kingdom. (Wide World Photos)

he had a big mouth, a flaw that sank his political career. In 1940, when he was ambassador to the United Kingdom, he blurted to a reporter, "Democracy is finished in England." With that remark and the firestorm of bad press it triggered, Kennedy's career in public service was over. He resigned under pressure and transferred his ambitions for political power to his children, Joseph Jr. and John, both of whom he could envision capturing the White House someday—with his help. When Joseph Jr. was killed on a combat mission in Europe, the mantle fell on John's shoulders.

During the Christmas holiday of 1948, at his beachfront mansion in Palm Beach, Florida, Joseph P. Kennedy held a series of intense, private discussions with his son John, a thirty-one-year-old U.S. Navy veteran and hero of service in the South Pacific during

World War II. After some reluctance, the shy son agreed to his father's master plan to thrust him into national politics.

"We're going to sell Jack like soap flakes," boasted the elder Kennedy, and over the next twelve years, Joseph acted as the behind-the-scenes CEO of JFK's stunning rise to the presidency. In each campaign—for the House of Representatives in 1946, the U.S. Senate in 1952, and the presidency in 1960—Joseph Kennedy, working in the shadows, took charge of JFK's campaign marketing, publicity, strategy, and research. His nearly unlimited checkbook paid for a vast amount of campaign literature, direct mailings, and broadcast advertising, as well as political payoffs.

JFK went on to become one of the most admired presidents in modern history. Privately, he said of his entrepreneur father, "He's the one who made all this possible."

One day in 1928, a train pulled out of New York City's Grand Central Terminal, heading for Hollywood.

On board the train was a twenty-six-year-old cartoon illustrator, high school dropout, and former World War I ambulance driver who had started an animation company with his brother in their uncle's California garage.

The young man had a pipe and a mustache in order to look suave and sophisticated. But on this day he was seething with anger, and acting, according to his wife, "like a raging lion."

His name was Walt Disney.

He had two failed companies and one bankruptcy behind him, and his latest venture, a movie cartoon series about his creation "Oswald the Lucky Rabbit," had just blown up in his face. At a meeting in New York, Disney had discovered that his distributor had taken the rights to the popular cartoon away from him, cut his pay, and swiped his employees to boot. Now he had no income, no job, no contract, and no staff. It also looked like he'd run out of adorable cartoon animals to draw for profit, since rabbits, dogs, cats, and bears were already taken.

It was a moment of pure personal and professional despair, the kind of moment that can sneak up and strike many an entrepreneur during their career, even multiple times. But it was a moment some of us are born to master. As Disney explained, "Disaster seemed right around the corner," and "I function better when things are going badly than when they're smooth as whipped cream."

As the cross-country train barreled westward, a furious Disney gathered his thoughts and did what he did best. He started doodling and sketching designs on a drawing pad. Then, Disney recalled, a creature "popped out of my mind" onto the paper.

By the time the train pulled into Kansas City, Disney had created a cute little mouse, a plucky rodent who wore red velvet pants and seemed born for adventure and hijinks.

Walt wanted to call the creature "Mortimer," but his wife hated the name. "Too sissy," she declared. They talked it over and settled on Mickey. "It's better than Mortimer," she said.

The new character, born in a moment of desperation, launched Disney's new studio and put it on a thirty-year path to become one of the world's leading entertainment companies. "Mickey Mouse is, to me, a symbol of independence," Disney remembered. "He was a means to an end. Born of necessity, the little fellow literally freed us of immediate worry. He provided the means for expanding our organization to its present dimensions and for extending the medium of cartoon animation toward new entertainment levels. He spelled production liberation for us." He added, "All we ever intended for him or expected of him was that he should continue to make people everywhere chuckle with him and at him. We didn't burden him with any social symbolism; we made him no mouth-piece for frustrations or harsh satire. Mickey was simply a little personality assigned to the purposes of laughter."

An epic series of movies, TV shows, theme parks, and entertainment products flowed out of Walt Disney Studios. They include *Snow White and the Seven Dwarfs*, *Fantasia*, *Dumbo*, *Pinocchio*, *Bambi*, *The Mickey Mouse Club*, *Mary Poppins*, Epcot, Walt Disney World, Walt Disney Parks and Resorts, and Disneyland, a project for which Disney mortgaged everything he had, including his personal insurance, to build in 1955. Today, more than fifty years after Walt Disney's death, the company he founded is a thriving media mega-powerhouse, with a market value of around $150 billion.

A U.S. postage stamp of Walt Disney. (USPS)

And it all started with one young man, a failed entrepreneur, and a little mouse on a drawing pad. "You may not realize it when it happens," Disney once said, "but a kick in the teeth may be the best thing in the world for you."

One day in 1939, two engineering students at Stanford University decided to create a start-up technology company in a humble garage at 367 Addison Avenue in Palo Alto, California.

They wound up creating much of what the world now calls Silicon Valley.

The two young men weren't sure whose name should go first

in the new company's name. So they flipped a coin. The winner of the toss was a humble and friendly man named William Hewlett, who was a brilliant mathematician and tinkerer who struggled with dyslexia as a child. By the time he was in high school he had built an electrical transformer and a crystal radio set.

The company he formed with David Packard, christened Hewlett-Packard (or "HP"), started off with $538 in working capital. Hewlett slept in a shed near the garage, Packard in a nearby apartment. The partnership of these two men changed the world of technology.

Hewlett-Packard's first product was an audio production device used by Walt Disney Productions in making the 1940 classic movie *Fantasia*. Over the next four decades, the company came out with a long series of innovative, breakthrough products that regularly outflanked its competitors. They included in 1951 the high-speed frequency counter that was used by radio stations to meet FCC requirements, in 1964 the cesium-beam standard clock that fixes international time standards, in 1968 and 1972 the first desktop and scientific hand-held calculators, in 1982 the first desktop mainframe computer, and the pacesetting HP LaserJet printer series. By 2009, HP had sales of $114.6 billion.

The company was based on "the HP Way," a set of principles that Bill Hewlett explained as "a deep respect for the individual [and] a dedication to affordable quality and reliability," in order to make products that help all of humanity.

But according to management expert Jim Collins, the HP Way was not just about benevolence and charity. "Packard and Hewlett demanded performance, and if you could not deliver, the HP Way held no place for you," Collins wrote. "Therein we find the hidden DNA of the HP Way: the genius of the And. Make a technical contribution and meet customer needs. Take care of your people and demand results. Set unwavering standards and allow immense operating flexibility. Achieve growth and achieve profitability. Limit growth to arenas of distinctive contribution and create new arenas of growth through innovation. Never compromise integrity and always win in your chosen fields."

The success of HP was an inspiration to other young entrepreneurs who launched digital ventures in the Silicon Valley–style "garage start-up culture," like Apple, Google, Cisco, Intel, Facebook, Uber, and Airbnb, along with so many others.

On April Fool's Day in 1976, twenty-one-year-old Steve Jobs and his twenty-five-year-old buddy Steve Wozniak started Apple Computer in Jobs's parents' garage in Los Altos, California. Under Jobs's charismatic, impassioned leadership, Apple went on to become the world's largest information technology company and a prime force behind the world's digital revolution, with culture-shaping products like the Macintosh computers line, the iPod, the iPhone, the Mac operating system, Final Cut Studio, iTunes, and the iPad. By 2010, Apple's market value had passed that of software and Internet colossus Microsoft, whose college-dropout entrepreneur founder Bill Gates has become one of the world's wealthiest people, with a net worth of some $80 billion.

Google was started in 1998 by Stanford University doctoral students Sergey Brin and Larry Page with an investment of only $100,000. Just ten years later, Google's parent company had reached $820 billion in market value as the world's largest search engine.

Today, the one-car garage where Bill Hewlett and Dave Packard launched both Hewlett-Packard and the Silicon Valley technology revolution is honored as a California historic landmark and is on the National Register of Historic Places.

Some modern-day American entrepreneurs have revolutionized their industries.

Take Alfred Sloan, for example—not a name you hear much

nowadays, but a man who was a founding father of American business. He was a ball-bearing company owner who sold his business to General Motors in 1916 for $100 million in today's dollars, eventually became GM's president, and had built it to annual revenues of $20.7 billion when he died. "Sloan was a business genius who turned GM into the largest company in the world," said author David Farber. "And he, more than any other individual, invented modern corporate management and created the form of consumer capitalism that characterized much of 20th century America."

Or consider Sam Walton, who started off as a small businessman and did more in his time to change the face of the world of retail than anybody else. In 1945, he opened his first general store with a $25,000 loan from his father-in-law. The first official Walmart was opened in Rogers, Arkansas, in 1962. Today, mass retailer Walmart is the world's largest company by revenue, has

The original Walton's Five and Dime in Bentonville, Arkansas, the store that spawned a multibillion-dollar empire. (Bobak)

over eleven thousand stores, and is the biggest private employer in the world.

In 1942, during World War II, industrialist Henry J. Kaiser founded Kaiser Permanente, the world's first health-care organization, to keep his employees productive and in good health. As a construction entrepreneur in the 1930s who overcame humble beginnings, Kaiser led companies that built some of the greatest projects of the twentieth century, including the Hoover Dam in Nevada, the San Francisco–Oakland Bay Bridge, and the Grand Coulee Dam in Washington. His more than one hundred companies made everything from ships to cars to houses. During World War II, Kaiser Shipyards produced nearly 1,500 ships, more than any other company.

His greatest legacy is Kaiser Permanente, which today is America's biggest health maintenance organization. "I make progress by having people around me who are smarter than I am and listening to them," he once explained. "And I assume that everyone is smarter about something than I am."

One day in 1952, a fifty-two-year-old traveling kitchen-product salesman named Ray Kroc walked into a family-operated burger joint in the desert outside Los Angeles—and had a vision of the future of the restaurant business.

What he saw that day in the McDonald brothers' San Bernardino restaurant—efficiency, cleanliness, fast assembly-line service, value prices, and a simple, short menu—inspired Kroc to buy the brothers out, franchise the concept, and launch the world's biggest restaurant chain, all based on a product that much of the world is still in love with: the hamburger. Kroc became the founding father of fast food and one of America's greatest entrepreneurs.

Kroc's success mirrored the rise of the franchise model of entrepreneurship, in which a small business owner joins a network of branded outlets and shares in their business format and marketing and operations power in exchange for paying a royalty fee. Franchising grew rapidly after World War II and expanded to the restaurant, gas station, print shop, and many other business segments, and by 2010, more than eight million Americans were employed by over 750,000 franchise units.

Many of these pioneers have been immigrants, who have always played a key role in American entrepreneurship ever since the days of people like French-born Stephen Girard, German-born John Jacob Astor, and Scotch-born Andrew Carnegie.

In Boston in 1951, Shanghai-born An Wang started Wang Laboratories with $600 and built it into a $3 billion business employing over 30,000 people before his death in 1990. Palestinian-born Jesse Aweida helped launch the data storage industry when he established Storage Technology in 1969. Hungarian-born Andrew Grove pioneered the semiconductor industry. Russian-born Sergey Brin cofounded Google in a rented garage in 1998. South African–born Elon Musk is transforming the businesses of space, energy, and automobiles.

Today immigrant entrepreneurs are achieving great things across the nation. Immigrants are more than twice as likely to launch a new business as citizens born in the United States. And while immigrants compose some 13 percent of the population, they currently start over 25 percent of new businesses in America.

As just one example, take the story of Asian immigrant Derek Cha. Forty years ago, twelve-year-old Cha came to America with his parents and three siblings. "In 1977, South Korea was a poor country," Cha recalled. "My parents were looking for better opportunities and education for us." His father worked as a janitor and dishwasher and his mother as a seamstress. Young Derek helped with his father's work, delivered newspapers, and at sixteen started his first job, at McDonald's.

In 2009, after an earlier business failure, and as the economy was recovering from a major recession, Cha launched the Richmond, Virginia–based SweetFrog chain of frozen yogurt shops. Today, the firm has over 340 locations in twenty-seven states and was named a top franchise for veterans by *Entrepreneur* magazine in 2017.

One of the most amazing American entrepreneurs of the twentieth and twenty-first centuries is a man from Omaha, Nebraska, by the name of Warren Buffett.

He started a company in his bedroom and went on to become the head of a multinational conglomerate, a global rock-star business guru, and one of the wealthiest people on the planet.

The son of a congressman and stockbroker, Buffett showed a keen aptitude for money and business from a very early age, including the striking ability to perform like a human Excel program, rattling columns of numbers off the top of his head.

When he was six years old, Buffett went to his grandpa's grocery store and bought six-packs of Coke and resold each bottle at a marked-up profit. He devoured a library book called *1000 Ways to Make $1000* and operated a lucrative paper route and a successful pinball machine business in high school. When he was eleven, Buffett bought his first stock, three shares of Cities Service Preferred at $38 per share, but sold them too soon and missed its eventual rise to $200. That experience, and a book about "value investing" he read at age nineteen titled *The Intelligent Investor*, taught him an important lesson: to invest patiently for long-term growth, not short-term profit.

After attending the University of Nebraska and Columbia Business School, Buffett went to work selling securities for his father's brokerage company in Omaha for three years. To save money, he and his new wife moved into a modest house and even made a bed for their newborn daughter in a dresser drawer. He was terrified of public speaking. "You can't believe what I was like if I had to give a talk," Buffett recalled. "I would throw up." He took a public speaking course taught at Dale Carnegie, the institute named for the author of *How to Win Friends and Influence People*, he overcame his fear, and eventually he became one of the world's most influential business speakers.

In 1956, Warren Buffett decided he was ready to become a full-time American entrepreneur. He launched his own investment company in one of his bedrooms, then moved to a little office with seven limited partners, including his aunt Alice and his sister Doris. His business boomed, and in five years his partnerships achieved a 251 percent profit, while the Dow Jones Industrial Average had increased only 74.3 percent. By 1962 he was a millionaire. That year he invested in troubled textile-manufacturing firm Berkshire Hathaway, which eventually became the parent company for his investment empire, which, despite periodic market downturns, has thrived remarkably over the last half century.

Today, the eighty-eight-year-old Buffett has a net worth of nearly $90 billion. In early 2018 a single share of Berkshire Hathaway stock was selling for $294,000. Buffett still lives in the modest house he bought in 1957 for $31,000, doesn't use a smartphone, and takes public transportation instead of private jets.

One of the greatest entrepreneurs in American history had a secret life.

He was the James Bond of charity, a mystery man who used a small army of lawyers, executives, and shell organizations to keep his identity totally secret and give away billions of dollars to worthy causes.

For twenty years, he was one of the richest men on earth, but almost no one knew who he was.

Unknown to all but a tiny handful of people, this quiet, humble, mega-rich, self-made man traveled the world on a highly covert mission—to give away almost all the money he made, and to stay completely anonymous.

And he almost got away with it.

Charles Feeney was born in Elizabeth, New Jersey, in 1931, the son of a nurse and an insurance man, and the grandson of Irish immigrants. As a boy, he hustled for jobs, shoveled snow, sold Christmas cards door-to-door, and caddied at golf courses. After serving in Korea in the U.S. Air Force, he attended the Cornell University School of Hotel Administration on the GI Bill.

As a college freshman, Feeney started a sandwich delivery business that serviced his fellow students. He shrewdly bought sandwich ingredients on a Friday with a check that wouldn't clear until Monday, and got his buddies and roommates to pitch in and make the sandwiches. On weekend nights, when convenient snacks and munchies were scarce and students were hungry, Feeney, known as "the Sandwich Man," blew a whistle outside fraternities and sororities to announce his arrival. He sold seven hundred sandwiches per week and bankrolled a trip to France.

In Europe, Feeney and his college buddy Robert Miller hit upon the idea of entering the duty-free liquor business and launched a venture that came to be known as DFS, or Duty Free Shoppers. In the late 1950s, reported journalist Mike Colman, "the two Americans began driving from port to port all over Europe, meeting U.S. Navy ships as they docked and taking orders. They expanded their range, adding perfume, watches and cars. There was a mail-order arm and duty-free sales to American tourists driving back over the

Canadian border. Almost as an afterthought, they picked up the duty-free concessions at new airport terminals in Honolulu and Hong Kong." Money rolled in, but it went out just as quickly, and by 1965 the company was so overextended that it faced bankruptcy.

Feeney and his partners reorganized just in time to catch a wave of new global tourist business that took off in 1966 when the Japanese government lifted travel restrictions on its citizens at the same time its economy boomed. This unleashed a massive pent-up demand for gift items like liquor and perfume, which DFS offered duty-free at a fraction of the prices in Japan. Feeney struck deals with tour guides to walk their Japanese tourist groups through DFS airport outlets around the world, which featured Japanese-speaking sales staff. "That's when the business kind of exploded," Feeney recalled. "We couldn't wait on the tables, we had so many customers. That's when I thought, oh my, this is a good business." As the first truly global chain of duty-free airport stores, Feeney and his partners quietly created an entirely new business category—and an incredibly profitable one.

It was a license to print hundreds of millions of dollars, and by the 1980s, DFS was a thriving, highly profitable, privately owned multinational company and the largest travel retailer in the world, making Feeney and Miller among the wealthiest people on earth.

Then, at the age of fifty-three, in what journalist Conor O'Clery called "one of the biggest single transfers of wealth in history," Feeney decided to do something no one else is known to have done before. He decided to give away billions of dollars, nearly all the money he had made, to charity—and to do it in total secrecy.

Chuck Feeney, it turns out, was a frugal, humble man, in the extreme sense of those words. He kept his name out of the media. He was deeply uncomfortable with the trappings of wealth. For decades, he traveled coach, took the New York City subway, wore off-the-rack clothes, held meetings in coffee shops, carried his newspaper in a plastic bag, and wore a Casio watch that cost less than fifteen dollars. He figured, "If I can get a watch for $15 with a five-year battery that keeps perfect time, what am I doing messing around with a Rolex?" On one occasion, Feeney explained simply, "I am not really into money. Some people get their kicks that way. That's not my style." Though he was, in his words, an "intensely competitive" businessperson, he explained that in life there has to be "a balance of business, family, and the opportunity to learn and teach." Feeney has also referred to himself as "the shabby philanthropist" and once noted, "It's the intelligent thing to be frugal."

After a brief encounter with Feeney in 2007, *New York Times* reporter Jim Dwyer described him as an anonymous face in the crowd. "Rumpled by habit, limping on old knees, smiling faintly after a night of celebration, Chuck Feeney stepped out of a building on Park Avenue Monday night and vanished, carried away on a river of passing strangers who knew nothing about him," Dwyer recounted. "Perfectly disguised as an ordinary man, Mr. Feeney, one of the most generous and secretive philanthropists of modern times, had dropped from sight once again. It is a skill he mastered over decades."

One of Feeney's first forays into philanthropy occurred in 1981, when he gave his alma mater Cornell University $700,000. This triggered a flurry of requests for money. Feeney thought about how much of a wider impact he could achieve if he treated philanthropy as a well-managed entrepreneurial and investment venture that selected and screened which causes and charities to support but kept the operation as secret as possible to avoid endless unsolicited pleas for money.

Over and over, Feeney read Andrew Carnegie's famous 1889 essay "The Gospel of Wealth," in which the super-tycoon argued not only that a man of wealth should set an example "of modest, unostentatious living, shunning display or extravagance," but that the best way to deal with wealth was to give it all away, to benefit "the ladders upon which the aspiring can rise," like libraries and universities. The more Feeney thought about it, he later explained, the more he realized "I did not want money to consume my life." Unlike Carnegie, though, who widely advertised his giving by name, Feeney would stay anonymous. "I just felt I didn't see the need for blowing a horn," he said when asked why he wanted to remain unknown. Family security was another factor. "Part of the consideration was I was married and had five kids. We lived in France at the time. I wanted to make sure that the kids didn't have security issues."

Gradually, Feeney came to a life-changing decision. Finally, after making fairly modest provisions for his wife and children, starting in 1982 he transferred all his assets, including his entire 38.75 percent interest in DFS, to a largely secret offshore foundation that eventually was named the Atlantic Philanthropies, dedicated to charitable giving in the United States and the world, especially in the fields of medicine and education. Feeney himself wound up with a personal net worth of less than $5 million. As part of a divorce settlement, his first wife received the family's seven homes, along with $60 million and funding for her own foundation.

Even Feeney's business partners did not know of his secret arrangements. For Feeney, it seemed, there would be no building plaques or black-tie dinners in his honor, no publicity machines spreading the word of his good deeds. "Strict rules were formulated for the conduct of the foundation," wrote O'Clery. "No solicitations would be entertained. Gifts would be made anonymously, and those who received them would not be told where they came from. The recipients, too, would have to sign confidentiality agreements. If they found out anything about the Atlantic Foundation or Chuck Feeney and made it public, the money would stop. The

Atlantic Foundation would be the biggest secret foundation of its size in the world."

For nearly fifteen years, it looked like Feeney would succeed in his covert mission of compassion on a global scale. Between 1994 and 1997, Feeney quietly also used his own personal funds to help broker peace in the northern part of his ancestral homeland of Ireland. Then, in 1997, a multibillion-dollar dispute between Feeney and his business partners over the sale of their company to giant luxury conglomerate LVMH triggered a lawsuit. Feeney knew that by forcing his name into the court system, the astonishing story of his philanthropy would be exposed. His project of secret giving was about to come to an end. So in an effort to preempt and manage the news, he called the *New York Times* and explained the whole story. After the story ran to the surprise of the business and charity worlds, Feeney receded into the shadows until O'Clery wrote his authorized biography in 2007, *The Billionaire Who Wasn't*.

By now, Feeney was in his seventies and his cover had already been blown, so he decided to talk publicly about his legacy on a number of occasions, as a way of encouraging other successful people to adopt a policy of "giving while living." As Feeney quipped, "It beats giving while you're dead."

In 2011, Feeney signed the "Giving Pledge" that was spearheaded by Warren Buffett and Bill Gates, who themselves were acting with the inspiration of both Carnegie and Feeney himself. The pledge calls on America's wealthiest individuals to promise to give at least half of their wealth to philanthropic and charitable causes. In Feeney's case it was a retroactively symbolic gesture, since he had already transferred most of his assets to the foundation decades earlier. Bill Gates described Feeney as "the ultimate example of giving while living," and Warren Buffett said Feeney was the "spiritual leader" for both him and Bill Gates, and that Feeney "should be everybody's hero."

By 2020, when the Atlantic Philanthropies is scheduled to cease operations, Feeney and his organizations will have given away almost everything he and his ventures ever earned, a grand total of more than $8 billion. Of that amount, $564 million was used to support the University of California, San Francisco, including a biomedical center and a cardiovascular complex. Additionally, Feeney's philanthropy helped disadvantaged and vulnerable people, especially youth and the elderly, through medical and education programs in the United States, South Africa, Australia, Ireland, Vietnam, and beyond.

Today, the eighty-seven-year-old Chuck Feeney lives a modest existence in a cramped rented apartment in San Francisco with his second wife, and he still does not own a car. His net worth is said to be less than $2 million.

More than perhaps any other American entrepreneur, Feeney strove to fulfill a challenge that St. Matthew tells us Jesus Christ made in the Sermon on the Mount.

Jesus said that when you give to the needy, "do not let your left hand know what your right hand is doing, so that your giving may be in secret. Then your Father, who sees what may be in secret, may reward you."

In 2016, a young man in Long Island, New York, wondered about his future.

John Cronin's high school graduation was coming up, and he figured that he needed to generate some income pretty soon.

He huddled up with his father, Mark, and they chewed over the options.

John adored his father and pretty soon they began talking about starting a business together. They wanted to become American entrepreneurs. But there were a million different business ideas out there, and they weren't sure which one would work for them. The twenty-one-year-old John had only one nonnegotiable requirement—whatever they did, it had to be fun.

Their first idea was a food truck.

This made sense, John recalled, because "both of us are good at eating." The trouble was, neither man could cook. They scratched that idea.

For most of his life, John loved wearing wild and crazy socks. His older brothers often asked their father to tone down their kid brother's wacky hosiery choices. John ignored their pleas. "They are not the fashion police," he explained. "Socks are fun and creative and colorful, and they let me be me."

John had another special personality characteristic. As he puts it, "I have Down syndrome and it never holds me back."

By November 2016, John Cronin and his father settled on a brainstorm idea that John, who studied retailing and customer service in high school, had suggested. They decided to open an online store to sell socks with fun and wacky designs.

Mark thought his son's idea was great. "Most of us wear some sort of uniform to work—it might be a suit, it might be khakis and a polo shirt, it might be an orange jumpsuit," he recalled. "Yet you can wear a pair of socks and express yourself, adding some color and flair, and you can do that for $10 or less." They decided to call the store "John's Crazy Socks."

Together they designed a logo and a website. "I came up with a catchphrase," John said. "Socks, socks, and more socks." They opened up a "pick-and-pack warehouse," eventually stocked with a curated collection of over 1,500 variations and designs of socks made by different manufacturers—everything from Abe Lincoln socks to socks featuring beer, astrological signs, and NFL quarterbacks. They launched a social media campaign featuring lots of videos starring John, the company's cofounder and CHO, or Chief Happiness Officer.

Their first month in business, they sold four hundred pairs of socks. After a little more than a year, they were selling eight hundred pairs of socks every day, had shipped more than 42,000 orders, and hit $1.4 million in revenue. News articles and TV segments profiled the business. Today John's Crazy Socks has thirty-two employees on the payroll, half of whom have learning disabilities.

The father-son team picked a good business to be in—the global sock market is expected to nearly double by the year 2025. They work hard together, often pulling ten- and eleven-hour days. Their great love for each other makes it easy, though. "I have the perfect partner," says the father. "It makes me happy because I like helping all the customers and I like working with my dad," says John.

John serves as the company spokesperson and brand ambassador, and loves acting as "sock wrangler," which means picking out socks and helping pack and ship them. Mark handles management, accounting, inventory, and human resources. The company takes a very personal approach. "In every box," explains John, "I put a handwritten note, some candy, and two discount cards for ten percent off." If an order comes in within driving distance, John frequently makes the delivery himself, knocking on doors and often getting hugs in return.

John sends socks to celebrities like former president George W. Bush and Canadian prime minister Justin Trudeau, and if he learns that a leading athlete has been injured, he sends them socks. John also makes monthly selections for the company's Monday Madness Mystery Bag and Sock of the Month Club. Five percent of profits are earmarked for donation to the Special Olympics. The company plans to expand its social media presence, offer custom-made socks, and start a wholesale line for other small businesses.

Mark says the company has "a social mission and a retail mission, and they're indivisible." He explains, "I don't think it's enough anymore to just produce a service or produce a product. I think there has to be values attached to that, and we have a model that's showing that." The company wants to inspire other businesses to hire more disabled people.

Says John, "We're spreading happiness. What's better than that?"

You can measure business success many ways. But if you measure the worth of a business by its ability to create love and happiness, I nominate John and Mark Cronin as true American Superstar Entrepreneurs.

Sometimes, with TV shows like *Shark Tank* and *The Apprentice*, and well-known stories like those of Steve Jobs and Bill Gates, it seems like entrepreneurs are the rock stars of the business world.

But you might be surprised to learn that over the last forty years, entrepreneurship has, in fact, taken a big hit in the United States. It's always been tough to be an entrepreneur—but recent decades have proven especially tough. By some estimates, three out of four venture-backed start-ups fail, over 95 percent of start-ups fall short of their initial projections, only about 30 percent of family businesses successfully pass to the second generation, and only 10 to 12 percent last into the third.

According to Jim Clifton, CEO and president of the Gallup, Inc., polling company, "The U.S. now ranks not first, not second, not third, but twelfth among developed nations in terms of business startup activity." U.S. Census Bureau data indicates that when measured in terms of start-ups per capita, we are actually behind countries like Denmark, Finland, New Zealand, Sweden, Hungary, Israel, and Italy. Clifton added, "You never see it mentioned in the media, nor hear from a politician that, for the first time in 35 years,

American business deaths now outnumber business births." In 2015, for example, start-ups totaled 414,000, which was, as the Census Bureau reported, "well below the pre–Great Recession average of 524,000 startup firms." Likely culprits: the lingering effects of the severe economic downturn and a sluggish recovery, and the disruption and severe competitive pressures caused by the rising market power of giant chain stores and websites.

The good news is that entrepreneurship is still alive, and in many ways well, in America.

We still have a highly innovative, competitive economy, which also happens to be the world's largest. Entrepreneurial growth is picking up from the depths of the Great Recession. New businesses continue to create an average of three million new jobs a year and have been responsible for almost all of the net new job creation in the United States in the last forty years.

A recent study by the Kauffman Foundation suggests that high-potential small firms, which have a disproportionate positive impact on employment and economic growth, are growing especially fast. The foundation's high-growth-entrepreneurship index, which has followed fast-growing start-up companies since 2005, has bounced back to its prerecession value. Political leaders in Washington, including a president who was himself once an entrepreneur and heir to a family business, are pursuing pro-business policies that hopefully will create conditions for a long-term boost to entrepreneurship.

Interest in entrepreneurship among young people is high, and the United States may be poised for a burst of new entrepreneurs in the near future. "The number of entrepreneurship classes on college campuses has increased by a factor of 20 since 1985, so it's possible that there are thousands of future startup founders who are currently employees sifting through ideas for their own firm," reported Derek Thompson of *The Atlantic* in 2016. "The Millennial generation may be like a dormant volcano of entrepreneurship that will erupt in about a decade."

As long as there is a United States, there will be American entrepreneurs. "The opportunities for people with ideas and a willingness to take risks are plentiful in America, and there is plenty of capital available to bring those ideas to life," said historian John Steele Gordon in 2013. "On top of that, mechanisms to bring ideas and capital together are more robust than they have been in the past. So the future of entrepreneurship in this most entrepreneurial of countries remains bright."

I have discovered the greatest book of business wisdom ever written.

It is the ultimate management book, an ancient guide to life and business that I refer to on a daily basis.

This book contains all the secrets to success, leadership, management, and prosperity in a thrilling collection of inspiring lessons and stories that have endured for thousands of years.

It is the perfect book of guidance for entrepreneurs.

It is called the Holy Bible.

I've got a copy of the book in my desk at the office, and I'll crack it open at the drop of a hat, to seek a joyful moment, a word of comfort, or a burst of wisdom to guide a personal, family, or business decision. Many days, I start off in a moment of prayer and reflection, heeding the challenge of Psalm 5:3: "In the morning, Lord, you hear my voice; in the morning I lay my requests before you and wait expectantly."

Whether or not someone believes as I do that the Bible is divinely inspired and that Jesus Christ is our savior and the son of God, there is a wealth of magnificent wisdom in the scriptures that can help the American entrepreneur, or anyone else, thrive through risk, danger, and adversity, and master the challenges of failure and success.

I believe that one of the reasons entrepreneurs have made such a powerful contribution to American history is that religion, spirituality, and the Bible are a part of so many of our lives. My family and I have always been connected to faith-based and Bible-based congregations, camps, charities, and volunteer groups, and in doing so we have joined a great American tradition, a bedrock of our democracy and our economy.

Religion itself is a huge American enterprise, and it has a massive impact on American economic life. A 2016 study by the Religious Freedom and Business Foundation estimates that religion contributes about $1.2 trillion of social and economic value annually to the U.S. economy. Of this, about 40 percent comes from religious congregations, the rest from other religious institutions such as universities, health systems, and charities, and from faith-inspired, faith-related, or faith-based businesses.

There are more than 344,000 religious congregations in America, including churches, chapels, temples, synagogues, and mosques. They buy billions of dollars of goods and services, often from local and small-town American entrepreneurs, and hire hundreds of thousands of American workers, both full-time and part-time. Schools that are connected to congregations educate 4.5 million students and have 420,000 full-time teachers on the payroll every year.

Religious congregations and faith-based schools have a long-term multiplier effect for America, too. The impact of faith-based schools in the United States is significant. For instance, St. Benedict's Prep in Newark, New Jersey, gets 530 largely minority and economically disadvantaged boys ready for their college and career journeys, and has a good record of college graduation and alumni achievement. One graduate, Uriel Burwell, came back to the community and launched an affordable housing campaign that raised $3 million and built dozens of affordable homes. Religiously inspired institutions are key players in the world of higher learning, like Jewish-affiliated Brandeis University, my alma mater of Christian-inspired Harding University, Catholic University, Liberty University, and many, many others.

Religious congregations support local and community nonreligious groups doing great work, from the American Red Cross and the United Way to Big Brothers and Big Sisters. The evangelical Christian mega-congregation of Saddleback Church in Orange County, California, has helped tens of thousands of citizens get back on track with church-hosted alcohol recovery programs. The Church of Jesus Christ of Latter-day Saints has set up employment service centers across the nation. One in six hospital patients in America is cared for in a Catholic facility. Adventist Health System has forty-six hospitals and employs over 78,000 people. Over 25,000 American congregations conduct active ministry to help folks coping with HIV/AIDS. Catholic groups like the Knights of Columbus and Catholic Charities address a wide range of human needs with hundreds of thousands of volunteers and multimillion-dollar budgets, as do charities inspired by many other faiths.

The net effect of all this great work is to make America a better and stronger nation, and to help create the conditions where entrepreneurs and everybody else will thrive.

Beyond all this good work and economic impact, religion is a guiding source of life inspiration for multitudes of American entrepreneurs. Consider, for example, the writings referred to by Christians as the "Old Testament" and the "Hebrew Scriptures" by the Jewish faith, and the writings that Christians call the "New Testament." These writings have many parallels in other world religions, too. They contain an amazing collection of prayers, devotions, parables and encouragements, gentle reminders and commandments, all of which are relevant not only to daily life, marriage, and parenthood, but to business as well. As 1 Timothy 6:12 challenges us, "Fight the good fight of the faith. Take hold of the eternal life to which you were called when you made your good confession in the presence of many witnesses."

One day not long ago, as I read the Bible from front to back, I realized to my surprise that both testaments contain a pattern of five great insights that you can call "the Entrepreneur's Code"—Wisdom, Courage, Compassion, Integrity, and Humility. These insights, I realized, have spoken directly over the years to everything I've experienced in business being an American entrepreneur.

The first insight in the Entrepreneur's Code is *Wisdom*.

Our business and personal lives are a journey in search of wisdom into ourselves and the world around us. As Proverbs 7:4 commands us, "Say to wisdom, 'You are my sister'; and to insight, 'You are my relative.'" And for me, the best source of wisdom is that contained in the Bible, which many of us believe is divine wisdom communicated to us in the voice of ancient prophets. As Job 12:12 says, "Is not wisdom found among the aged? Does not long life bring understanding?"

In many Bible passages, such as Proverbs 4:5–9, you can find a road map of inspiration to achieve the wisdom necessary for success in both life and business:

Get wisdom, get understanding;
*   do not forget my words or turn away from them.*
Do not forsake wisdom, and she will protect you;
*   love her, and she will watch over you.*
The beginning of wisdom is this: Get wisdom.
*   Though it cost all you have, get understanding.*

Cherish her, and she will exalt you;
  embrace her, and she will honor you.
She will give you a garland to grace your head
  and present you with a glorious crown.

The second insight of the Entrepreneur's Code is *Courage*.

To succeed as an entrepreneur, you must marshal your courage, embrace risk, and be ready to push through the inevitable trials and storms of business, with boldness and diligence. This includes the courage to take action and work very hard. In the words of Proverbs 28:1, "The righteous are as bold as a lion."

In my own career, I feel that these biblical encouragements toward courage and diligence have helped me tremendously. "The fear of the Lord is the beginning of wisdom," proclaims Psalm 111:10 in a passage that helps form the foundation of my life's mission; "all who follow his precepts have good understanding."

As Ecclesiastes 9:10 puts it, "Whatsoever your hand finds to do, do it with all your might," and in the words of Proverbs 22:29, "Do you see someone skilled in their work? They will serve before kings." And as Galatians 6:7 cautions, "A man reaps what he sows." The way of the entrepreneur is often the path of those who outhustle, outthink, and simply outwork the competition. "By the sweat of your brow you will eat your food," declares Genesis 3:19.

I've never had the pleasure of "standing before kings," or queens, for that matter, but I have spent some quality time with the last two presidents of the United States!

The third insight of the Entrepreneur's Code is *Compassion*.

If you make compassion your personal and business goal, I believe you can move mountains and achieve miracles, as well as have material success. Compassion, to me, means showing mercy, love, understanding, and positive actions to your family, your co-workers, your employees and partners, your customers, people in the community who are in trouble or disadvantaged, even your competitors.

In the words of Proverbs 20:28, "Love and faithfulness keep a king safe; through love his throne is made secure." And as Proverbs 10:12 puts it, "Hatred stirs up conflict, but love covers over all wrongs." Job 27:4 declares, "My lips will not say anything wicked, and my tongue will not utter lies."

You don't see too many business books written about love, but I think it's the entrepreneur's secret weapon. Many of America's great entrepreneurs were motivated at one time or another by authentic love—for innovations that helped the world, for their family, their employees and customers, and for the millions of people who would benefit from their philanthropic work. As 1 Corinthians 13 declares,

If I speak in the tongues of men or of angels, but do not have love, I am only a resounding gong or a clanging cymbal . . . Love is patient, love is kind. It does not envy, it does not boast, it is not proud. It does not dishonor others, it is not self-seeking, it is not easily angered, it keeps no record of wrongs. Love does not delight in evil but rejoices with the truth. It always protects, always trusts, always hopes, always perseveres. Love never fails.

Throughout our history, American entrepreneurs like Stephen Girard, Andrew Carnegie, John D. Rockefeller, Chuck Feeney, and countless others have heeded the words of Psalm 112:9: "They have freely scattered their gifts to the poor, their righteousness endures forever."

The Bible actually promises us, in Proverbs 3:3–10, that if you guide your life by love, mercy, and truth, and place your honor and trust in God, "you will win favor and a good name in the sight of God and man," "he will make your paths straight," you will "bring health to your body and nourishment to your bones," and "your barns will be filled to overflowing, and your vats will brim over with new wine."

The power of compassion and charity extends to the ways we entrepreneurs manage our employees and team members. Proverbs 3:27 proclaims, "Do not withhold good from those to whom it is due, when it is in your power to act." Proverbs 27:23 urges us to "be sure you know the condition of your flocks, give careful attention to your herds."

The Bible is filled with sayings that I see as encouragements for us to show leadership through positive reinforcement, supportiveness, and recognizing and complimenting our staff, such as Proverbs 16:24, "Gracious words are a honeycomb, sweet to the soul and healing to the bones," and Proverbs 17:22, "A cheerful heart is good medicine, but a crushed spirit dries up the bones."

The Bible also urges us to control our anger, which is excellent advice for the entrepreneur in dealing with rough-and-tumble decisions, crises, and employees. "Do not be quickly provoked in your spirit," says Ecclesiastes 7:9, "for anger resides in the lap of fools." Proverbs 21:23 points out that "those who guard their mouths and their tongues keep themselves from calamity." And likewise, Proverbs 14:29 and 16:32 point out that "whoever is patient has great understanding, but one who is quick-tempered displays folly"; and "better a patient person than a warrior, one with self-control than one who takes a city."

The fourth insight in the Entrepreneur's Code is *Integrity*, which to me means being honest and righteous with the world, including the world of business.

Integrity, honesty, and fair dealings come up again and again in the Bible. Leviticus 19:13 reads, "Do not defraud or rob your neighbor. Do not hold back the wages of a hired worker overnight." Psalm 25:21 challenges us, "May integrity and uprightness protect me, because my hope, Lord, is in you." Job 27:5 includes the resolute phrase "till I die, I will not deny my integrity." Proverbs 11:1 declares, "The Lord detests dishonest scales, but accurate weights find favor with him."

As Isaiah 33:15–16 puts it, "Those who walk righteously and speak what is right, who reject gain from extortion and keep their hands from accepting bribes . . . they are the ones who will dwell on the heights, whose refuge will be the mountain fortress. Their bread will be supplied, and water will not fail them."

I believe that integrity as an entrepreneur also means being honest with your employees and business partners, and constructively and respectfully pointing out their mistakes and areas of improvement as a way of helping them. Proverbs 25:12 tells us, "Like an earring of gold or an ornament of fine gold is the rebuke of a wise judge to a listening ear."

The final insight in the Entrepreneur's Code is *Humility*.

This means being honest with yourself—admitting your weaknesses and limitations, and reaching out for help when you need it.

The Bible tells us that we must seek out the advice and opinions of others. As Proverbs 11:14 advises, "For lack of guidance a nation falls, but victory is won through many advisers."

We must also acknowledge our mistakes, and, as hard as it is, welcome and even seek out criticism. "The purposes of a person's heart are deep waters," reads Proverbs 20:5, "but one who has insight draws them out."

As an entrepreneur, a father, and a husband, I make mistakes on a fairly regular basis, but the words of the Bible teach me that it's my responsibility to learn from them and try not to repeat them. The entrepreneur needs to understand that, in the words of Proverbs 6:23, "correction and instruction are the way to life."

"Teach me, and I will be quiet; show me where I have been wrong," reads Job 6:24, "and cause me to understand wherein I have erred." As Ecclesiastes 7:5 points out, "It is better to heed the rebuke of a wise person than to listen to the song of fools."

In 1925, an entrepreneur named Bruce Barton wrote a book that became one of the bestselling books of the twentieth century.

Titled *The Man Nobody Knows*, it told the story of Jesus Christ, a young religious leader who "picked up twelve men from the bottom ranks of business and forged them into an organization that conquered the world," and in only three years, defined a mission, carried it out, and launched the most successful start-up in human history.

Barton, who cofounded a company later known as BBDO, which today is one of the largest advertising agencies in the world, saw Jesus as a strong, tough, decisive, and charismatic leader who chopped wood and swung an ax as a successful carpenter, who "slept outdoors and spent his days walking around his favorite lake," and whose "muscles were so strong that when he drove the money-changers out, nobody dared to oppose him." In fact, Barton saw Jesus as nothing less than "the founder of modern business."

In the midst of the Roaring Twenties, when the United States was enjoying a dizzying economic boom and social mores were changing rapidly, Barton's book struck a powerful chord. Barton wrote that Jesus was a model of leadership in any age. "First of all he had the voice and manner of the leader—the personal magnetism which begets loyalty and commands respect." He wrote, "The essential element in personal magnetism is a consuming sincerity—an overwhelming faith in the importance of the work one has to do . . . that quality of conviction." Jesus was a superb organizer, communicator, and motivator, and the ultimate "servant-leader" who led by the inspiration of his personal example. In one extreme act of humility, Jesus went so far as to wash the feet of his own disciples.

All his leadership qualities, noted Barton, helped Jesus forge a motley collection of followers into a world-changing vanguard of inspiration whose influence is felt centuries later in the lives of billions of people. The original group of his followers, Barton pointed out, featured "[n]obody who had ever made a success of anything, a haphazard collection of fishermen and small-town businessmen, and one tax collector—a member of the most hated element in the community. What a crowd!"

With that bunch of misfits, losers, and sinners, Jesus changed the destiny of the human race for the better. If ever there was a person who personified the qualities of Wisdom, Courage, Compassion, Integrity, and Humility, He was it.

As I look back at the history of American entrepreneurs both big and small, I have come to realize that, above all, these are the qualities that will help us persevere through trials and tribulations, to weather the storms of failure, chaos, and uncertainty, and to achieve success in our business and personal lives.

These are the secrets that will truly help us build a golden age of success for ourselves, our families, and our fellow human beings.

I believe in the Lord. I believe He has set up you and me for success. And I believe that if we remain true to our vision of a better life for our families and community, He will come through for us when times are the toughest.

One day a number of years ago, when our family business was in its early years, we ran out of money.

We had run out of credit. We had literally nothing in the bank, but an $800 banknote was due. My father was at the end of his financial rope, totally out of ideas, and my mother was in tears of despair, seeing the whole future of what we had scraped and built together as a family come crashing to an end.

My father said, "Well, I might as well go down to the mailbox and see if anybody's sent us any checks."

My mother replied, "There are no checks due! We've deposited and spent all the money we're due for every order we've gotten!" He went to the mailbox anyway.

When he opened up the mailbox, he found an envelope in there that had a whole lot of international postage on it.

It was a letter all the way from Japan, and enclosed was a check for exactly $800 to prepay for a bulk shipment of duck calls.

Now, I don't remember any orders from Japan before then, and I don't remember too many at all since then, but this was for real. The check cleared, and we were able to make our bank payment.

That envelope saved our family business. The postmark may have been from Japan, but I think it really came from an address far, far above us.

The Lord truly does work in mysterious and beautiful ways. He certainly has for this American entrepreneur and his family.

As you experience the struggles and joys of your own business and career, I pray that He will do the same for you, too.

ACKNOWLEDGMENTS

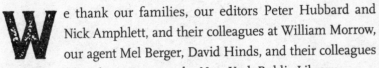e thank our families, our editors Peter Hubbard and Nick Amphlett, and their colleagues at William Morrow, our agent Mel Berger, David Hinds, and their colleagues at WME, and Melanie Locay at the New York Public Library.

APPENDIX A

My Favorite Quotes on Entrepreneurship and Success

Ever since the first settlement of Europeans in the New World, America has been a magnet for people seeking adventure, fleeing from tyranny, or simply trying to make a better life for themselves and their children.

Milton Friedman

Aim for success, not perfection. Never give up your right to be wrong, because then you will lose the ability to learn new things and move forward with your life. Remember that fear always lurks behind perfectionism.

David M. Burns

Don't limit yourself. Many people limit themselves to what they think they can do. You can go as far as your mind lets you. What you believe, remember, you can achieve.

Mary Kay Ash

If you want to be happy, set a goal that commands your thoughts, liberates your energy, and inspires your hopes.

Andrew Carnegie

If there is no struggle, there is no progress.

Frederick Douglass

You build on failure. You use it as a stepping-stone. Close the door on the past. You don't try to forget the mistakes, but you don't dwell on it. You don't let it have any of your energy, or any of your time, or any of your space.

Johnny Cash

I learned that courage was not the absence of fear, but the triumph over it. The brave man is not he who does not feel afraid, but he who conquers that fear.

Nelson Mandela

Only those who dare to fail greatly can ever achieve greatly.

Robert F. Kennedy

Courage, then, and patience! Courage for the great sorrows of life, and patience for the small ones. And then when you have laboriously accomplished your daily task, go to sleep in peace. God is awake.

Victor Hugo

All our dreams can come true if we have the courage to pursue them.

Walt Disney

The best revenge is massive success.

Frank Sinatra

The successful warrior is the average man, with laserlike focus.

Bruce Lee

Would you like me to give you a formula for success? It's quite simple, really: Double your rate of failure. You are thinking of failure as the enemy of success. But it isn't at all. You can be discouraged by failure or you can learn from it, so go ahead and make mistakes. Make all you can. Because remember that's where you will find success.

Thomas J. Watson

The ultimate measure of a man is not where he stands in moments of comfort, but where he stands at times of challenge and controversy.

Martin Luther King, Jr.

The greatest leader is not necessarily the one who does the greatest things. He is the one that gets the people to do the greatest things.

Ronald Reagan

The test of success is not what you do when you are on top. Success is how high you bounce when you hit the bottom.

George S. Patton, Jr.

The thing that motivates me is a very common form of motivation. And that is, with other folks counting on me, it's so easy to be motivated.

Jeff Bezos

Motivation is simple. You eliminate those who are not motivated.

Lou Holtz

"What day is it?" asked Pooh.

"It's today," squeaked Piglet.

"My favorite day," said Pooh.

A. A. Milne

Energy and persistence conquer all things.

Benjamin Franklin

You shouldn't focus on why you can't do something, which is what most people do. You should focus on why perhaps you can, and be one of the exceptions.

Steve Case

Do not be embarrassed by your failures, learn from them and start again.

Richard Branson

You've got to come up with the most positive things that can be said about the business and what you're doing, even in the most adverse times. And you've got to believe. Only then can your team believe in you.

Charles Schwab

Failure is only the opportunity more intelligently to begin again. There is no disgrace in honest failure; there is disgrace in fearing to fail. What is past is useful only as it suggests ways and means for progress.

Henry Ford

Success is not the key to happiness. Happiness is the key to success. If you love what you are doing, you will be successful.

Albert Schweitzer

You can't connect the dots looking forward; you can only connect them looking backward. So you have to trust that the dots will somehow connect in your future. You have to trust in something—your gut, destiny, life, karma, whatever. This approach has never let me down, and it has made all the difference in my life.

Steve Jobs

Failure is an option here. If things are not failing, you are not innovating enough.

Elon Musk

An entrepreneur is someone who jumps off a cliff and builds a plane on the way down.

Reid Hoffman

What I know for sure is this: The big secret in life is that there is no big secret. Whatever your goal for this year is, you can get there—as long as you're willing to be honest with yourself about the preparation and work involved. There are no back doors, no free rides.

Oprah Winfrey

You must be very patient, very persistent. The world isn't going to shower gold coins on you just because you have a good idea. You're going to have to work like crazy to bring that idea to the attention of people. They're not going to buy it unless they know about it.

Herb Kelleher

The very first company I started failed with a great bang. The second one failed a little bit less, but still failed. The third one, you know, proper failed, but it was kind of okay. I recovered quickly. Number four almost didn't fail. It still didn't really feel great, but it did okay. Number five was PayPal.

Max Levchin

Out of life's school of war: What does not destroy me, makes me stronger.

Friedrich Nietzsche

Develop success from failures. Discouragement and failure are two of the surest stepping-stones to success.

Dale Carnegie

If you work just for money, you'll never make it, but if you love what you're doing and you always put the customer first, success will be yours.

Ray Kroc

I am not a product of my circumstances. I am a product of my decisions.

Stephen Covey

Every great dream begins with a dreamer. Remember, you have within you the strength, the patience, and the passion to reach for the stars to change the world.

Harriet Tubman

Success is doing the thing that you want to do every single day and being around the people that you want to be around. It's also knowing that you define who you are. That you don't need anyone else's validation, unless the validation is out of love.

Daymond John

Indomitable perseverance in a business, properly understood, always ensures ultimate success.

Cyrus McCormick

With engineering, I view this year's failure as next year's opportunity to try it again. Failures are not something to be avoided. You want to have them happen as quickly as you can so you can make progress rapidly.

Gordon Earle Moore

If your only goal is to become rich, you will never achieve it.

John D. Rockefeller

When you're surrounded by people who share a passionate commitment around a common purpose, anything is possible.

Howard D. Schultz

The greatest real thrill that life offers is to create, to construct, to develop something useful. Too often we fail to recognize and pay tribute to the creative spirit. It is that spirit that creates our jobs.

Alfred Pritchard Sloan, Jr.

There is only one boss. The customer. And he can fire everybody in the company from the chairman on down, simply by spending his money somewhere else.

Samuel Moore "Sam" Walton

A man can succeed at almost anything for which he has unlimited enthusiasm.

Charles M. Schwab

Competition brings out the best in products and the worst in people.

David Sarnoff

When something is important enough, you do it even if the odds are not in your favor.

Elon Musk

If you think you can do a thing or think you can't do a thing, you're right.

Henry Ford

All business is personal. . . . Make your friends before you need them.

Robert Louis Johnson

One piece of advice that always stuck in my mind is that people should be respected and trusted as people, not because of their position or title.

Herb Kelleher

There is an immutable conflict at work in life and in business, a constant battle between peace and chaos. Neither can be mastered, but both can be influenced. How you go about that is the key to success.

Phil Knight

Dollars have never been known to produce character, and character will never be produced by money. I'll invest my money in people.

Will Kellogg

The two most important requirements for major success are: first, being in the right place at the right time, and second, doing something about it.

Ray Kroc

You can't do it unless you can imagine it.

George Lucas

Success seems to be connected with action. Successful people keep moving. They make mistakes, but they don't quit.

Conrad Nicholson Hilton

Give them quality. That's the best kind of advertising in the world.

Milton Hershey

The biggest competitive advantage is to do the right thing at the worst time.

William Hewlett

It's important to give a better country to your children, but it is more important to give better children to your country.

Carlos Slim Helú

I have this ability to find this hidden talent in people that sometimes even they didn't know they had.

Berry Gordy, Jr.

My deeds must be my life.

Stephen Girard

Success is a lousy teacher. It seduces smart people into thinking they can't lose.

Bill Gates

People ask me all the time, "How can I become a successful entrepreneur?" And I have to be honest: It's one of my least favorite questions, because if you're waiting for someone else's advice to become an entrepreneur, chances are you're not one.

Michael Dell

Thought, not money, is the real business capital.

Harvey Samuel Firestone

I have had all of the disadvantages required for success.

Larry Ellison

Our greatest weakness lies in giving up. The most certain way to succeed is always to try just one more time.

Thomas Edison

Everyone has an invisible sign hanging from their neck saying, "Make me feel important." Never forget this message when working with people.

Mary Kay Ash

I think if you look at people, whether in business or government, who haven't had any moral compass, who've just changed to say whatever they thought the popular thing was, in the end they're losers.

Michael Bloomberg

Obviously everyone wants to be successful, but I want to be looked back on as being very innovative, very trusted and ethical, and ultimately making a big difference in the world.

Sergey Brin

It takes twenty years to build a reputation and five minutes to ruin it. If you think about that, you'll do things differently.

Warren Buffett

It is better to fail in originality than to succeed in imitation.

Herman Melville

Success usually comes to those who are too busy to be looking for it.

Henry David Thoreau

Try not to become a man of success. Rather become a man of value.

Albert Einstein

Stop chasing the money and start chasing the passion.

Tony Hsieh

I owe my success to having listened respectfully to the very best advice, and then going away and doing the exact opposite.

G. K. Chesterton

The only limit to our realization of tomorrow will be our doubts of today.

Franklin D. Roosevelt

Character cannot be developed in ease and quiet. Only through experience of trial and suffering can the soul be strengthened, ambition inspired, and success achieved.

Helen Keller

The way to get started is to quit talking and begin doing.

Walt Disney

There are no secrets to success. It is the result of preparation, hard work, and learning from failure.

Colin Powell

If you really want to do something, you'll find a way. If you don't, you'll find an excuse.

Jim Rohn

I cannot give you the formula for success, but I can give you the formula for failure—it is: Try to please everybody.

Herbert Bayard Swope

Fall seven times and stand up eight.

Japanese proverb

Many of life's failures are people who did not realize how close they were to success when they gave up.

Thomas Edison

I failed my way to success.

Thomas Edison

I never dreamed about success, I worked for it.

Estée Lauder

Just when the caterpillar thought the world was ending, he turned into a butterfly.

Proverb

Whenever you see a successful person you only see the public glories, never the private sacrifices to reach them.

Vaibhav Shah

If you don't value your time, neither will others. Stop giving away your time and talents—start charging for it.

Kim Garst

A successful man is one who can lay a firm foundation with the bricks others have thrown at him.

David Brinkley

No one can make you feel inferior without your consent.

Eleanor Roosevelt

The whole secret of a successful life is to find out what is one's destiny to do, and then do it.

Henry Ford

If you're going through hell, keep going.

Winston Churchill

The ones who are crazy enough to think they can change the world are the ones that do.

Anonymous

What seems to us as bitter trials are often blessings in disguise.

Oscar Wilde

Happiness is a butterfly, which when pursued, is always beyond your grasp, but which, if you will sit down quietly, may alight upon you.

Nathaniel Hawthorne

If you can't explain it simply, you don't understand it well enough.

Albert Einstein

Your problem isn't the problem. Your reaction is the problem.

Anonymous

You can do anything, but not everything.

Anonymous

If you want to achieve excellence, you can get there today. As of this second, quit doing less-than-excellent work.

Thomas J. Watson

You may only succeed if you desire succeeding; you may only fail if you do not mind failing.

Philippos

Courage is resistance to fear, mastery of fear—not absence of fear.

Mark Twain

Only put off until tomorrow what you are willing to die having left undone.

Pablo Picasso

People often say that motivation doesn't last. Well, neither does bathing—that's why we recommend it daily.

Zig Ziglar

We become what we think about most of the time, and that's the strangest secret.

Earl Nightingale

The best reason to start an organization is to make meaning; to create a product or service to make the world a better place.

Guy Kawasaki

Success is liking yourself, liking what you do, and liking how you do it.

Maya Angelou

A real entrepreneur is somebody who has no safety net underneath them.

Henry Kravis

Whenever you find yourself on the side of the majority, it is time to pause and reflect.

Mark Twain

Take up one idea. Make that one idea your life—think of it, dream of it, live on that idea. Let the brain, muscles, nerves, every part of your body, be full of that idea, and just leave every other idea alone. This is the way to success.

Swami Vivekananda

The number one reason people fail in life is because they listen to their friends, family, and neighbors.

Napoleon Hill

Success does not consist in never making mistakes but in never making the same one a second time.

George Bernard Shaw

You must expect great things of yourself before you can do them.

Michael Jordan

Most of the important things in the world have been accomplished by people who have kept on trying when there seemed to be no help at all.

Dale Carnegie

You measure the size of the accomplishment by the obstacles you had to overcome to reach your goals.

Booker T. Washington

Real difficulties can be overcome; it is only the imaginary ones that are unconquerable.

Theodore N. Vail

Fortune sides with him who dares.

Virgil

Little minds are tamed and subdued by misfortune; but great minds rise above it.

Washington Irving

Failure is the condiment that gives success its flavor.

Truman Capote

A man can be as great as he wants to be. If you believe in yourself and have the courage, the determination, the dedication, the competitive drive and if you are willing to sacrifice the little things in life and pay the price for the things that are worthwhile, it can be done.

Vince Lombardi

Success is simple. Do what's right, the right way, at the right time.

Arnold Glasow

Rest satisfied with doing well, and leave others to talk of you as they please.

Pythagoras

We mount to heaven mostly on the ruins of our cherished schemes, finding our failures were successes.

Amos Bronson Alcott

Along with success comes a reputation for wisdom.

Euripides

Success rarely brings satisfaction.

Baltasar Gracián

He that succeeds makes an important thing of the immediate task.

William Feather

In most things success depends on knowing how long it takes to succeed.

Montesquieu

Be kind to everyone on the way up; you'll meet the same people on the way down.

Wilson Mizner

The most important single ingredient in the formula of success is knowing how to get along with people.

Theodore Roosevelt

APPENDIX B

Great Moments in the History of the American Entrepreneur

hen the Constitution was ratified in 1788, the United States was a bankrupt, failing start-up venture. Today it is the world's greatest economy, producing almost one-third of the goods and services on earth.

How did we do it?

In large part, through the sweat and brainpower of millions of American entrepreneurs who have written true tales of daring, courage, and triumph across the pages of business history. Here are just a few of our greatest achievements and turning points, which are moments that will echo through the halls of time:

Between 500 and 200 BCE: Native peoples of America establish vital regional trade networks across the continent, buying and selling flint, knives, arrowheads, animal products, vegetables, copper, marine shells, pottery, and countless other goods. They are the spiritual godfathers and godmothers of today's American entrepreneurs.

1600s: English American settlements and colonies are set up as for-profit entrepreneurial ventures in Massachusetts Bay, Plymouth, and Virginia. Cod fishing takes off in the waters of New England, kicking off a long economic boom for the region. The unofficial motto of these new ventures might as well be "Let's make deals, let's build, make, and sell things—let's make as much money as we can. Cash is king!"

1618: The West Indian tobacco crop takes off as a highly profitable business, making Virginia wealthy. The tragic downside is tobacco's link to cancer, which won't be definitively proven until the 1960s.

1624: The Dutch West India Company sets up a beaver-pelt trading post in present-day New York. "New Amsterdam" is a colony of entrepreneurial go-getters, hustlers, wheeler-dealers, and speed-talkers, setting the pace for the modern American metropolis.

1646: John Winthrop establishes the Saugus Iron Works in Massachusetts, representing the arrival of heavy industry in America. Unable to turn a profit, it collapses and fails by the 1670s amid management squabbles and lawsuits. It's a familiar tale for American entrepreneurs. Sometimes you've got to try three, four, or more times to make a business click.

1671: New England ships six million pounds of dried cod to international markets. Cod is tasty, profitable, and abundant. Fortunes are made and mansions are built in Boston. Let's face it, there's nothing like a good down-home backyard fish fry. Pass me the tartar sauce!

1700s: Lumber for shipbuilding becomes New England's first great industry and a lucrative cash crop. Sawmills blossom along the area's rivers.

1775: Virginia entrepreneur and agribusinessman George Washington takes charge of the colonial rebellion against the British. He's a tall, sturdy horseman whose executive skills have been honed by many years in the world of business as a land speculator and as the operator of a diversified, for-profit agro-industrial enterprise at Mount Vernon that includes a fishery, meat processing facility, textile and weaving manufactory, distillery, gristmill, blacksmith shop, brickmaking kiln, cargo-carrying schooner, and fields of grain. Washington's black slaves provide the muscle power.

1776: The Declaration of Independence is signed by a group of fifty-six men that includes many entrepreneurs and self-made businessmen like Benjamin Franklin, Samuel Adams, Philip Livingston, and John Hancock.

1776: The Continental Congress, fearing capture by British forces, flees Philadelphia, leaving entrepreneur Robert Morris behind to finance and run the revolutionary government as the de facto CEO for three months. Morris rescues General Washington and his freezing, starving troops with emergency supplies in the nick of time to complete their historic crossing of the Delaware on Christmas Day 1776. In 1781, Morris comes to the rescue again, running Washington's army finances and the American revolutionary government's budget out of his own pockets, juggling a blizzard of credit and paperwork. Morris again rushes food, supplies, and payments to the rebels in the nick of time. Great work! Lesson learned: if you want something impossible done, call in an entrepreneur.

1781: In a bold, risky campaign financed by Robert Morris and Philadelphia bond broker and Jewish American entrepreneur Haym Salomon, George Washington leads thousands of French and American troops on an epic march down the Atlantic coast from New York to Yorktown, Virginia, and knocks the British out of the war. To finance the operation, Morris uses his own personal credit and currency ("Morris notes"), juggled with loans and supplies from Spain, France, and Cuba. Independence is formally achieved in 1783.

1784: A group of American investors launches *The Empress of China*, which sails from New York to Asia loaded with furs and ginseng root, which it trades for tea, silks, china and porcelain, exotic plants and birds, and other luxury goods. The venture makes a huge profit, kicking off the era of large-scale American commerce with Asia.

1785: George Washington launches America's first trade development company, the Potomac Company, a partnership of private and public capital.

1790: The Philadelphia-Lancaster Turnpike is authorized and generates immediate profits for the company that built it. Commerce booms along the route, which inspires similar road and turnpike projects throughout the mid-Atlantic and New England states, including the Cumberland Road, which eventually extends all the way from Maryland to Illinois.

1792: Twenty-four stockbrokers gather under a sycamore tree in lower Manhattan and sign the Buttonwood Agreement, the beginning of the New York Stock Exchange.

1793: America's first multimillionaire entrepreneur, French immigrant Stephen Girard, risks his life to spearhead the rescue and treatment of yellow fever victims in Philadelphia.

1780s–90s: Robert Morris's idea for a national bank is approved by Congress and helps stabilize the postcolonial economy. Thomas Jefferson designs a currency system for the new nation. Morris turns down the post of secretary of the Treasury, so Washington appoints young Alexander Hamilton, who proves to be a brilliant choice, and, in 2015, the star of a smash-hit Broadway musical. By 1795, six years after taking charge of the bankrupt United States, George Washington's government restores America's credit to a level that international bankers declare is better than that of any European power. Government bonds sell at a premium in European markets. Washington puts the nation on a path toward strong tax and customs powers and an effective monetary system, which unleashes the entrepreneurial and free market destiny of the new nation. The Bank of the United States circulates notes throughout the nation, creating a reliable money supply for the nation's entrepreneurs and citizens.

1797: George Washington returns to Mount Vernon to be a full-time entrepreneur at age sixty-five, expands to breeding sheep, hogs, cattle, and deer for profit, and launches a whiskey distillery, which soon becomes one of the biggest in the new nation.

1807: Inventor and entrepreneur Robert Fulton builds a flat-bottom paddle-wheel steamboat, inaugurating a new age of reliable public and commercial transportation.

1807: Eli Whitney's cotton gin is patented and ignites the South's production of cotton, which soars from 1 percent of the world's total in 1793 to almost 70 percent of the world's total in 1850. The machine allows a single worker to do in one day what used to take fifty. A tragic consequence is the expansion and strengthening of human slavery in the United States.

1811: Boston merchant Francis Cabot Lowell takes a tour of English textile mills, makes mental notes of the equipment and processes, and clones the technology when he returns to the United States by building the world's first fully integrated textile mill in Waltham, Massachusetts. This sneaky act of industrial espionage helps trigger the wave of American mass-production manufacturing that transforms the nation.

1818: New York starts the first scheduled shipping service with Europe, and transatlantic trade begins booming.

1825: Rebecca Lukens takes over her family's near-bankrupt Brandywine Iron Works and Nail Factory in Pennsylvania. She becomes the first prominent American female CEO by leading a successful steel enterprise that operated into the twenty-first century. In 1994, *Fortune* calls her "America's first female CEO of an industrial company" and inducts her into the National Business Hall of Fame.

1825: The Erie Canal is completed ahead of schedule and under budget, becomes one of the first successful government-funded mega-projects and a business superhighway for entrepreneurial activity, and launches a business boom all along its 363-plus-mile route. Until then it took three weeks and $120 to ship a ton of flour from Buffalo to New York City. Now it takes eight days and only costs $6. By connecting the Hudson with the Great Lakes, New York is now linked with the Midwest, which unleashes a tidal wave of new business activity.

1830: There are twenty-three miles of railroad track in the nation. By the time of the Civil War, there are more than 30,000, and by 1900, there are nearly 200,000.

1830s: Former fur mogul and German immigrant entrepreneur John Jacob Astor gobbles up huge amounts of New York City real estate, betting that land values will skyrocket as the city moves north. They do, and he becomes the wealthiest man in early America.

1825–40: The annual Rocky Mountain Rendezvous trade fair is held in present-day Utah and Wyoming, bringing together Native Americans, white trappers, and their families.

1833: After years of experimentation and failure, New England entrepreneur Frederic Tudor manages to ship a 180-ton load of ice from Boston all the way to Calcutta—a 16,000-mile, four-month trip—in the days before electricity and refrigeration. The British population in Calcutta rejoices with chilled wine and beer parties to celebrate. An international ice-shipping empire is born. Profits roll in and the refrigerated foundation of the modern food industry is born.

1835: Young entrepreneur Samuel Colt creates the Patent Arms Manufacturing Company in Paterson, New Jersey, and registers his first patent, launching the age of reliable, mass-produced guns.

1844: Inventor-entrepreneur Samuel Morse introduces the blockbuster technology of instant long-distance communication with a test message of his telegraph machine between Washington and Baltimore, with the biblical phrase "What hath God wrought!"

1848: A pèa-shaped object catches the attention of a worker at John Sutter's mill near Sacramento, California. He feels his heart thump and exclaims, "Boys, by God, I believe I have found a gold mine," and the California Gold Rush begins, kicking off a wave of economic and entrepreneurial growth in California and the American West.

1850: Isaac Singer invents the Singer sewing machine and builds America's first multinational consumer product company with it.

1856: Cyrus McCormick's factory is making four thousand mechanical reapers a year for domestic and foreign markets, leading to a global revolution: the mechanization of agriculture. He makes a fortune.

1858: Rowland Hussey Macy, who has failed at five different business ventures, opens up the R. H. Macy Dry Goods store on the corner of Sixth Avenue and Fourteenth Street in New York City. Through clever merchandising, he builds it into the world's first "department store," and by 1866 the store employs four hundred people, including women in leadership roles. In 1902, Macy's opens its world-famous flagship megastore on Herald Square, occupying an entire city block. The brand grows to become a household name, with over eight hundred retail locations.

1861: Entrepreneur Cornelius Vanderbilt achieves dominance of the transatlantic and transcontinental steamship lines and later becomes the nation's leading railroad operator, exerting major influence on the financial and transportation markets. Big railroad ventures are powering the commerce of the nation.

1864: At age twenty-five, John D. Rockefeller and partners make one of the best business investments in history by buying Cleveland's biggest oil refinery. It is the beginning of a saga that will create the world's first great modern multinational corporation and make Rockefeller the wealthiest man in modern history.

1872: Jewish immigrant and San Francisco store owner Levi Strauss invents blue jean pants and waist-high work overalls made of rivet-reinforced, sturdy denim cotton. They take the clothing and fashion world by storm.

1875: Teenage entrepreneur Milton Hershey borrows $150 from his aunt and opens a candy shop in Philadelphia. It fails. He tries again in Chicago and fails. He comes to New York and fails again. Years go by. Still convinced he can build a successful candy company, and eager to build a factory to mass-produce and mass-distribute milk chocolate candy, he moves to Pennsylvania and eventually opens up the Hershey Chocolate Company. A global brand is born, along with Hershey's Kisses, Almond Joy, Mounds, and Reese's. Hershey became a philanthropist and set up a model community that endures to this day, including housing, churches, schools, parks, recreational facilities, cultural activities, and a hotel and trolley, all for his employees and community members.

1883: William Procter and James Gamble, two Ohio brothers-in-law who started the Procter & Gamble Company, launch their first major brand, Ivory Soap. The company grows to become a global consumer product powerhouse.

1880s: After the Civil War, America booms into a vast, vibrant national market for entrepreneurs. Real gross domestic product (GDP) increases more than seven times between 1865 and 1920, and real per capita product doubles.

1889: Andrew Carnegie writes "The Gospel of Wealth," arguing that the rich have a moral obligation to give away most of their money, and that personal wealth should be considered as a trust fund to create economic opportunity for the less fortunate. A century later, Chuck Feeney, Bill Gates, Warren Buffett, and other entrepreneurial super-tycoons use the Carnegie article as inspiration for the "Giving Pledge."

1898: John Merrick launches the North Carolina Mutual Life Insurance Company, catering to the lucrative, underserved African American market.

1898: In an accidental baking discovery, brothers John and Will Kellogg create a tasty wheat cereal flake. The brothers squabble and split, and Will winds up creating the company behind Kellogg's Corn Flakes, becoming one of America's wealthiest men and greatest philanthropists in the process. Pass the milk, please.

1900: America's population grows to 76 million, nearly doubling in the last quarter century. One-third of the increase comes from immigration.

1900: Black leader Booker T. Washington builds the National Negro Business League into six hundred chapters, encouraging African Americans to uplift themselves and their communities by launching their own business ventures.

1906: Madam C. J. Walker starts her own line of hair-care and beauty products aimed at the African American market, including the top-selling "Madam Walker's Wonderful Hair Grower," forming the basis of a national business network. Walker will become one of her era's greatest black philanthropists.

1907: Financial entrepreneur J. P. Morgan rescues Wall Street during a major financial crisis.

1908: William "Billy" Crapo Durant, a horse-buggy manufacturer and the favorite grandson of Michigan timber mogul and Michigan governor Henry Crapo (now there's a name I wouldn't wish on anybody), pulls together car manufacturers Cadillac, Buick, and Oldsmobile and creates General Motors Company, the world's first automotive conglomerate. He soon loses control of the company, then founds the Chevrolet Motor Company, then takes over General Motors in 1915. In 1920, he is booted out by the board of directors and devotes his life to being a gambler, drinker, and bowling alley operator, losing his fortune in auto stock in the Great Depression.

1900–09: Powered by immigration, the U.S. population jumps from 76 million to 92 million, by far the fastest rate of growth in the century, creating vast new markets for entrepreneurs.

1922: Juan Trippe starts the company that will eventually become Pan American Airways. The son of a Wall Street banker, he watched Wilbur Wright's 1909 flight around the Statue of Liberty and was inspired to become an aviator. After World War I, he bought scrapped seaplanes from the navy and started giving rides at Coney Island, then began an air taxi and mail-carrying service, as well as an international passenger service throughout the Caribbean and the Americas that became the world's largest commercial airline. In 1935, Pan Am inaugurated the first "China Clipper" flight with a flying boat packed with 111,000 letters, taking off from San Francisco and bound for Manila, and cheered by a throng of 150,000 people. In World War II, Pan Am planes shuttle American troops to war zones. In 1958, Pan Am launches the era of commercial jets with a nonstop flight from New York to Paris.

1928: On board a train from New York to Hollywood, illustrator and failed entrepreneur Walt Disney draws a rodent on a piece of paper. Mickey

Mouse is born, and Disney's company eventually soars to become a global media and entertainment powerhouse.

1937: Margaret Rudkin, a broke Connecticut housewife whose family lost everything in the Great Depression (including a 125-acre farm and a Tudor-style mansion with a five-car garage and a twelve-horse stable), makes a batch of her Pepperidge Farm bread in her kitchen and sells it to a local grocery store. The bread is hailed as a sensation through word of mouth and local media, and, with the help of an ad campaign showing a friendly older man delivering bread in a horse-drawn wagon, becomes a classic American food brand. Rudkin, who originally baked the wholesome bread to help her sickly son's allergies, sold her company to Campbell Soup in 1961 and served on Campbell's board of directors. "There isn't a worthwhile thing in the world that can't be accomplished with good hard work," she once said. "You've got to want something first and then you have to go after it with all your heart and soul."

1939: The symbolic birth of Silicon Valley and the Information Age occurs when Stanford University students William Hewlett and David Packard start a technology company in a garage at 367 Addison Avenue in Palo Alto, California, paving the way for other garage-style start-ups like Apple, Google, Cisco, Intel, Facebook, Uber, and Airbnb.

1945: World War II ends and consumer demand takes off like a rocket. American entrepreneurs enjoy a golden age.

1948: Estée Lauder starts selling her kitchen-brewed skin cream concoctions at a counter at New York City's Saks Fifth Avenue luxury superstore. By 1998, *Time* magazine ranks her the only woman on their list of the twentieth century's "most influential business geniuses," and when she dies six years later, her company's sales exceed $5 billion.

1959: Ruth Handler invents the Barbie doll, which powers her Mattel company to global leadership in the toy business, reaching the Fortune 500 in the 1960s, and today achieving global sales of over $5 billion.

1968: Robert Noyce and Gordon Moore start Intel, which in 1971 introduces the world's first commercial microprocessor chip, a foundation of the modern computer industry.

1971: The first Starbucks coffee shop opens in Seattle, Washington.

1974: Sandra Kurtzig starts a business in her spare bedroom that becomes

ASK Computer Systems, one of the fastest-growing computer software companies in the United States. In 1981, she becomes the first woman to lead a technology company public stock offering.

1975: Fred Smith's start-up overnight delivery service Federal Express is running out of money and down to its last $5,000 after a critical business loan was denied. Smith hops on a plane to Las Vegas, sits down at a black-jack table, and wins $27,000, enough to meet the next week's payroll and help keep the company afloat. Today FedEx is a $60 billion global company and Fred Smith is still chairman.

1977: The Apple II is introduced, launching the age of the personal computer.

1978: Ben Cohen and Jerry Greenfield start Ben & Jerry's Homemade Holdings, Inc., and open their first shop in Burlington, Vermont.

1980: IBM signs a contract with start-up software company Microsoft to create an operating system for its new PC. In one of the most brilliant business moves of all time, the twenty-six-year-old Microsoft cofounder Bill Gates inserts a clause in the agreement that permits Microsoft to sell the operating system to other computer manufacturers. Gates foresaw that other companies would clone IBM's hardware. IBM, apparently, did not fully grasp this. The clause shapes the course of technology history, allowing Microsoft to become a dominant force in the technology industry. By 1983, one-third of the world's PCs are running Microsoft software, and by 1986 Gates is a billionaire.

1984: Steve Jobs unveils the Apple Macintosh computer, unleashing a torrent of products that transform the world of consumer technology, media, communications, and entertainment.

1987: Reginald Lewis stages the $985 million takeover of the international division of Beatrice Foods, creating the first black-owned billion-dollar company and representing the then-biggest leveraged buyout of overseas assets by an American company in history.

1988: Oprah Winfrey launches her multimedia company, Harpo Studios, and later becomes the cofounder of Oxygen Media and is named by *Businessweek* as the greatest African American philanthropist in American history.

1995: Jeff Bezos opens Amazon.com on the Web, launching the age of consumer e-commerce.

1998: Google is started by Stanford University doctoral students Larry Page and Sergey Brin with an investment of only $100,000. Just ten years later, Google's parent company reaches $820 billion in market value as the world's largest search engine.

2004: Mark Zuckerberg launches Facebook and drops out of Harvard University. By 2018, his personal wealth is estimated to be about $72 billion.

2011: African American–owned businesses total some two million and enjoy the highest largest growth rate in minority-owned companies from 2002 to 2011.

2012: The Latino share of American entrepreneurs grows to almost 20 percent in 2012, up from 10.5 percent in 1996.

2014: Almost 30 percent of companies are majority-owned by women, and they generate more than $1 trillion in revenues and employ more than seven million people.

SOURCE NOTES

PROLOGUE: AN AMERICAN FAMILY BUSINESS

2   "the individual willing to embark on adventure": in Joe Carlen, *A Brief History of Entrepreneurship: The Pioneers, Profiteers, and Racketeers Who Shaped Our World* (New York: Columbia University Press, 2016), p. 1.

2   "the act that endows resources with a new capacity to create wealth": in "Innovation," *The Economist*, August 17, 2012.

2   "The first patent awarded to an American resident": John Steele Gordon, "Entrepreneurship in American History," *Imprimis*, February 2014.

20   "get into nutty situations": Erik Hedegaard, "Redneck, Inc: The Duck Dynasty Story," *Men's Journal*, October 10, 2013.

CHAPTER 1: THE FOUNDING ENTREPRENEURS

27   "What kept them going was the knowledge": Mourning Dove, *Mourning Dove: A Salishan Autobiography*, ed. Jay Miller (Lincoln: University of Nebraska Press, 1994), p. 69.

28   "by between 500 and 200 BCE": in Samuel Western, "Trade Among Tribes: Commerce on the Plains Before Europeans Arrived," Wyoming State Historical Society, April 26, 2016, https://www.wyohistory.org/encyclopedia/trade-among-tribes-commerce-plains-europeans-arrived.

28   "We think that the Shoshone were among": Ibid.

29   "the manufacture of very powerful bows": Ibid.

30   "The Shoshone, it seems, traded": Ibid.

30   "If we wanted to trade with them": in David Quinn, Alison Quinn, and Susan Hillier, *America from Concept to Discovery: Early Exploration of North America* (New York: Arno Press, 1979), p. 287.

31   "The high tide in typical Plains culture": Clark Wissler, "The Influence of the Horse in the Development of Plains Culture," *American Anthropologist*, January 1914.

31   "For the Sioux, corn was more important than blood": in Western, "Trade Among Tribes."

33   "I want some recompense": in John Steele Gordon, "Entrepreneurship in American History."

33   "By limiting liability": Ibid.

35   "The Dutch founded New Amsterdam": John Steele Gordon, "New York City: Built to Earn," *Barron's*, January 14, 2012.

35   "more a mole-hill than a fortress": in Stephen Brown, *Merchant Kings: When Companies Ruled the World, 1600–1900* (New York: Macmillan, 2010), p. 84.

36   "didn't care what people there thought": John Jeremiah Sullivan, "New Amsterdam's New Hero: A Stubborn, Brainy Young Lawyer," *Observer*, March 8, 2004.

36   "If what made America great": Russell Shorto, *The Island at the Center of the World: The Epic Story of Dutch Manhattan and the Forgotten Colony That Shaped America* (New York: Vintage, 2005), p. 3.

37   "They talk loud, very fast": in John Tierney, "What's New York the Capital of Now?," *New York Times*, November 20, 1994.

37   "the emporium of commerce, the seat of manufacture": Ibid.

37   "tongue that is licking up the cream": in Thomas Kessner, *Capital City: New York City and the Men Behind America's Rise to Economic Dominance, 1860–1900* (New York: Simon & Schuster, 2004), p. 30.

38   "By the time the 13 colonies declared": Gordon, "Entrepreneurship in American History."

CHAPTER 2: THE REBEL ENTREPRENEURS

41   "Building the national prosperity": in Ilan Mochari, "5 Surprising Business Lessons from This Entrepreneur-Turned-U.S. President," *Inc.*, May 2, 2016.

42   "in modern wars the longest purse": in Joseph Ellis, *His Excellency: George Washington* (New York: Vintage, 2005), p. 125.

42 "We are at the end of our tether": George Washington, *The Writings of George Washington* (Boston: American Stationers, 1835), p. 7.

42 "the first country in the world in which business people got involved": in Jan Norman, "As in 1776, Small Business Is the Backbone of the Nation," *The Orange County Register*, July 4, 1994.

43 "From the earliest American settlements": Carl Prince, "Colonial Commerce," *Dictionary of American History*, 2003, http://www.encyclopedia.com/history/dictionaries-thesauruses-pictures-and-press-releases/colonial-commerce.

43 "By the 18th century, regional patterns": in Robert McCan, William H. Peterson, and Stewart Ramsey, "Outline of American Economy," USIA, 1991, http://www.let.rug.nl/usa/outlines/economy-1991/.

44 media mogul: "Isaacson on Benjamin Franklin Book: Ben Franklin, Unbound," CNN, July 1, 2003.

44 "Remember that time is money": Benjamin Franklin, *Works of the Late Doctor Benjamin Franklin* (P. Wogan et al., 1793), p. 188.

44 "Credit is money": Benjamin Franklin, *The Works of Benjamin Franklin*, Volume 2 (New York: Putnam, Knickerbocker Press, 1904), p. 235.

44 "depends chiefly on two words": Benjamin Franklin, *The Works of the Late Dr. Benjamin Franklin* (New York: E. Duyckinck, 1807), p. 175.

44 "was not only one of the first": Blaine McCormick, "Benjamin Franklin: Founding Father of American Management," *Business Horizons*, January 2001.

44 "a crafty and diligent entrepreneur": Edward G. Lengel, *First Entrepreneur: How George Washington Built His—and the Nation's—Prosperity* (Boston: Da Capo Press, 2016), p. 4.

45 "a relatively small tobacco plantation into a diversified agro-industrial enterprise": Harlow Giles Unger, *"Mr. President": George Washington and the Making of the Nation's Highest Office* (Boston: Da Capo Press, 2013), p. 95.

46 "was up before dawn, forever on horseback supervising the plantation": James Thomas Flexner, "George Washington, Businessman," *American Heritage*, October 1965.

47 "Nothing should be bought": Lengel, *First Entrepreneur*, p. 238.

47 "A penny saved": Ibid.

47 "The man who does not estimate": George Washington, *The Writings of George Washington from the Original Manuscript Sources, 1745–1799*, Volume 36: August 4, 1797–October 28, 1798 (New York: Best Books, 1939), p. 112.

47 "System in all things is the soul": George Washington letter to James Anderson, December 21, 1797, "Washington Quotes," http://www .mountvernon.org/george-washington/quotes/.

47 "By 1766": in John Berlau, "Founding Father, Entrepreneur," *Reason*, February 12, 2009.

48 "well supplied with various kinds": George Washington letter to Arthur Young, December 12, 1793, National Archives Founders Online, https://founders.archives.gov/documents/Washington/05-14-02-0337.

48 "Since American merchants had to deal": John Dos Passos, "Robert Morris and the 'Art Magick,'" *American Heritage*, October 1956.

50 "The commonest things become intricate": Ibid.

50 "He spread his stock among various": Charles Rappleye, *Robert Morris: Financier of the American Revolution* (New York: Simon & Schuster, 2010), p. 202.

50 "He carried the art of kiting checks": Dos Passos, "Robert Morris and the 'Art Magick.'"

51 "mixing business and pleasure": Rappleye, *Robert Morris*, p. 24.

51 "He was tall. He was wide": "Robert Morris: America's Founding Capitalist," NPR, December 20, 2010.

53 "the most powerful man in America": in Rappleye, *Robert Morris*, p. 4.

54 "I must entreat you, if possible": in United States Department of State, *The Revolutionary Diplomatic Correspondence of the United States*, Volume 4 (Washington, DC: U.S. Government Printing Office, 1889), p. 665.

55 "He was beset by Continental officers": Dos Passos, "Robert Morris and the 'Art Magick.'"

57 "between 25 & 29 Sail of the line & 3200 land Troops": in William Spohn Baker, ed., *Itinerary of General Washington from June 15, 1775, to December 23, 1783* (Philadelphia: J. B. Lippincott, 1892), p. 231.

57   "to consider, to calculate": Eleanor May Young, *Forgotten Patriot: Robert Morris* (New York: Macmillan, 1950), p. 104.

57   "I am sorry to inform you that I find": in United States Department of State, *The Revolutionary Diplomatic Correspondence of the United States*, Volume 4, p. 650.

58   "We are on the Eve of the most Active Operations": Ibid., p. 651.

58   "It seems as if every Person": Ibid., p. 650.

59   "The late Movements of the Army have so entirely drained me": in John Sanderson, *Sanderson's Biography of the Signers to the Declaration of Independence* (Philadelphia: Thomas, Cowperthwait & Company, 1847), p. 359.

59   band played "The World Turned Upside Down": There is some dispute over whether this really happened, as there are no eyewitnesses or contemporary accounts of it.

60   "The American and French flags": in James Parton, *Revolutionary Heroes, and Other Historical Papers* (Boston: E. Maynard & Company, 1890), p. 46.

62   "laid the foundation that set America": Charles Rappleye, *Robert Morris, Financier of the American Revolution* (New York: Simon & Schuster, 2010), p. 2.

62   "I can recommend a far cleverer fellow than I am": in Rappleye, *Robert Morris*, p. 454.

62   "monster"; "impossible to decide": "Some Visits and Adventures of B. H. Latrobe," *Appleton's Booklovers Magazine*, August 1905.

63   "Who in God's name has all the Money?": in Ellis Paxson Oberholtzer, *Robert Morris: Patriot and Financier* (New York: Macmillan, 1903), p. 330.

63   "His complicated system of paper juggling": Albert Southwick, "Robert Morris, Con Man," *Worcester Telegram & Gazette*, June 18, 2009.

64   "any European power whatever": Alexander Hamilton, *The Papers of Alexander Hamilton*, Volume 18 (New York: Columbia University Press, 1973), p. 357.

65   "drank freely"; "kept bad company"; "was a very debauched person": in Lengel, *First Entrepreneur*, p. 238.

65   for being an "intolerable sot": Ibid., p. 243.

65 "rye, malted barley and corn were mixed": in Berlau, "Founding Father, Entrepreneur."

66 "In his new buff uniform and his spanking new epaulets": in Southwick, "Robert Morris, Con Man."

CHAPTER 3: THE PIONEERS

67 "The Americans always display a free, original": Alexis de Tocqueville, *Democracy in America*, Volume 3 (London: Saunders and Otley, 1840), p. 79.

67 "Boone was an entrepreneur": Roger McGrath, "Daniel Boone's Empire," *New York Times*, May 5, 1985.

68 "mirth, songs, dancing, shouting": James Pierson Beckwourth, *The Life and Adventures of James P. Beckwourth, Mountaineer, Scout, and Pioneer, and Chief of the Crow Nation of Indians* (New York: Harper & Brothers, 1858), p. 107.

68 "It's a great sight to see a large train get underway": in Peter Myers, Robert Hines, and Rex Field, *Life in the American Past* (American Heritage, 1997), p. 162.

69 "You talk of making a canal": in Robert J. Samuelson, "Republic of Turmoil," *Washington Post*, November 24, 2004.

69 "In 1839 only eighty bushels of wheat": Ibid.

70 "the most perfect weapon in the World": in Craig Boddington, *America, the Men and Guns that Made Her Great* (Los Angeles: Petersen, 1981), p. 33.

70 "The world is going too fast": in John Steele Gordon, *An Empire of Wealth: The Epic History of American Economic Power* (New York: Zondervan, 2009), p. 151.

73 "Many young boys who served": Robert Wright and David Cowen, *Financial Founding Fathers: The Men Who Made America Rich* (Chicago: University of Chicago Press, 2006), p. 148.

73 "Fearlessly, audaciously and defiantly": in Scott Smith, "Stephen Girard Built Massive Wealth via Bold Trading," *Investor's Business Daily*, October 20, 2014.

73 "His sailors were among the healthiest": Ibid.

74 "It was a simple but brilliant plan": Ibid.

75   "No Joke, Ship Full of Ice Sets Sail": in Leon Neyfakh, "How a Massachusetts Man Invented the Global Ice Market," *Boston Globe*, December 19, 2014.

76   "assumed the absolute novelty of ice": in Scott Smith, "Fred Tudor's Cold Calculus Put Ice in Summer Drinks," *Investor's Business Daily*, July 22, 2015.

76   "The object is to make the whole population": in Neyfakh, "How a Massachusetts Man Invented the Global Ice Market."

78   "The sweltering inhabitants of Charleston": Henry David Thoreau, *The Writings of Henry David Thoreau* (Boston: Houghton Mifflin, 1894), p. 459.

78   "Tudor's big idea ended up": Neyfakh, "How a Massachusetts Man Invented the Global Ice Market."

80   "The father of the American Industrial Revolution": Howard Anderson, "20 People Who Changed Tech: Francis Cabot Lowell," *Information Week*, March 4, 2013.

81   "John Jacob was a canny trader": Axel Madsen, *John Jacob Astor: America's First Multimillionaire* (New York: Wiley, 2002), p. 24.

82   "His innovation": in Dennis Drabelle, "Astoria: John Jacob Astor and Thomas Jefferson's Lost Pacific Empire," *Washington Post*, March 21, 2014.

82   "relentless in the pursuit of wealth": in William L. Lang, "John Jacob Astor (1763–1848)," Oregon Encyclopedia, https://oregonencyclopedia.org/articles/astor_john_jacob/#.WiXln7Y-JhA.

83   "The beaver became a factor of empire": James Stokesbury, "John Jacob Astor: Wealthy Merchant and Fur Trader," *American History*, December 1997.

83   "a most excellent man": in Ellen Terrell, "A Fortune Made from Fur: John Jacob Astor," Library of Congress blog, July 23, 2012, https://blogs.loc.gov/inside_adams/2012/07/a-fortune-made-from-fur-john-jacob-astor/.

84   "By the end of the war": Stokesbury, "John Jacob Astor."

85   "Astor was able to recognize": Ibid.

85   "All he touched turned to gold": in Eric Jay Dolin, *Fur, Fortune, and Empire: The Epic History of the Fur Trade in America* (New York: Norton, 2011), p. 282.

86   "Could I begin life again": Ibid., p. 194.

86   "Every dollar": in Owen Moritz, "Poor Immigrant Started It All," *New York Daily News*, December 28, 1997.

86   "one of the ablest, boldest, and most successful operators": James Parton, *Famous Americans of Recent Times* (Boston: Ticknor and Fields, 1867), p. 453.

86   "ingenious powers": in Stokesbury, "John Jacob Astor."

87   "The scene of sufferance was excruciating": John Quincy Adams, *Memoirs of John Quincy Adams: Comprising Portions of His Diary from 1795 to 1848*, Volume 9 (Philadelphia: Lippincott, 1876), p. 31.

88   "to accomplish a great work": in T. J. Stiles, *The First Tycoon: The Epic Life of Cornelius Vanderbilt* (New York: Knopf, 2009), p. 93.

88   "As a self-taught, self-made": Michael Kazin, "Ruthless in Manhattan," *New York Times*, May 7, 2009.

89   "Gentlemen: You have undertaken to cheat": in Amity Shlaes, "An Age of Creative Destruction," *Wall Street Journal*, October 29, 2010.

90   "I am not afraid of my enemies": in Stiles, *The First Tycoon*, p. 434.

90   "thought every man could stand watching": Ibid., p. 404.

90   "never placed confidence in anyone": Ibid., p. 223.

90   "Don't tell anybody what you're going to do": *Pacific Rural Press*, September 16, 1899, p. 191.

90   "looked like a conqueror": Louis Auchincloss, *The Vanderbilt Era: Profiles of a Gilded Age* (New York: Collier Books, 1990), p. 15.

90   "Corporate ethics, however": Kazin, "Ruthless in Manhattan."

90   "Contemporaries, too, often hated or feared Vanderbilt": in John Skipper, *Roosevelt's Revolt: The 1912 Republican Convention and the Launch of the Bull Moose Party* (Jefferson, NC: McFarland, 2018), p. 23.

92   "was a paradox": Stiles, *The First Tycoon*, p. 222.

92   "Every movement of his will": *New York Times*, January 5, 1877.

93   "The Fifth Avenue mansions, alas, are long gone": Arthur T. Vanderbilt II, *Fortune's Children: The Fall of the House of Vanderbilt* (New York: HarperCollins, 2013), p. x.

93 "the dismembered bodies of men": Christopher Gray, "The Curious Travels of the Commodore," *New York Times*, March 19, 2006.

93 "stands a hostage, in a haze": Ibid.

94 "It's a contraption that is seemingly a cross": in Scott Smith, "Cyrus McCormick's Reaper Revolutionized Farming," *Investor's Business Daily*, December 28, 2012.

94 "In this hour of debt and defeat": Ibid.

96 "The reaper is to the North what slavery is to the South": in Scott Smith, "Cyrus McCormick Revolutionized Farming Worldwide with the Reaper," *Investor's Business Daily*, April 14, 2016.

96 "While the cotton gin had made slavery profitable": Smith, "Cyrus McCormick's Reaper Revolutionized Farming."

97 "his invention made farmers' lives better": in Smith, "Cyrus McCormick Revolutionized Farming Worldwide with the Reaper."

97 "Work, work!": in Smith, "Cyrus McCormick's Reaper Revolutionized Farming."

CHAPTER 4: THE SUPER-TYCOONS

99 "found it more attractive on average": Gerald Gunderson, "The Founding Entrepreneurs: America's Prosperity," National Council for the Social Studies, The Free Library, 2007, https://www.thefreelibrary.com/The+founding+entrepreneurs%3a+America%27s+prosperity.-a0162455059.

101 "The half-century or so following the Civil War was a period": in David Landes, Joel Mokyr, and William Baumol, *The Invention of Enterprise: Entrepreneurship from Ancient Mesopotamia to Modern Times* (Princeton, NJ: Princeton University Press, 2012), p. 367.

102 "I began to learn what poverty meant": in Elizabeth Grice, "The Man Who Gave $350 Million to Charity," *Telegraph* (UK), June 29, 2006.

103 "I have made millions since": Andrew Carnegie, *Autobiography of Andrew Carnegie* (Boston: Houghton Mifflin, 1920), p. 34.

103 "There was scarcely a minute": Ibid., p. 39.

103 "As the steel pen embossed the dots and dashes": Peter Krass, *Carnegie* (New Jersey: Wiley, 2011), p. 33.

104 "ride in their carriage": Carnegie, *Autobiography of Andrew Carnegie*, p. 56.

104 "the management skills, the financial dealings": Krass, *Carnegie*, p. 12.

104 "I shall remember that check as long as I live": in David Nasaw, *Andrew Carnegie* (New York: Penguin, 2007), p. 60.

105 "to go entirely contrary to the adage": Ibid., p. 176.

105 "Andrew Carnegie was a brilliant cost analyst": in David Saito-Chung, "Andrew Carnegie Ignited America's Steel Industry Drive," *Investor's Business Daily*, February 28, 2013.

106 "The installation of the 12-hour workday": Nasaw, *Andrew Carnegie*, p. 261.

106 "Tell him I'll see him in hell": Len Barcousky, "'Meet You in Hell' by Les Stanford," *Pittsburgh Post-Gazette*, May 29, 2005.

107 "set an example of modest, unostentatious living": Andrew Carnegie, *The Gospel of Wealth Essays and Other Writings* (New York: Penguin, 2006), p. 10.

107 "Mr. Carnegie, I want to congratulate you": John Thornhill, "The Story of Skibo, Andrew Carnegie's Scottish Estate," *Financial Times*, September 19, 2014.

109 "It's the best kind of philanthropy I can think of": in Grice, "The Man Who Gave $350 Million to Charity."

109 "Maybe with the giving away of his money": Carnegie Museums of Pittsburgh, *Carnegie* (journal), Volume 69, Part 1, 2005, p. 128.

110 "a purple bulb": Jean Strouse, *Morgan: American Financier* (New York: Random House, 2014), p. xii.

110 "like an over-ripe pomegranate": William French, "J. Pierpont Morgan Had a Nose for Money," *Globe and Mail*, August 8, 1981.

111 "part of the American business structure": in "Business Profile: America's Saviour Had Midas Touch," *Telegraph* (UK), August 23, 2007.

111 "[d]uring the 1870s, Pierpont began to style himself": Ron Chernow, *The House of Morgan* (New York: Grove/Atlantic, 2010), p. 15.

112 "America's most powerful man": Ibid., p. 18.

112 "Pierpont differed from most of the Gilded Age": Ibid., p. 24.

113 "Morgan not only collects Old Masters": in Douglas Burgess, *Seize the Trident* (New York: McGraw-Hill, 2005), p. 51.

114 "In the absence of an income tax": Daniel Alef, *J. P. Morgan: America's Greatest Banker* (California: Titans of Fortune Publishing, 2009), p. 6.

114 "if people will keep their money in the banks": in "Lessons from Wall Street's Panic of 1907," *All Things Considered*, NPR, August 28, 2007.

115 "the greatest financial genius this country": in Chernow, *The House of Morgan*, p. 32.

116 "Morgan's supreme moment": in Daniel Gross, *Forbes Greatest Business Stories of All Time* (New Jersey: Wiley, 1997), p. 60.

116 "With his financial power": Donald Miller, "'Morgan' by Jean Strouse," *Pittsburgh Post-Gazette*, September 19, 1999.

116 "a beefy, red-faced, thick-necked financial bully": in Strouse, *Morgan: American Financier*, p. x.

116 "in cycles of expansion and contraction": Ibid., p. 11.

116 "had drafted him to do what he could": Ibid.

118 "And to think he wasn't even a rich man": in Miller, "'Morgan' by Jean Strouse."

119 "I cheat my boys every chance I get": in Carl O'Donnell, "The Rockefellers: The Legacy of History's Richest Man," *Forbes*, July 11, 2011.

119 "It was at this moment": "The Rockefellers," *American Experience*, PBS documentary, 2000.

120 "God gave me the money": in Anthony Sampson, *The Midas Touch* (New York: Plume, 1991), p. 18.

120 "all the methods and systems of the office": in Ron Chernow, *Titan: The Life of John D. Rockefeller, Sr.* (New York: Random House, 1998), p. 46.

120 "All my future seemed": Ibid., p. 45.

120 "I was almost always present": John D. Rockefeller, *Random Reminiscences of Men and Events* (New York: Doubleday, 1909), p. 37.

121 "He developed a reputation among bankers": Scott Smith, "Rockefeller Struck It Rich Creating Standard Oil," *Investor's Business Daily*, September 27, 2012.

121 "He always had a plan and a clear-sighted goal": Ibid.

122 "Business came in upon us so fast": Rockefeller, *Random Reminiscences*, p. 45.

122 "By that time, whale oil had become": Smith, "Rockefeller Struck It Rich."

122 "Never one to do things halfway": Chernow, *Titan*, p. 79.

123 "I shall never forget how hungry I was": Ibid., p. 101.

123 "from a semi-tropical wilderness": Gordon, "Entrepreneurship in American History."

124 "the most cruel, impudent": in Chernow, *Titan*, p. 292.

124 "Rockefeller and other industrial captains": Ibid., p. 148.

125 "if we did not sell out": Ibid., p. 143.

125 "Rockefeller may have been unique": Smith, "Rockefeller Struck it Rich."

125 "revealed both his finest and most problematic": Ibid.

125 "All the fortune that I have made": in Daniel Yergin, *The Prize: The Epic Quest for Oil, Money and Power* (New York: Simon & Schuster, 1992), p. 6.

125 "By the early 1890s, Standard Oil had achieved": Robert Cherny, "Entrepreneurs and Bankers: The Evolution of Corporate Empires," The Gilder Lehrman Institute of American History, undated, https://ap.gilderlehrman .org/essays/entrepreneurs-and-bankers-evolution-corporate-empires.

126 "the kind of place that God would have built": "The Rockefellers," PBS documentary.

126 "Four-fifths of these letters": in Chernow, *Titan*, p. 300.

127 "About the year 1890 I was still following": Rockefeller, *Random Reminiscences*, p. 156.

127 "You must keep up with it!": in Chernow, *Titan*, p. 563.

127 "It is a great problem": Ibid., p. 468.

127 "The only thing which is of lasting benefit": Rockefeller, *Random Reminiscences*, p. 152.

127 "the best investment I ever made": in Chernow, *Titan*, p. 325.

129 "The best philanthropy": Rockefeller, *Random Reminiscences*, p. 177.

131 "Her judgment was always better than mine": in Chernow, *Titan*, p. 93.

CHAPTER 5: THE WINNERS

133 "Entrepreneurship has no age or time limits": in Kristin Chessman, "16 Legendary Women Entrepreneurs," *Entrepreneur*, August 6, 2008.

134 "I married at the age of 14": in Margo Jefferson, "Worth More Than It Costs," *New York Times*, April 1, 2001.

134 "That's when she began to envision herself": in Raquel Laneri, "Manse Built by America's First Self-Made Millionairess Seeks New Life," *New York Post*, February 18, 2017.

135 "I was at my washtubs one morning": in Tiffany M. Gill, *Beauty Shop Politics: African American Women's Activism in the Beauty Industry* (Champaign: University of Illinois Press, 2010), p. 20.

135 "He answered my prayer": in A'Lelia Bundles, *On Her Own Ground: The Life and Times of Madam C. J. Walker* (New York: Simon & Schuster, 2001), p. 60.

136 "Madam Walker fit into a whole pattern of women": "Bundles Tells True Tales of Walker's Life," *Boston Globe*, February 28, 2001.

136 "But what was interesting about Walker": Ibid.

138 "without regard to cost": in Patrick Sisson, "Preservationists Hope the Awe-Inspiring Home of Entrepreneur Madam C. J. Walker Gets a Second Life," curbed.com, December 28, 2016.

138 "I am building this home so that I can show": "A Black Woman Who Meant Business," CBSNews.com, February 10, 2001.

139 "I want to live to help my race": in Bundles, *On Her Own Ground*, p. 273.

139 "It is given to few persons to transform a people": W. E. B. Du Bois, *Crisis: A Record of the Darker Races*, May 1919.

139 "I am a woman who came from the cotton fields": in Chime Edwards, "What Madame C. J. Walker Really Did for Black Women," *Essence*, February 18, 2015.

139 "From there I was promoted to the washtub": in Sharon Jarvis, "American Rags-to-Riches Mythos: The Madam C. J. Walker Saga," New York Public Library, January 24, 2011, https://www.nypl.org/blog/2011/01/24/madam-c-j-walker-part-1.

140 "I got my start by giving myself a start": in Bundles, *On Her Own Ground*, p. 68.

140 "Don't sit around waiting for opportunities": in Sylvia Moreno, "Inspired by Madam C. J. Walker," *Washington Post*, February 12, 1998.

140 "There is no royal flower-strewn path to success": Tachelle Wilkes, "Preserving Madam C. J. Walker's Legacy," *Ebony*, October 1, 2014.

142 "He was a beacon for African American entrepreneurs": in Clay Latimer, "John Merrick: From Slavery to Insurance Magnate," *Investor's Business Daily*, January 12, 2015.

142 "He was a beacon for African American uplift": Ibid.

142 "There is in this small city a group": Ibid.

142 "complex, organized, and structured market economies": Juliet E. K. Walker, *The History of Black Business in America: Capitalism, Race, Entrepreneurship* (Chapel Hill: University of North Carolina Press, 2009), p. 1.

142 "propelled by a high degree of both individual": Ibid., p. 9.

143 "The world is a market, the market is the world": Ibid.

144 "When I was growing up, we had black laundromats": in Joel Kotkin, "The Reluctant Entrepreneurs," Inc.com, September 1, 1986.

144 "It was like an insurmountable trade barrier had dissolved": Ibid.

145 "Well, maybe it will be different for him": Reginald F. Lewis and Blair S. Walker, *Why Should White Guys Have All the Fun? How Reginald Lewis Created a Billion-Dollar Business Empire* (Baltimore: Black Classic Press, 2005), p. xvii.

146 "I quit football after my freshman year": Lewis and Walker, *Why Should White Guys Have All the Fun?*, p. 40.

146 "He always had a purpose": Ibid., p. 42.

147 "I did the usual work doled out to beginning associates": Ibid., p. 74.

148 "after selling off assets in Latin America and Asia": Irene Silverman, "Widow of First Black Billionaire Keeps His Memory Alive," Regi-

nald F. Lewis website, http://reginaldflewis.com/reginaldflewis.com/news
-media/080708-Widow-of-First-Black-Billionaire-Keeps-His-Memory
-Alive.html.

148 "I'm trying not to take it too seriously": in Andrew Kupfer, "Reginald Lewis: The Newest Member of the LBO Club," *Fortune*, January 4,
1998.

149 "Unfortunately, when we label people it tends to circumscribe":
in Kathleen Teltsch, "Record Gift for Harvard Law Is Milestone for
Blacks," *New York Times*, July 8, 1992.

149 "Reginald Lewis accomplished more in half a century": in Wolf-
gang Saxon, "Reginald Lewis, Financier, Is Honored at Service," *New York
Times*, January 26, 1993.

149 "Keep going, no matter what": in Sean Yoes, "Reginald Lewis,
Another Shining Chapter in Black Baltimore's History," AFRO.com, December 14, 2017.

150 Oprah Winfrey quotes: in Grace Bluerock, "24 Quotes on Success
from Oprah Winfrey," *Entrepreneur*, January 29, 2016.

151 "I started working from the time": Daymond John as told to Oc-
tavio Blanco, "Daymond John on His Mom, Hip-Hop, and Making It Big,"
CNNMoney.com.

152 "You need to outthink, out-hustle, outperform": in Michael Mink,
"'Shark' Daymond John Wrapped His Apparel Brand in Hip-Hop Mystique," *Investor's Business Daily*, May 15, 2017.

152 "I notice a common trait in the super successful people": Ibid.

152 "The choice of whether to succeed—or not": Ibid.

152 "We pushed our guys onto bank boards": in Douglas Martin, "J.
Bruce Llewellyn, Who Forged a Path for Blacks in Business, Is Dead at
82," *New York Times*, April 9, 2010.

153 "For an African American businessman to receive": Ibid.

153 "Llewellyn consolidated plants and warehouses": Dyan Machan,
"Working the System," *Forbes*, December 13, 1999.

153 "Yes, I was the first minority bottler": Ibid.

153 "nerve-wracking, gut-wrenching and pain inducing": in Martin,
"J. Bruce Llewellyn."

153   "Minorities have to understand that the world revolves": Ibid.

154   "[t]he last thirty years also have brought": Brian Feldman, "The Decline of Black Business," *Washington Monthly*, March/April/May 2017.

154   "a virtual bloodbath": Joyce Jones, "Seeking a New Policy for Growth," *Black Enterprise*, June 1, 1999.

156   "Rebecca was able to build the company up": Kat Michels, "Heroines of History: Rebecca Lukens—An Ironclad Matriarch," *Business Heroine*, March 14, 2014.

157   "Confidence was instilled in me": in Carrie Hammer, "Nina Vaca Shows Small Businesses Are Big Players," *Forbes*, December 2, 2017.

157   "The future of entrepreneurship continues to be very bright": Ibid.

158   "The soothsayers prophesied that I was doomed": Mary Kay Ash, *The Mary Kay Way: Timeless Principles from America's Greatest Woman Entrepreneur* (New York: Wiley, 2009), p. 34.

159   "If you let people know you appreciate them and their performance": Ibid., p. 62.

159   "She made everyone feel important whether it was the maintenance man": Ibid., p. 45.

159   "We fall forward to success": Ibid., p. 103.

159   "Don't limit yourself": in Jacquelyn Smith and Emmie Martin, "105 Inspirational Quotes from Some of the World's Most Successful People," *Business Insider*, March 6, 2016.

160   "I have never worked a day in my life without selling": in Tatiana Morales, "Cosmetics Mogul Estee Lauder Dies," CBSNews.com, April 12, 2004.

160   "If I believe in something, I sell it, and I sell it hard": "Cosmetics Queen Estee Lauder Dies," BBC News, April 25, 2004.

160   "She was devastatingly sincere and insistent": in Scott Smith, "Estee Lauder Built a Cosmetics Empire on High Quality," *Investor's Business Daily*, January 7, 2014.

160   "Good was not good enough": Estée Lauder, *Estée: A Success Story* (New York: Random House, 1985), p. 24.

161   "the Golden Age for women": Elaine Pofeldt, "Why Women En-

trepreneurs Will Be the Force to Be Reckoned With in 2017," CNBC.com, February 28, 2017.

163 "In 1760, for example": Ibid.

164 "As leading actors in the U.S. economy": Dilawar Syed, "Asian American Entrepreneurship: An Asset to the Nation's Economy," White House archive, November 22, 2011, https://obamawhitehouse.archives.gov /blog/2011/11/22/asian-american-entrepreneurship-asset-nation-s-economy.

CHAPTER 6: THE GOLDEN AGE OF THE AMERICAN ENTREPRENEUR

165 "Forget the ZZ Top beards": Bill Carter, "A Calculated Push into Entertainment Lifts 'Duck Dynasty' Family Fortunes," New York Times, August 25, 2013.

166 "ranks up there with that of Cain and Abel": "Will Keith Kellogg: The Cornflake King," Entrepreneur, October 10, 2008.

167 "I feel kind of blue"; "Am afraid that I will always be a poor man": in Howard Markel, The Kelloggs: The Battling Brothers of Battle Creek (New York: Pantheon Books, 2017), p. 108.

167 "Will was a serious student of the emerging science"; "a massive, modern, beautiful and luxurious medical": in Scott Smith, "Viewed as a Flake, W. K. Kellogg Ended Up Redefining Breakfast," Investor's Business Daily, March 4, 2017.

168 "I sort of feel it in my bones": in Horace Powell, The Original Has This Signature: W. K. Kellogg (New York: Prentice-Hall, 1956), p. 121.

169 "He had no capital to rebuild": in Smith, "Viewed as a Flake."

169 "Mr. Kellogg appreciated the power of the new force": Powell, The Original Has This Signature, p. 131.

169 "Visualizing his foods on breakfast tables": Ibid.

171 "ruthless businessman and investor": Jacob Heilbrunn, "The Patriarch: Joseph Kennedy Sr.'s Outsized Life," Daily Beast, November 21, 2012.

171 "From the beginning, Joe knew": Richard Whelan, "Profile of Joseph P. Kennedy," Fortune, January 1963.

172 "operated just like Joe Stalin": in Cari Beauchamp, Joseph P. Kennedy Presents: His Hollywood Years (New York: Vintage, 2010), p. 307.

172   "He's a charmer": in Cari Beauchamp, *Without Lying Down: Frances Marion and the Powerful Women of Early Hollywood* (Berkeley: University of California Press, 1998), p. 156.

172   "Kennedy was the first and only outsider to fleece Hollywood": in Beauchamp, *Joseph P. Kennedy Presents*, p. 403.

172   "a smart, rough competitor": Whelan, "Profile of Joseph P. Kennedy."

174   "We're going to sell Jack like soap flakes": in John Davis, *The Kennedys: Dynasty and Disaster* (Paris: SP Books, 1993), p. 151.

174   "He's the one who made all this possible": in Gretchen Craft Rubin, *Forty Ways to Look at JFK* (New York: Ballantine Books, 2005), p. 71.

174   "like a raging lion": Walt Disney, *Walt Disney: Conversations*, Part 52 (Jackson: University of Mississippi Press, 2006), p. 51.

175   "Disaster seemed right around the corner": in Russell Schroeder, *Walt Disney: His Life in Pictures* (New York: Disney Press, 1996), p. 21.

175   "I function better when things are going badly": in Neal Gabler, *Walt Disney: The Triumph of the American Imagination* (New York: Vintage, 2007), p. 568.

175   "popped out of my mind": in Lewis Howes, "20 Lessons from Walt Disney on Entrepreneurship, Innovation, and Chasing Your Dreams," *Forbes*, July 17, 2012.

175   "Too sissy"; "It's better than Mortimer": in Linda Rottenberg, "Walt Disney Created His Most Famous Character in a Fit of Rage," *Business Insider*, October 28, 2014.

175   "Mickey Mouse is, to me, a symbol of independence": in Gross, *Forbes Greatest Business Stories of All Time*, p. 129.

176   "You may not realize it when it happens": in Nina Zipkin, "16 Inspirational Quotes from Walt Disney," *Entrepreneur*, December 5, 2016.

177   "a deep respect for the individual": in Steve Strauss, "Big, Bold Visions: Does Every Entrepreneur Need One?," CBSNews.com, August 17, 2011.

177   "Packard and Hewlett demanded performance": Jim Collins, "The HP Way," jimcollins.com, May 2005.

180   "I make progress by having people around me": in Scott Stod-

dard, "Industrialist Henry Kaiser Made Just About Everything His Business," *Investor's Business Daily*, August 20, 2016.

181 "In 1977, South Korea was a poor country": in Adam Bluestein, "The Most Entrepreneurial Group in America Wasn't Born in America," Inc.com, January 12, 2015.

184 "the two Americans began driving from port to port": Mike Colman, "The Bearable Lightness of Giving," *Courier Mail* (Australia), June 12, 2012.

185 "one of the biggest single transfers of wealth in history": Conor O'Clery, "In 1984 This Man Was a Billionaire. Then He Decided to Give Away Most of His Wealth," *Irish Times*, August 25, 2007.

186 "If I can get a watch for $15 with a five-year battery": in Conor O'Clery, "The Silent Giver," *Irish Times*, October 4, 2003.

186 "I am not really into money": in O'Clery, "In 1984 This Man Was a Billionaire."

186 "intensely competitive": Ibid.

186 "a balance of business, family": in Conor O'Clery, *The Billionaire Who Wasn't: How Chuck Feeney Secretly Made and Gave Away a Fortune* (New York: PublicAffairs, 2007), p. 98.

186 "the shabby philanthropist": Ibid., p. 128.

186 "It's the intelligent thing to be frugal": in Margot Roosevelt, "Passing Along His Good Fortune," *Los Angeles Times*, March 8, 2008.

186 "Rumpled by habit, limping on old knees": Jim Dwyer, "Out of Sight, Till Now, and Giving Away Billions," *New York Times*, September 26, 2007.

187 "I did not want money to consume my life"; "Part of the consideration was": in O'Clery, "The Silent Giver."

187 "Strict rules were formulated": O'Clery, *The Billionaire Who Wasn't*, p. 120.

188 "It beats giving while you're dead": in Conor O'Clery, "The Irish-American Billionaire Who Gave Away His Fortune," *Irish Times*, January 3, 2017.

188 "the ultimate example of giving while living": Ibid.

188 "spiritual leader": in Gregory Lamb, "Giving Pledge: A Big-Hearted Billionaires Club, Led by Bill Gates and Warren Buffett, Keeps Growing," *Christian Science Monitor*, May 11, 2011.

188 "should be everybody's hero": in Tom Lyons, "Forbes Award: Buffett Cites Chuck Feeney as 'My Hero,'" *Irish Times*, June 19, 2014.

190 "They are not the fashion police": in Meghan Holohan, "Man with Down Syndrome Starts Million-Dollar Sock Company," Today.com, January 24, 2018.

190 "Socks are fun and creative and colorful, and they let me be me": in Joshua Cheetham, "The Million Dollar Sock Entrepreneur with Down's Syndrome," BBC News, January 13, 2018.

190 "I have Down syndrome and it never holds me back": in Holohan, "Man with Down Syndrome Starts Million-Dollar Sock Company."

190 "Most of us wear some sort of uniform": in Cheetham, "The Million Dollar Sock Entrepreneur."

190 "I came up with a catchphrase": in Holohan, "Man with Down Syndrome Starts Million-Dollar Sock Company."

191 "I have the perfect partner"; "It makes me happy": in Cheetham, "The Million Dollar Sock Entrepreneur."

191 "In every box": in Veronica Quezada, "How This 21-Year-Old with Down Syndrome Is Making Six Figures Selling Socks," *Time*, April 25, 2017.

192 "a social mission and a retail mission": in Cheetham, "The Million Dollar Sock Entrepreneur."

192 "We're spreading happiness. What's better than that?": in Larry Kim, "Meet John—the 21-Year-Old Entrepreneur Whose Inspiring Story Will Make You Cry Tears of Joy," Inc.com, January 31, 2018.

192 "The U.S. now ranks not first, not second": Jim Clifton, "American Entrepreneurship: Dead or Alive?", *Gallup Business Journal*, January 13, 2015.

193 "The number of entrepreneurship classes": Derek Thompson, "The Myth of the Millennial Entrepreneur," *The Atlantic*, July 6, 2016.

194 "The opportunities for people with ideas": John Steele Gordon, speech to Hillsdale College free market forum, November 15, 2013.

195 A 2016 study by the Religious Freedom and Business Foundation: Brian Grim and Melissa Grim, "The Socio-Economic Contributions of Religion to American Society: An Empirical Study," Religious Freedom and Business Foundation, 2016.

APPENDIX A: MY FAVORITE QUOTES ON
ENTREPRENEURSHIP AND SUCCESS

207 "Ever since the first settlement": Milton Friedman and Rose Friedman, *Free to Choose: A Personal Statement* (Boston: Houghton Mifflin Harcourt, 1990), p. 1.

207 "Aim for success, not perfection": in William Safire, *Words of Wisdom* (New York: Simon & Schuster, 1990), p. 248.

207 "Don't limit yourself": "Success Quotes from Accomplished People," *Business Insider*, September 22, 2014.

207 "If you want to be happy": "18 Motivational Quotes About Successful Goal Setting," Inc.com, December 29, 2016.

207 "If there is no struggle": in Philip Sheldon Foner and Robert J. Branham, *Lift Every Voice: African American Oratory, 1787–1900* (Tuscaloosa: University of Alabama Press, 1998), p. 310.

207 "You build on failure": "Cowboy's Log," *American Cowboy*, March 2007, p. 32.

207 "I learned that courage": "Mandela in His Own Words," CNN International, June 26, 2008.

207 "Only those who dare to fail": Robert F. Kennedy, Day of Affirmation Address, University of Capetown, Capetown, South Africa, June 6, 1966.

208 "Courage, then, and patience!": Victor Hugo, *The Letters of Victor Hugo, from Exile, and After the Fall of the Empire* (Boston: Houghton Mifflin, 1898), p, 23.

208 "All our dreams can come true": in Howes, "20 Lessons from Walt Disney."

208 "The best revenge is massive success": in Sean Hotchkiss, GQ.com, November 21, 2011.

208 "The successful warrior": in Rob Berger, "Top 100 Money Quotes of All Time," Forbes.com, April 30, 2014.

208 "Would you like me": in Adam Cutler, "Good Design Is (Still) Good Business," IBM Design blog, July 3, 2014, https://www.ibm.com/design/blog-state.shtml.

208 "The ultimate measure of a man": in Aaron Couch, "Martin Luther King Day: 10 Memorable Quotes," *Christian Science Monitor*, January 17, 2011.

208 "The greatest leader is not necessarily": in Mike Wallace, "Ronald Reagan Remembered," *60 Minutes*, CBS News, June 6, 2004.

208 "The test of success": in Jeffrey Hirsch, *Stock Trader's Almanac 2015* (Hoboken, NJ: Wiley, 2014), p. 105.

208 "The thing that motivates me": in Robert Hof, "Online Extra: Q&A with Amazon's Jeff Bezos," *Bloomberg Businessweek*, May 14, 2001.

208 "Motivation is simple": in Dick Harmon, "Lou Holtz, ESPN Part Ways but His Quotes, Personality Will Endure," *Deseret News*, April 13, 2015.

208 "What day is it?": "10 Quotes on Life from Winnie the Pooh," *New York Daily News*, October 14, 2015.

209 "Energy and persistence conquer all things": "7 Must-Read Life Lessons from Benjamin Franklin," *Business Insider*, June 1, 2011.

209 "You shouldn't focus": in Rose Leadem, "9 Steve Case Quotes to Help Launch Every Entrepreneur's Career," Entrepreneur.com, September 27, 2017.

209 "Do not be embarrassed": in Marcel Schwantes, "Richard Branson Reveals 3 Important Lessons," Inc.com, September 23, 2017.

209 "You've got to come up": "Charles Schwab Makes Investing Safer for Americans," *Investor's Business Daily*, March 26, 2014.

209 "Failure is only the opportunity": Henry Ford with Samuel Crowther, *My Life and Work* (New York: Garden City Publishing Company, 1922), pp. 19–20.

209 "Success is not the key": in Deep Patel, "25 Quotes to Inspire Your Entrepreneurial Journey," *Entrepreneur*, April 23, 2017.

209 "You can't connect the dots": Steve Jobs, Commencement Address at Stanford University, June 12, 2005.

209 "Failure is an option here": in Rich Wiley, "Entrepreneurs: 5 Things We Can Learn from Elon Musk," Forbes.com, October 8, 2015

209 "An entrepreneur is someone": in John Brandon, "22 Inspiring Quotes from Famous Entrepreneurs," Inc.com, October 8, 2014.

209 "What I know for sure is this": "What I Know for Sure," Oprah.com, http://www.oprah.com/omagazine/what-i-know-for-sure-hard-work.

210 "You must be very patient": "Herb Kelleher on the Record, Part 3," Bloomberg.com, December 24, 2003.

210 "The very first company": Max Levchin, interview with Renee Montagne, "FailCon: Failing Forward to Success," Morning Edition, NPR, October 29, 2009.

210 "Out of life's school of war": in Daniel Slotnik, "Friedrich Nietzsche, a Philosophical Renegade Whose Ideas Endured," New York Times, August 25, 2016.

210 "Develop success from failures": in Berger, "Top 100 Money Quotes of All Time."

210 "If you work just for money": in Thomas Heath, "Value Added," Washington Post, January 8, 2012.

210 "I am not a product of my circumstances": in Jeff Haden, "50 Top Motivational Quotes to Inspire You to Achieve Your Goals," Inc.com, April 28, 2017.

210 "Every great dream begins": in Bill Murphy, Jr., "Here Are the Best Inspirational Quotes for 2018," Inc.com, December 29, 2017.

210 "Success is doing the thing": in Mink, "'Shark' Daymond John Wrapped His Apparel Brand in Hip-Hop Mystique."

210 "Indomitable perseverance in a business": in Smith, "Cyrus McCormick Revolutionized Farming Worldwide with the Reaper."

210 "With engineering, I view this year's failure": "Up to Date," NASA Educator Resource Center Newsletter, January 2013.

211 "If your only goal": in Edwin Lefevre and Jon Markman, Reminiscences of a Stock Operator: With New Commentary and Insights on the Life and Times of Jesse Livermore (Hoboken, NJ: Wiley, 2010), p. 11.

211 "When you're surrounded by people": in Carmine Gallo, "What Starbucks CEO Howard Schultz Taught Me About Communication and Success," Forbes.com, December 19, 2013.

211 "The greatest real thrill": Alfred P. Sloan Foundation, 1997 Annual Report, p. 2.

211 "There is only one boss": "Tip of the Day—There Is Only One Boss," *Business Insider*, July 21, 2010.

211 "A man can succeed": in Norman Vincent Peale, *Enthusiasm Makes the Difference* (New York: Simon & Schuster, 2003), p. 4.

211 "Competition brings out the best": in *Esquire*, January 1964, p. 36.

211 "When something is important enough": in Luis Romero, "Elon Musk's 4 Success Mantras from SpaceX and Tesla," Forbes.com, October 17, 2017.

211 "If you think you can": in Travis Bradberry, "8 Ways Smart People Use Failure to Their Advantage," Forbes.com, April 12, 2016.

211 "All business is personal": in Derek T. Dingle, *Black Enterprise Titans of the B.E. 100s: Black CEOs Who Redefined and Conquered American Business* (Hoboken, NJ: Wiley, 1999), p. 28.

211 "One piece of advice": "Quotes of the Day," *Investor's Business Daily*, November 10, 2014.

211 "There is an immutable conflict": in Larry Kim, "25 Billionaire Quotes About Success in Business and Life," Inc.com, April 13, 2015.

211 "Dollars have never been known": in Tony Osuwu, "Inspirational Quotes from Top Business Leaders to Get You Through Tough Times," TheStreet.com, September 9, 2017.

212 "The two most important requirements": "Become a Better Leader: Ray Kroc, McDonald's, and His Ten Recipes for Success," Forbes.com, January 14, 2014.

212 "You can't do it unless": in Stephen Covey, *Everyday Greatness: Inspiration for a Meaningful Life* (Nashville, TN: Thomas Nelson, 2009), p. 96.

212 "Success seems to be connected with action": in Priyannkaa Dey, "Inspiring Quotes to Deal with Failure," Entrepreneur.com, November 7, 2015.

212 "Give them quality": "Milton S. Hershey: The Candy Man," Entrepreneur.com, October 8, 2008.

212 "The biggest competitive advantage": in Phil McKinney, "10 Quotes from Bill Hewlett and David Packard That Every Executive Should Read," Forbes.com, October 3, 2011.

212 "It's important to give": "Carlos Slim: The Richest Man You Never Heard Of," *Good Morning America*, ABC News, October 8, 2007.

212 "I have this ability": in Kevin Daum, "21 Inspiring Quotes from Black Business Leaders," Inc.com, July 13, 2017.

212 "My deeds must be my life": in Henry Ingram, "The Life and Character of Stephen Girard" (privately published, 1896), p. 152.

212 "Success is a lousy teacher": in Murphy, "Here Are the Best Inspirational Quotes for 2018."

212 "People ask me all the time": Michael Dell, "Michael Dell's Rules for Winning Startups," Inc.com, May 5, 2014.

212 "Thought, not money": in David Saito-Chung, "Harvey Firestone's Strategy, Innovation Boosted Tires," *Investor's Business Daily*, November 30, 2012.

212 "I have had all of the disadvantages": in Joe Curtis, "10 Brilliant Facts About Larry Ellison," *Computer Business Review*, September 19, 2014.

212 "Our greatest weakness": in Murray Newlands, "20 Motivational Quotes to Inspire Your Next Business Idea," Entrepreneur.com, October 17, 2017.

213 "Everyone has an invisible sign": in Lee Colan, "Ignite True Commitment with Appreciation," Inc.com, July 12, 2017.

213 "I think if you look at people": in Geoffrey James, "15 Essential Quotes from Billionaire Mike Bloomberg," Inc.com, January 12, 2016.

213 "Obviously everyone wants to be successful": in Rose Leadem, "28 Quotes on Success," Entrepreneur.com, December 14, 2017.

213 "It takes twenty years": in James Berman, "The Three Essential Warren Buffett Quotes to Live By," Forbes.com, April 20, 2014.

213 "It is better to fail in originality": Herman Melville, "Hawthorne and His Mosses," *The Literary World*, August 1850, p. 146.

213 "Success usually comes": in *IBD* staff, "Wisdom to Live By: Quotes of the Week," *Investor's Business Daily*, July 10, 2017.

213 "Try not to become": in William Miller, "Death of a Genius," *Life*, May 2, 1955.

213 "Stop chasing the money": "7 Lessons from a Multimillionaire CEO's Book," *Business Insider*, May 30, 2017.

213   "I owe my success": in Jayson DeMers, "51 Quotes to Inspire Success in Your Life and Business," Inc.com, November 3, 2014.

213   "The only limit to our realization": in Joseph McAuley, "FDR and the Words He Never Got to Speak," *American Magazine*, April 12, 2016.

213   "Character cannot be developed": in Virgie Townsend, "What Doesn't Kill You Doesn't Necessarily Make You Stronger," *Washington Post*, January 2, 2015.

213   "The way to get started": in Haden, "50 Top Motivational Quotes."

213   "There are no secrets": "Living: Career Advice from Iconic Leaders," CNN, April 4, 2011.

214   "If you really want to do something": in Harvey Deutschendorf, "7 Habits of Highly Persistent People," *Fast Company*, April 1, 2015.

214   "I cannot give you the formula": in Ilya Pozin, "16 Leadership Quotes to Inspire You to Greatness," Forbes.com, April 10, 2014.

214   "Fall seven times": in Murphy, "Here Are the Best Inspirational Quotes for 2018."

214   "Many of life's failures": in Gordon Tredgold, "65 Quotes That Will Motivate You to Reach Success," Inc.com, February 28, 2017.

214   "I failed my way": in Kate Burgess, "Biotech Investment Fraught with Pitfalls as Wofford Discovers," *Financial Times*, April 29, 2018.

214   "I never dreamed about success": in *IBD* staff, "Quotes of the Week," *Investor's Business Daily*, September 3, 2017.

214   "Just when the caterpillar": in Zach Cutler, "8 Motivational Quotes for 2016," Entrepreneur.com, December 31, 2015.

214   "Whenever you see a successful person": in Haden, "50 Top Motivational Quotes."

214   "If you don't value your time": "Top 100 Money Quotes of All Time," Forbes.com, April 30, 2014.

214   "A successful man is one who can": in Newlands, "20 Motivational Quotes to Inspire Your Next Business Idea."

214   "No one can make you": in Jeff Haden, "51 Motivational Quotes to Inspire Willpower, Determination, and Success," Inc.com, March 6, 2018.

214   "The whole secret of a successful life": in Lolly Daskal, "100 Motivational Quotes," Huffington Post, January 1, 2014.

214 "If you're going through hell": in Geoff Loftus, "If You're Going Through Hell, Keep Going—Winston Churchill," Forbes.com, May 9, 2012.

215 "The ones who are crazy enough": in Carmine Gallo, "5 Personality Traits Apple Looks For in Job Candidates," Forbes.com, December 21, 2015.

215 "What seems to us": in Daskal, "100 Motivational Quotes."

215 "Happiness is a butterfly": Ibid.

215 "If you can't explain it simply": in Jeff Haden, "13 Motivational Quotes," Inc.com, August 4, 2017.

215 "Your problem isn't the problem": in Daskal, "100 Motivational Quotes."

215 "You can do anything": in Bruce Kasanoff, "You Can Do Anything, But Not Everything," Forbes.com, March 13, 2017.

215 "If you want to achieve": in Robert Reiss, "Great Entrepreneurs Share Quotes About Their Business Breakthroughs," Forbes.com, July 27, 2015.

215 "You may only succeed": in Daskal, "100 Motivational Quotes."

215 "Courage is resistance to fear": in Jayson DeMers, "Things Every Courageous Leader Knows," Forbes.com, February 19, 2014.

215 "Only put off until tomorrow": in Hugo Greenhalgh, "Life After Death: Ensuring an Artist's Legacy," *Financial Times*, March 10, 2016.

215 "People often say that motivation": in Kristi Hedges, "How to Make Yourself Care," Forbes.com, July 2, 2015.

215 "We become what we think": in Daskal, "100 Motivational Quotes."

215 "The best reason to start": Ibid.

215 "Success is liking yourself": in Shana Lebowitz, "12 Rich, Powerful People Share Their Surprising Definitions of Success," *Independent* (UK), March 5, 2018.

216 "A real entrepreneur": in Berger, "Top 100 Money Quotes of All Time."

216 "Whenever you find yourself": in Pamela Yellen, "5 Pieces of Free Financial Advice You Can't Afford to Take," Forbes.com, November 14, 2017.

216　"Take up one idea": in John Rampton, "50 Quotes with the Power to Motivate You to Do Anything," Entrepreneur.com, August 23, 2016.

216　"The number one reason": in Chris Gaborit, "What Do All Mentally Tough People Do?," *Sydney Morning Herald*, July 29, 2014.

216　"Success does not consist": in Jacquelyn Smith, Emmie Martin, and Jenna Goudreau, "88 Quotes on Success from the World's Most Accomplished People," *Business Insider*, September 22, 2014.

216　"You must expect great things": in Jacquelyn Smith and Emmie Martin, "101 Inspirational Quotes from Super-Successful People," *Business Insider*, August 18, 2014.

216　"Most of the important things": in Daskal, "100 Motivational Quotes."

216　"You measure the size": in Rampton, "50 Quotes with the Power to Motivate You to Do Anything."

216　"Real difficulties can be overcome": in Matthew James, "5 Tips to Defeat Autumn Anxiety," Huffington Post, September 25, 2015.

216　"Fortune sides with him": in Berger, "Top 100 Money Quotes of All Time."

216　"Little minds are tamed": in Daskal, "100 Motivational Quotes."

216　"Failure is the condiment": in Timothy Sykes, "5 Inspiring Quotes Perfect for When You Are Ready to Just Give Up on Your Business," Entrepreneur.com, August 23, 2017.

216　"A man can be": Vince Lombardi, *What It Takes to Be #1: Vince Lombardi on Leadership* (New York: McGraw-Hill Professional, 2003), p. 105.

217　"Success is simple": in Michael Gerber, "Why There's Only One Exactly Right Way to Do Everything," Inc.com, January 7, 2016.

217　"Rest satisfied with doing well": in Tryon Edwards, *The World's Laconics: Or, the Best Thoughts of the Best Authors* (New York: M. W. Dodd, 1853), p. 71.

217　"We mount to heaven": in Tryon Edwards, *A Dictionary of Thoughts: Being a Cyclopedia of Laconic Quotations from the Best Authors of the World, Both Ancient and Modern* (Detroit: F. B. Dickerson Company, 1908), p. 119.

217　"Along with success comes": in Steven Stavropoulos, *The Begin-*

ning of All Wisdom: Timeless Advice from the Ancient Greeks (Boston: Da Capo Press, 2003), p. 123.

217 "He that succeeds makes": in John Marks Templeton, *Wisdom from World Religions: Pathways Toward Heaven on Earth* (Pennsylvania: Templeton Foundation Press, 2008), p. 263.

217 "In most things success depends": in Edwards, *A Dictionary of Thoughts*, p. 551.

217 "Be kind to everyone": "Directs Traveler on the Road to Fame," *San Francisco Chronicle*, July 5, 1932.

217 "The most important single ingredient": in Smith, Martin, and Goudreau, "88 Quotes on Success from the World's Most Accomplished People."

INDEX